The Medway Valley
a Kent landscape transformed

An England's Past for Everyone paperback

Other titles in this series:

The Medway Valley
a Kent landscape transformed

ANDREW HANN

with contributions from John Newman,
John Vigar and Sandra Dunster

Phillimore

First published 2009
A Victoria County History publication
Published by Phillimore & Co. Ltd, Chichester, West Sussex PO20 2DD,
England in association with the Institute of Historical Research at the
University of London.
www.phillimore.co.uk

ISBN 978-1-86077-600-7

British Library Cataloguing in Publication Data. A cataloguing record for this
book is available from the British Library.

Typeset in Humanist 521 and Minion

We wish particularly to thank the following EPE and VCH staff for their efforts
during the production of this volume:

John Beckett – Director of the Victoria County History
Matthew Bristow – Historic Environment Research Manager
Sarah Byrne – Production Assistant
Catherine Cavanagh – Project Manager
Jessica Davies – Publications Manager
Skye Dillon – Education and Skills Manager
Nafisa Gaffar – Finance and Contracts Officer
Mel Hackett – Communications Manager
Nick Hall – Administrator
Dmitri Nemchenko – Web Manager
Alan Thacker – Executive Editor of the Victoria County History
Elizabeth Williamson – Architectural Editor of the Victoria County History

Printed and bound in Great Britain

Front cover: Burham Brickworks, 1885. Courtesy of Lafarge Cement UK
Back cover: A view of the Medway. Courtesy of English Heritage (Derek
Kendell)

Contents

List of Panels:

Foreword

Kent has a rich variety of natural resources, and when those resources come to be valued in some fresh way, people develop them, and adapt their lives to accommodate them. This new volume of Kent's history tells the story of one such energetic phase that transformed the Lower Medway Valley. From around 1750, industries used its many minerals to make cement, bricks, and paper; the farmland was exploited for more hops, fruit, and market gardening; rape and hemp seeds were crushed for oil; barges and ships were built, and goods began to be transported by canal and rail. It all gave much new work to its people, whose lifestyles in country and town were transformed.

So a colourful, human story is sympathetically told here, adorned with numerous, evocative illustrations; we see the landscape changing, and new technologies looming everywhere. I write this Foreword in a building where, in the late 1790s, septaria stones were dug up, first on Sheppey, and then south of the Swale estuary, making what was called 'Roman cement'. That mortar covered the facades of innumerable houses in Kent, London and further afield, which now are deemed 'historic buildings'. Yet within fifty years that technology was superseded by 'Portland cement'. But now, in 2009, we research the old technology again, recognising fresh merits in 'Roman cement', and bringing the same old stones from Grenoble in the Alps to restore and conserve those old buildings to the same standard. 'Roman cement' will become a familiar term again as we revive our memories of past achievements.

We welcome this vivid account by a new generation of historians, partnered with volunteers who live in Medway. All are equipped with the most varied skills, and display the insights of the local historian at their best.

Joan Thirsk

Joan Thirsk

Preface

This book is about industrial change in the Lower Medway Valley, an area of Kent distant from the heartlands of the industrial revolution. It tells the story of eight parishes that were part of Kent's 'garden of England' in 1750, but had been transformed by the mid-19th century, with the emergence of papermaking, cement, brickmaking, brewing, ship and barge building, seed crushing and engineering. It is the story of the development of a distinctive industrial region with its own clear identity, which differed markedly from that of surrounding rural districts.

Although this book owes a great debt to earlier studies of the Medway Valley's industrial past, it draws upon original research, much of it carried out by volunteers, and differs from its predecessors in two important ways. Firstly, it offers not a standard chronological overview, but rather a detailed exploration of the relationship between environment, economy and people. The approach adopted throughout has been to combine a close reading of the buildings and landscape with documentary research into the people who lived there and their everyday activities.

Secondly the project has been collaborative, involving both professional historians and volunteers. More than forty people contributed to the project in some way in a voluntary capacity. Volunteers were responsible for both architectural survey work and archival research. They also contributed text for the website and for panels in the book. Two volunteers, Roger Smoothy and Nigel Randell, photographed all pre-1914 properties in the three villages. Andrew Ashbee, Pam Doolin, Dean Jones and a number of others transcribed over 60,000 entries from the censuses; Margaret Crowhurst, Gina Beswarick and Pauline Weeds looked at wills and estate documents; Dean Jones and Ray Sturgeon provided valuable insights into life in Eccles; Brian Joyce, Odette Buchanan, Linda Brinklow, Stephen de Winton and Peter Lyons searched the local newspapers for relevant material; while Catharina Clement, John Basley, Vic and Astrid Salmon and Pauline Pullen researched topics as wide-ranging as apprentices, religious nonconformity, shipbuilding in the Medway and Malling Union workhouse.

John Newman, as architectural consultant, researched the buildings of Aylesford, Eccles and Snodland and wrote chapter 7. John Vigar worked with the village survey volunteers and wrote part of chapter 7 on the Established Church; Sandra Dunster, contributed to chapter 4. The Kent Management Committee offered comments on early drafts of chapters and provided helpful advice and support throughout the project.

Andrew Ashbee provided access to the large collection of old photographs and ephemera in Snodland Museum, while Halling School allowed us to borrow a valuable collection of glass side negatives, which were digitised by Roger Smoothy, and to a collection of original documents assembled by Halling historian Ted Gowers. Staff at Medway Archives and Local Studies Centre (MALSC) and the Centre for Kentish Studies (CKS) were helpful and supportive throughout, providing guidance on sources, and scanning and photocopying documents. Jim Preston, Jean Stirk, Alan Watkins, Mike Peevers, Christopher Chalklin and Joan Thirsk gave valuable help and advice. Both the Kent Archaeological Society and City of Rochester Society provided funds to support the project.

Many of the photographs in the book were taken by members of the project team, including volunteers. Thanks are due to Medway Archives and Local Studies, Centre for Kentish Studies, Snodland Museum, Halling School and The National Archives for allowing material to be reproduced. Other photography is by Matthew Bristow and Derek Kendall of English Heritage.

Some of the source material on which this book draws is being made available on the EPE website, which is designed to complement the paperback series. We hope it will encourage readers to carry out their own research into the industrial history of their own localities.

Andrew Hann

Introducing the Lower Medway Valley

Chapter 1

Introducing the Lower Medway Valley

Figure 1 The river Medway viewed from Rochester Bridge looking south-west. Just visible in the middle is the Medway viaduct, built in the 1960s to carry the M2 motorway across the valley. In 2003 a second viaduct was built adjacent to it to widen the motorway, and in 2007 a further bridge to the south-west was constructed to carry the high speed rail link between London and the channel tunnel.

In the middle of the 18th century the Lower Medway Valley in Kent, lying between the county town of Maidstone, and the Medway towns of Rochester and Chatham at the mouth of the estuary, was a prosperous area of mixed commercial farming and small scale industry, which owed its prosperity in no small part to the river itself. The landscape was typical of north Kent, with small villages and scattered farmsteads linked by a dense network of tracks and minor roads, which wound their way across the valley sides. This was Kent's 'Garden of England', and the villages along either side of the river were farming communities.

The eight riverside parishes, which are the focus of this study, are Frindsbury, Strood, Cuxton, Halling, Snodland, Aylesford, Burham and Wouldham. In the 18th century they were distinct, separate communities, with their own peculiarities and traditions, in spite of a shared farming heritage. Charles Dickens described the scene from Rochester Bridge in the early 19th century through the eyes of Mr Pickwick:

> On either side the banks of the Medway, covered with cornfields and pastures, with here and there a windmill or a distant church, stretched away as far as the eye could see, presenting a rich and varied landscape. The river, reflecting the clear blue of the sky, glistened and sparkled as it flowed noiselessly on; and the oars of the fishermen dipped into the water with a clear and liquid sound as the heavy but picturesque boats glided slowly down the stream.'[1]

Over the decades that followed, the settlements in the parishes grew so that by 1901 their combined population at 27,283 was five times greater than in 1801 when just 5,394 people lived in the valley. In this process of growth the parishes came to share a common sense of identity which differentiated them from the surrounding areas of rural Kent. This new identity was grounded in their shared experience of industrialisation. Here is Cox, writing of the Medway in 1913:

> Immediately to the south of Rochester, the beauty of the Medway is for several miles much marred by the long succession of cement works with their aggressively tall chimney shafts on

Figure 2 The county of Kent in the south east of England.

1

the eastern bank. Small railway lines carry the chalk from the hill-side quarries in the background. Nevertheless there is much compensation in the sight of the great barges, with their various shades of ruddy brown sails, gliding up or down the waters with a placid stately dignity.[2]

Compensation there may have been – for a few – but one common feature of this new world was smoke and dust. An 1893 account talked of the 'mingled smoke and steam throwing a haze'

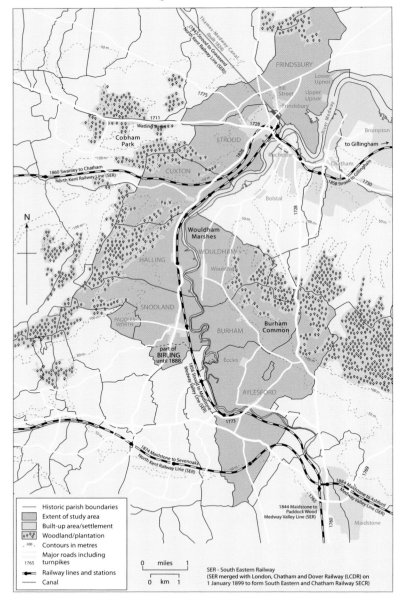

Figure 3 The eight riverside parishes of the Lower Medway Valley shown in relation to major towns, roads, railways, canals and topography.

Figure 4 Population figures for the Lower Medway parishes, 1801-1901

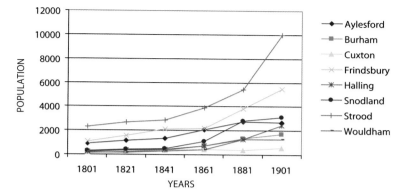

Figure 4 Population figures for the Lower Medway parishes, 1801-1901

Figure 5 Halling High Street *c.*1910 looking north towards the Hilton, Anderson and Co. cement works. Such was the close proximity of the works to the houses that their roofs were often covered in cement dust.

over Strood; W. and M. Wyllie noted the 'impalpable white powder' which covered the neighbourhood, and Edwin Harris recalled workers inhaling so much dust that were they to drink water their stomachs would be coated with cement. One consequence of this dusty environment was an absence of colour. Buildings close to the works became coated in a layer of cement giving them a uniform grey appearance; the air was made 'heavy with the suspended smoke belched from countless chimneys'. Cement Land was clearly a world apart, and recognised as such by locals and visitors alike.[3]

In his book *Unknown Kent*, published in 1921, the author Donald Maxwell described the Lower Medway Valley as 'Cementium', and in doing so he encapsulated the view that this was an agricultural landscape transformed by cement. It was more than this of course, because cement was accompanied by papermaking, brickmaking, brewing, ship and barge building, seed

Figure 6 The Rugby cement works in Halling, seen here in 2008, is the last operating cement works in the Lower Medway Valley.

crushing and engineering. This range of activities was recorded in 1938 by John (Sonny) Hanson Richardson and his wife, when they took a trip down the river Medway from its source at Turners Hill to the sea at Sheerness recording on cinematic film the various places they passed. The opening scenes show fields, woodland and picturesque villages, but along the river between Maidstone and Rochester the film captures an industrialised landscape which is scarcely imaginable today. The river is a hive of activity, with heavily laden barges and busy steam tugs plying their trade. On the banks are forests of cranes, wharves stacked with cargo, and factory chimneys. Everywhere there are people going about their business.[4]

But for how much longer? As early as 1921 Donald Maxwell described the 'ruined kilns and tottering chimneys' along the river, and the numerous quarries 'in which red-rusted machinery and decrepit trains of trucks lie abandoned as by a plague-stricken people'. By the 1950s Goodsall could write of the 'grim remains of disused lime-kilns and cement works' which he found scattered in the marshlands of Burham.[5]

The cement industry was transitory, a passing phase in the much longer history of change and development in the Lower Medway Valley. Today, by comparison with the scenes shot in 1938, the river is a picture of tranquillity along much of its course. Patches of industry remain such as the paper-mills at New Hythe and Snodland, while the one remaining cement works at Halling stands rather forlornly, set back from the river. An occasional pleasure craft passes by, but the overriding sense is one of quiet dereliction.

A CHANGING LANDSCAPE

Over time the landscape of the Lower Medway Valley has been shaped by the movement of people and goods along its numerous routeways, each of which has carved out its own highly visible legacy. The most important of these is the river Medway itself, which for centuries has been a vital link between the interior of Kent and the sea. It has, of course, been modified to improve navigation, alleviate flooding, and harness its flowing waters as a source of power. Evidence of this intervention can be seen everywhere along its course. North of Aylesford lines of embankments reveal attempts to limit the flooding of riverside meadows. These became necessary in the early 19th century when silting increased following the introduction of locks upstream at Allington to improve the navigation of the river. The Earl of Aylesford's land agent R.K. Summerfield reckoned in 1805 that these flood defences could raise the value of meadow land by as much as 25s. per acre.[6]

A little further north opposite the Aylesford Newsprint paper-mill at New Hythe the river straightens significantly, and a number of marshy inlets can be seen along the eastern bank. These mark the location of a series of cuts dug by the Lower Medway Navigation Company in an effort to improve the channel. The quay at the former Burham brick, lime and cement works now lies on the curve of a silted meander separated from the main watercourse by these improvements. At Strood the river banks have been raised and many of the old creeks culverted to counter the serious flooding which frequently afflicted the town

Figure 7 An early 20th-century view of the Medway looking across the river from Strood to the cathedral city of Rochester. In the foreground, the distinctive conical roofed oasthouses provide a reminder that agriculture continued to prosper alongside industry in the Lower Medway. To their left is the large Temple brickfield and in the distance the smoking chimneys of the cement works that lined the Frindsbury peninsula.

during exceptionally high tides. Smetham, in his *History of Strood*, described the damaging impact of flooding, recalling particularly 29 November 1898 when boats could be rowed up the High Street and the Temple Street area was left festering in a foul-smelling lake for several months.[7]

On the western bank of the river beyond Rochester bridge a low lying area covered in modern housing marks the location of Strood Dock, the southern terminus of the Thames and Medway Canal, opened in 1824. Originally proposed in 1799, the canal was designed to shorten the passage to London with a direct route across the Hoo peninsula. The intention was to save barge captains the 47-mile sea journey around the Isle of Grain. The canal proprietors promised carriage from Maidstone to London in only 24 hours. Much of the route lies hidden from view in a seven-mile-long tunnel under the North Downs emerging at Higham, but its alignment can be traced on the surface from evidence of the dozen or more shafts opened during tunnelling.

According to a report of 1844 the shafts were covered over and partly infilled shortly after the canal opened, although some have since subsided. The shaft at the junction of Frindsbury Road and Mill Road lay within an existing chalk pit. Today this forms a landscaped area behind English Martyrs Roman Catholic Church, but a small section of exposed cliff face is still visible. One substantial opening remains north of Dillywood Lane where the tunnel was opened to the surface in 1830 and widened to create a passing place for barges at a cost of £13,000.[8]

Despite these teething problems the new rail venture proved profitable. In 1845 the proprietors sold the line to the South Eastern Railway Company, which drained the canal and installed double tracks through the tunnel. These are still in use today on the route between Strood and Gravesend, with the brick entrance to the tunnel close to Strood station serving as a reminder of this impressive feat of Victorian engineering. This was to be the first of many lines which criss-crossed the area during the second half of the 19th century. Since the companies needed to avoid steep gradients, rail lines were incised into the landscape, cutting through hillsides and across ancient field boundaries and long-established pathways.[9]

To the people of the Lower Medway Valley the coming of the railway must have been a potent symbol of change. The route from Strood to Maidstone opened in 1856, and curves along the western bank of the Medway through Cuxton, Halling, Snodland, New Hythe and Aylesford. The line had a direct link on to London, and transformed the prospects for local industry, which previously depended on river transport. The alignment was largely determined by the local topography. At Aylesford, the influence is apparent of Edward Ladd Betts, railway contractor and proprietor of nearby Preston Hall. To limit the impact of the railway on his property he insisted that the line should skirt round the edges of his estate, rather than taking a more direct route, hence the location of the station somewhat anomalously about half a mile from the village centre. This is also why the line curves sharply here leading to a 15mph speed limit.[10]

The London, Chatham and Dover Railway, was built in stages between 1858 and 1863. At Strood, the high brick embankments upon which the track sits cut right through the town, separating it into two parts. On one side were the town centre and the industrial areas along the riverside, on the other the residential districts rising up Strood hill and across towards Frindsbury. Entrances to the town from the north and west along London Road, Gun Lane, North Street and Station road were now framed by majestic arches carrying the railway overhead, though many thought the viaduct carrying the railway over the Medway marred the view of and from Rochester Bridge.

Roads also had a profound impact on the landscape. Watling Street had been the main routeway between London and Continental Europe from at least Roman times and determined the strategic importance of Rochester Bridge. Indeed, it is said that the description of Kent as 'the garden of England' stemmed from the fact that most travellers' experiences of the county were confined to the fertile tracts of land which bordered this road. A second major route ran from London to Hythe via Footscray, Aylesford, Maidstone and Ashford.[11]

Figure 8 Entrance to the Medway tunnel, Frindsbury, to the north of Strood station. Opened in 1824 as part of the Thames and Medway Canal, the tunnel, which runs for 3,595 metres under the North Downs, was converted in 1844 for rail use and is still in use today.

Each of these strategic routes attracted development along its course, particularly at places such as Strood and Aylesford which grew wealthy because of their importance as bridging points over the Medway. From the early 18th century the improvement of roads by turnpike trusts set up with government legislation, brought further changes. Existing major routes and some minor ones were improved. At Snodland, the opening of the Strood to Malling turnpike in 1826 led to the creation of Malling Road which became the main thoroughfare to the south of the village in place of the road to Birling. In time this altered the whole configuration of the village. A further alteration of the route took place at Holborough in 1850, when William Lee diverted the road across a field in front of his residence, Holloway Court, to avoid the narrow lane past the old mill and enable him to add an extended driveway, wall and gatehouse to his property. Today the former line of the road is marked by Court Cottage which now lies within the grounds of Holborough Court, some distance from the present road.[12]

These many individual features make up a landscape dripping in history. As we see it today, the valley has been forged by the activities of generations of farmers, the decisions made by landowners, the role of the river as a link between inland Kent and the wider world and, perhaps all too briefly, an industrial phase which has been – and largely gone. But what was it like to live in the Lower Medway Valley through this remarkable period? In what follows we have painted a picture of the valley from the late 18th century until the 20th century. We have traced the pattern of change and development, of the rise, decline, and fall of an industrial area well away from the heartlands of industrial revolution England, and we have tried to reconstruct the life of the community through this period. Who lived in the valley, and what was life like for them? How did they make a living? Where did they live? And how did this rural Kentish landscape come to be transformed into an industrial area in the space of less than a century, and why did it take only half that time for it to decline, to return almost to its rural roots?

Chapter 2

Land and Farming

Common fields, so widespread in the midland counties, had largely disappeared by the beginning of the 17th century.[13] By the mid-18th century farms in Kent were large by comparison with other parts of the country. This was a result, or so it is usually claimed, of the popularity of gavelkind, a particular form of land tenure unique in England to Kent, by which all the sons of someone dying without making a will received an equal share of the estate (a 'partible' inheritance system). Gavelkind also produced a relatively open market in land, as it could be exchanged, bought or sold by partible inheritees. In turn, this ensured that estates remained relatively small.

During the 18th and 19th centuries Kentish farmers were at the forefront of innovation. Commercial opportunities arising from proximity to the large London market had encouraged specialisation from an early date. The marshes of the Thames and Medway

Figure 9 A section of I.J. West's 1849 map of the Preston Hall Estate, Aylesford, showing the winding lanes and isolated farmsteads which characterised the landscape of the Lower Medway Valley.

estuaries were renowned for their sheep by the 17th century, while the fertile loams on the lower dip slopes of the North Downs were highly regarded for their cereal crops and dairy cattle.[14]

As the Medway valley cut through a number of the county's main agricultural belts, land use and farming practices varied significantly. Most of the Lower Medway Valley parishes contained an area of high downland whose cold, heavy flinty-clay soils were reserved largely for woodland and the grazing of sheep. On the valley slopes the relatively thin chalky soils made productive corn land if properly manured. The best land, however, was in the valley bottoms, where fertile loams were to be found along with patches of brickearth, while near to the river's edge tidal flooding produced extensive salt marshes.[15]

FARMING PATTERNS AND PRACTICES

At the end of the 17th century around two-thirds of land in the valley was devoted to arable production. Evidence in probate inventories suggests that wheat and barley were the main crops, with wheat increasingly dominant due to the higher prices it could command. The importance of wheat probably helps to explain the adoption of new crop rotations from the early 1700s incorporating peas, beans and nitrogen fixing leguminous crops such as sainfoin, cinquefoil and clover. These enabled farmers to reduce the land fallowed each year while providing nutritious fodder for livestock so that stocking densities could be increased.[16]

Clover was grown mostly in Frindsbury, where there were extensive tracts of good loamy soil on the lower lying land. Sainfoin was found on the chalky downland slopes of Halling, Snodland and Wouldham. Mary Wingate of Snodland listed among her chattels in 1763 a ten-acre field recently sown with oats, barley and sainfoin. Turnips were also used in arable rotations on lighter land. They helped to clean the soil of weeds and pests, and provided animal fodder. John Dibly of Halling had nine acres sown with turnips in 1731.[17]

The planting of leguminous grasses encouraged the extension of sheep grazing onto the high downland pastures. Flocks were folded on fallow land, particularly where soils were thin and chalky, hence the regular appearance of hurdles and 'sheep gates' in inventories. In this way farmers were able to increase the size of their flocks. By the mid-18th century the average flock size was around eighty, although some of the larger farmers in Aylesford, Wouldham and Halling had more than two hundred. These figures can be compared with those in the early 18th century of only 45 to 50 for the county as a whole.[18]

Figure 10 A Southdown ram from John Boys' *General View of Agriculture of the County of Kent*. Southdowns, introduced to the Medway Valley in the 18th century, were particularly well suited to coarse downland pastures.

Selective breeding of sheep meant that varieties were available particularly suited to the different types of local environment. The renowned Romney Marsh sheep, which fattened easily and produced very long fine wool, did best on the riverside marshes; Southdowns, Wiltshires and Dorsetshires were more suited to the coarser downland pastures.

Cattle were kept by valley farmers but not in great numbers. The majority were milking cows supplying dairy produce for local consumption. A few bullocks and steers were fattened on the marshes during the summer, or fed on hay and turnips in the farmyard. Edmund Pearson of Strood had three cows 'in the marsh', while William Charlton kept 'ten steer runts and two country steers' in the regularly flooded meadows that bordered the river at Aylesford. Most farms also had two or more horses, which were used for a variety of farm work including carting and ploughing. Oxen were rarely employed as draught animals in the valley by the 18th century, although they were commonly found on the heavy clay soils of the Weald.[19]

Over the course of the 18th and 19th centuries subtle changes occurred in the patterns of cropping, and the balance between crops and livestock. The late 18th century was a period of poor harvests and rapidly rising grain prices under wartime conditions, encouraging an intensification of arable production. The 1801 crop returns show the continued advance of wheat at the expense of barley, and an extension in the cultivation of oats, which grew well on poor chalky downland soils and were mainly used as fodder for horses. Turnips were also now more widely cultivated, and made up around 10 per cent of the sown acreage. Small areas of land were also devoted to potatoes, which again were used mainly for fodder.

John Boys, writing a general account of Kent's agriculture in 1794, which he expanded in 1805, described in detail the most common rotations in use. On the better land in the valleys he advocated a system of six courses: turnips, barley, clover, wheat, beans and wheat. The poorer chalky soils of the high Downs should be cropped with turnips, barley, clover and wheat for one, two or three courses (years), then laid down to sainfoin or rye-grass for a few years to recover.[20]

One area of agricultural change that gathered pace through the 19th century was the introduction of new tools and equipment designed to raise labour productivity. Before 1800 there had been small incremental improvements in basic farm implements. Seed drills had come to be widely used, and scythes had replaced sickles for mowing barley and oats. In 1805, however, Boys was still able to complain that the heavy Kentish turn-wrest plough was 'almost the

Figure 11 The cultivation of arable land by steam plough was firmly established by the 1860s and was usually achieved by pulling a plough between two stationary steam engines using windlasses and wire rope. These steam engines, of which John Fowler's design was the most popular, were subsequently harnessed to power threshing machines, as shown here in this 20th-century photograph from Westerham, Kent.

only one used or known in the county'.[21] Lighter two-horse 'Dutch ploughs' used across much of eastern England had not been widely introduced due to the heavy soils in many parts of Kent.

The shortage of workers during the Napoleonic wars provided an incentive for the introduction of labour saving technology, particularly horse-powered threshing machines. The major step change came in the 1840s and 1850s with the introduction of steam powered machinery. This was eagerly adopted by the larger landowners and farmers in the valley. A sale of agricultural implements from the Home Farm on the Preston Hall estate in 1867 included 'an excellent 12-horse power portable steam engine, by Clayton, Shuttleworth, and Co., with Howard's patent 6-share iron plough', four patent reaping and mowing machines, a thrashing machine on wheels, a cog wheel clod-crusher and a Bentall's patent broadshare. In the same year the *Kent and Sussex Gazette* reported on a fire at the estate caused by the malfunction of a steam thrashing machine.[22]

By the later decades of the 19th century specialist contractors moved from farm to farm with traction engines performing labour intensive tasks such as threshing and ploughing. Several farm workers were described in the 1881 census as 'steam plough man' or 'plough engine driver'.

The Lower Medway Valley was also at the forefront of the agricultural machine-making industry. Thomas Aveling was producing steam ploughing equipment and self-propelled portable engines from his works in Rochester by the late 1850s. In 1861 he moved to Strood, and with Richard Porter established a large works which employed close to a thousand people by 1900. Other machine makers in the area included Cuthbert Russell, who made 'horizontal engines' suitable for 'agriculturalists' amongst other users at the Eagle Iron Works in Strood, and Balls Garrett of Maidstone, whose product range included seed drills, ploughs, thrashing machines and oil-cake crushers.[23]

Hops

Among the more significant developments in Kentish agriculture during the 18th century were the spread of hop and fruit growing, and market gardening. Many new orchards were planted in the Medway valley in the early 18th century, although acreages remained small by later standards. Apples were the most important crop, although pears, cherries and filberts, a type of cultivated hazelnut, were widely grown. Richard Hayes, farming at Owletts near Cobham, focused on cherries and walnuts. He followed the common practice of selling his fruit on the tree to contractors for a lump sum, though his uncle, who farmed nearby, picked and marketed the fruit himself. Inventory evidence of fruit growing in the valley is patchy: John Dibly of Halling had 'some apples' in the malthouse, and Edward Squibbs of Snodland had an orchard next to his oasthouse.[24]

The cultivation of hops was more widespread. Introduced from the Low Countries in the early 16th century, the crop was well suited to Kentish conditions and soon became commercially important. Hop gardens were initially concentrated just south of the Lower Medway Valley, along the Upper Medway Valley and to the east of Maidstone. Here the combination of small enclosed fields, plentiful

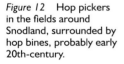

Figure 12 Hop pickers in the fields around Snodland, surrounded by hop bines, probably early 20th-century.

supplies of coppice wood for hop poles, and a thriving local brewing industry, provided ideal conditions for cultivation.

By the early 18th century production had spread northwards into all the eight parishes of the valley. Oasthouses, used to dry the hops, are listed in 12 inventories including those of John Wingate of Snodland and Joseph Brown of Frindsbury, while hop poles or hops themselves appear in 16 inventories. Some hop growers appear to have been operating on a relatively large scale: Francis How of Wouldham had 10 acres of hop ground in 1783, and William Charlton had 50 hundredweight of new hops in his oasthouse valued at £165.

Government statistics compiled from the early 19th century for taxation purposes reveal the continued expansion of hop cultivation across the study area. In 1800 the greatest acreage of hop gardens was in Aylesford, which lay on the fringes of the main hop-growing belt around Maidstone, but from around 1835, production increased significantly in the northern part of the valley, in Frindsbury, Cuxton, and later Strood. Growing hops was, however, a risky business since they were easily damaged by bad weather and disease, and sharp fluctuations in output occurred from year to year: from a similar acreage 636,093 pounds were harvested in 1858, but only 397,826 pounds in 1861.[25]

In the second half of the 19th century hops were one of the few profitable branches of agriculture. The agricultural census of

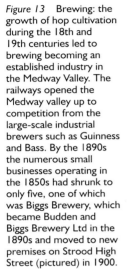

Figure 13 Brewing: the growth of hop cultivation during the 18th and 19th centuries led to brewing becoming an established industry in the Medway Valley. The railways opened the Medway valley up to competition from the large-scale industrial brewers such as Guinness and Bass. By the 1890s the numerous small businesses operating in the 1850s had shrunk to only five, one of which was Biggs Brewery, which became Budden and Biggs Brewery Ltd in the 1890s and moved to new premises on Strood High Street (pictured) in 1900.

Figure 14 Manor farm oasthouse, Frindsbury, 1860s. The distinctive conical roofs were a relatively late development, introduced around 1835 by John Read. Prior to this, oasts were generally rectangular barn-like structures with kilns in the middle and storage space at each end. Many farmers also used malt kilns to dry their hops.

1877 recorded 250 acres in Aylesford, 150 in Frindsbury, 143 in Strood and 88 in Cuxton. Some hop planters were now operating on a large scale. For instance, Mary Simmonds of the Friars in Aylesford, described as a 'hop planter', farmed 165 acres in 1861 and employed 56 labourers.

It was not to last. By the 1890s, the acreage under hops was beginning to fall away as consumers turned increasingly to light, bitter ales that required fewer hops. Production countywide was no more than half the levels achieved in the boom years of the 1870s, and many smaller growers had to abandon cultivation.[26]

Hop cultivation has left an indelible mark on the local landscape. The most obvious reminders of this once widespread activity are the round oasthouses that are scattered across the valley. Surviving examples include those at Ranscombe and Dean farms in Cuxton; Court Farm, Upper Halling; Hale Farm, Burham; and Cossington Farm, Aylesford, all of which have been converted into private houses.[27]

Another sign of hop growing is the widespread evidence of coppicing in woodland across the valley. Coppice wood, particularly larch, chestnut and ash, was used for hop poles, which were in great demand as they needed replacing every four years or so: each acre of hops required over 3,500 poles. Parts of the chalk downland overlain with clay-with-flints remained heavily wooded throughout the 18th and 19th centuries, and were carefully managed to produce various types of timber including hop poles. Eventually, coppicing declined because of the introduction of American wire-setting techniques, which used fewer hop poles. The Earl of Aylesford stocked his woodland with 30,000 ash and chestnut saplings from a nursery in Aylesford during the early

Figure 15 Hop pickers' huts, School Lane, Wouldham. Thought to date from around 1887, these huts survive as dog kennels. They are of rendered brick or shuttered concrete construction and would originally have been covered by a corrugated iron roof.

1820s. They produced an income for him of between £1,200 and £2,000 a year from the sale of underwood.[28]

The harvesting of hops and fruit relied on a large army of migrant workers, who descended on the valley each autumn. Migrants were often housed in communal lodgings or 'hopper houses', although tents were sometimes used. These hopper houses were little more than long sheds partitioned into ten or more compartments, each with its own entrance, but no window or furniture. Each compartment was allotted to a hop-bin's company; the organisation was left to make its own sleeping arrangements. The accommodation was basic, but it was preferred to the barrack blocks and tented encampments that were a common sight until the 1880s.[29]

Overcrowding was frequent with ten or twelve men, women and children often sleeping together in a single compartment of no more than 14 feet square. Unsurprisingly, complaints of disorderly behaviour were commonplace. Pickers were variously accused of drunkenness, petty pilfering, begging and prostitution as they made their way across Kent to the hop gardens.[30]

Stratton reported one incident of disorder in 1881 when a train failed to stop at Aylesford station to pick up a party of hoppers who had been working on the Preston Hall estate. Realising they were unlikely to get away that day, 'they speedily made their way to the nearest public-house, with the inevitable result of drunkenness and ill-humour, getting off late at night in disorderly fashion'.[31]

Market Gardening

Frindsbury and Strood were important centres for market gardening by the mid-18th century. Both parishes had plenty of rich loamy soils suitable for vegetable growing as well as good links with London by road and water. Flowers, carrots, cabbages, onions, garden peas, parsnips, turnips and asparagus were among the crops grown, and profits were such that, as early as the 1650s, gardeners were prepared to pay from £2 to £9 a year per acre for plots at a time when farmland rarely rented for more than 10-20s.[32]

By 1792 there was a public house in Cage Lane, Strood, called the *Three Gardeners*, and Finch's directory of 1803 lists two gardeners in the parish. A further 16 can be identified from early 19th-century parish registers, 11 in Strood and five in Frindsbury. Garden plots in Frindsbury were concentrated on the Thanet sands and brickearth around Bill Street and Wainscott where the soils were particularly productive. William Beadle worked a nursery ground here from at least 1835, producing young fruit trees and seeds for restocking local orchards. By mid-century gardens and nurseries had become a vital part of the local economy, and one that was to see further growth over following decades. The 1877 agricultural census recorded 82 acres of turnip and swedes, 17 acres of cabbages, 36 acres of kohl-rabi and three acres of carrots in Frindsbury, far more than in any of the other seven parishes.[33]

INSTITUTIONAL CHANGE

Enclosure and Engrossment

A central element of institutional change was enclosure, and in Kent this was mainly enclosure of common wastes, as common field farming had never been widespread in the county. Much of this was barren heathland used for rough grazing and gathering fuel. Burham Downs were noted for their poor soils and 'uninclosed pastures, much covered with low scrubby bushes, heath, and furze.' Along the riverbanks there were also common meadows and salt marshes. The latter were particularly extensive in Wouldham and Snodland, where Edward Hasted described them as 'offensive' and 'unhealthy'.[34]

From the late 18th century this remaining common land was steadily eroded through piecemeal enclosure, often at the behest of the larger landowners. The Earl of Aylesford secured a Parliamentary Act to enclose Burham Common in 1813. The common, which extended for upwards of 300 acres along the tops of the Downs, was described as 'entirely covered over with scrub oaks and brambles'. According to the Earl's agent, the people who held customary grazing rights mostly lived at a distance, and it provided little feed of any consequence. He claimed that the farmers and cottagers with 'privilege of cutting bushes' apparently thought it hardly worth their while due to 'the great length of carriage'. The agent reckoned the common, if cleared, would make good farmland. Though clearly a polemic, these arguments illustrate the widely perceived benefits of enclosure. In this case the Earl received an allotment of 131 acres in lieu of his common rights, which was combined with land purchases in the vicinity to form Burham Street Farm, which was let in 1815 to a Mr Bishop.[35]

Elsewhere in the valley enclosure acts were obtained in East Malling and Teston (1805), and Birling (1814), and by the 1840s few of the parishes had any substantial tracts of common land remaining. In Wouldham there were 140 acres of rough pasture and 29 acres of common salting, while in Snodland 75 acres remained in common ownership. Halling and Cuxton had small areas of common amounting to no more than 25-30 acres, but elsewhere it had completely disappeared. Much of this remaining common land had been enclosed by the 1880s.

Another element of structural change in agriculture was engrossment, the amalgamation of holdings to produce larger farms. Already by 1750 most farmers in the Lower Medway Valley were farming relatively large holdings. John Wingate of Snodland was probably typical. In 1752 he had 57 acres under crops (wheat, oats, barley and peas), and a further 24 acres laid down to sainfoin. His goods and chattels were valued at £424 5s. Other farmers operated at an even larger scale. William Charlton of Aylesford had over 230 sheep, 26 cattle, four acres of hop poles, 65 acres of ploughed land and almost 200 quarters of grain in the barn and granary at his death in 1761.[36]

Consolidation had progressed furthest in Aylesford and Cuxton, where one or two aristocratic families held most of the land. In Cuxton the Earl of Darnley was the main landowner, and his property was divided into 11 substantial farms by the 1760s. In contrast, there were many smaller holdings in Frindsbury where there was no dominant landowner. Here fields were often scattered in different parts of the parish because competitive bidding for leases made farm consolidation and enlargement more difficult.[37]

By the 1840s most land in the valley was in the hands of substantial tenant farmers: in Cuxton and Wouldham over 80 per cent of land was in holdings of over 100 acres, although the comparable figure for Burham was only 55 per cent. Smaller farms did survive, particularly in Burham, Frindsbury and Aylesford, but these were frequently occupied by specialist producers such as hop planters or market gardeners, or people combining agriculture with another activity. George Baker, who held 27 acres in Frindsbury, was a substantial brickmaker, while James Westbrook, who had 11 acres in Aylesford, was a shoemaker. The process of

Figure 16 Whornes Place, Cuxton, one of the 11 farms leased by the Earl of Darnley, was once a far grander residence. The main house and stable block erected in the early 17th century for Sir John Leverson were demolished in 1872 after falling into disrepair and being 'infested by evil characters'. Only the granary (pictured), later converted into a farmhouse, now survives, facing onto the A228 south of Cuxton village.

consolidation continued through the 19th century as commercial pressures squeezed out the small farmer. Evidence from the 1861 and 1881 censuses shows that the number of farms over 100 acres was rising, and the average number of labourers employed on each farm was also increasing.[38]

Land was also enclosed for parkland. The remains of parks and gardens are visible in the landscape, often long after the country house with which they were associated has been swept away. Holborough Court, north of Snodland, was demolished in 1932, but the gate-house remains along with sections of the boundary wall, and the 'footprint' of the park can still be discerned from the shape of the surrounding woodland.[39]

Today the different elements of this managed landscape can most readily be seen at Preston Hall in Aylesford. Edward Ladd Betts laid out an expansive landscaped deer park, richly planted with elms, chestnuts, ash, larch, oaks and cedars on what had formerly been flat meadowland. He created sumptuous gardens, wide gravel terraces, and to the south west of the estate an artificial lake, sheltered by trees and flowering shrubs. Much of this landscape has now disappeared under buildings, but a hint of past glories remains. To the north-east of the former mansion patterns in the lawn mark the location of an orangery, demolished in 1953, while the extent of the deer park is defined by a scattering of mature trees, although many have been felled in recent years. The lake was still clearly visible in the 1940s: today only a slight depression behind the southern gate house marks its former site.[40]

Tenure

Tenants of the larger estates, including those of the Earls of Aylesford and Earls of Darnley, mostly occupied farms held on leases for terms of seven to 21 years. Many other farmers held their lands 'at will' from minor gentry families such as the Boghursts of Frindsbury and Goldings of Aylesford and Burham. By contrast tenants on the extensive estates of the Dean and Chapter of Rochester in Frindsbury, Wouldham and Aylesford benefited from 21 year leases, renewable every seven years. Here the customary practice of levying a large initial fine and low annual rents survived. In most cases the land was then sublet at a commercial rate so that the occupying tenants were in a similar position to those renting from private landlords.

The failure of the Dean and Chapter to manage their estates on a commercial basis enabled a number of enterprising tenants to reap large rewards from mineral resources. George Hankey, the lessee of land next to the river in Frindsbury, instigated large-scale

extraction of chalk, brickearth and sand in the early 19th century
by issuing sub-leases to other operators without the permission
of the ecclesiastical authorities. These operations earned him over
£900 a year in royalties, little of which was passed on to the Dean
and Chapter until 1867 when professional agents appointed by the
Ecclesiastical Commissioners took charge of administration.[41]

Tenurial change during the 19th century was largely associated
with the expansion of the larger estates, which continued the
process of buying out smaller freeholders. The Earl of Aylesford
purchased land from Sir Samuel Chambers, Mrs Lane and the
late Mr Dunning in 1815 to help constitute Burham Street Farm
at a cost of £5,400. These estates were managed in an increasingly
professional manner by agents such as R.K. Summerfield who
produced a detailed atlas of the Earl of Aylesford's Kentish holdings
in 1805 to assist efficient administration.[42]

One aspect of this professionalisation was the use of leasing
agreements to control farming practices. Clauses were often
included in these documents specifying certain activities and
prohibiting others. The tenant of Court Lodge Farm in Aylesford
was instructed in 1887 to leave at least one-fifth of the arable
land fallow each year and not to 'grow two white straw crops in
succession, but sow intervening green and pulse crops'.[43]

Landowners, including the Earl of Aylesford, found themselves
having to reduce rents and abandon attempts at improvement in
difficult economic circumstances following the downturn in grain
prices from 1812. The tenant of Burham Court Farm was forced
to give it up in 1822 due to 'the low price of landed produce'. His
replacement, a Mr Ward, took the farm at a reduced rent of £420
with a promise to pay more if times got better. After a return to
prosperity in the 1840s and 1850s, depressed conditions returned
around 1870. Kent's gross farm output fell by around 19 per cent
between 1873 and 1911 during the agricultural depression of the
late 19th century. Across the county rents fell steadily, reflecting
the financial weakness of existing tenants and a shortage of new
ones. In the Lower Medway Valley the impact of falling agricultural
prices was to some extent offset by the variety of alternative
economic activities, though the prolonged malaise significantly
reduced the income of many of the larger landowners and
weakened their position within local society.[44]

EMPLOYMENT AND WAGES

Farmers pressed by falling incomes struggled to retain their
employees, particularly from the mid-19th century when new
industries began to offer alternatives to agricultural employment

in the north of the county. In the Lower Medway Valley wages were consistently above the county average. Labourers working on the Cobham Hall estate, for instance, were paid 9s. a week in the 1750s, rising to between 9s. and 12s. in the 1790s, 12s. to 14s. in the 1830s and 15s. to 16s. in the 1870s.[45]

These figures disguise significant variations in wage levels, reflecting the hierarchical structure of the agricultural labour force. At the top of this hierarchy were farm servants – skilled workers hired yearly to fulfil specific roles as ploughmen, waggoners, shepherds or carters. John Smith was hired by the Aylesford farmer, Thomas Hildash, in 1810 'to serve him as waggoner for a year at the wages of eighteen guineas'. In the 1790s male farm servants in west Kent were paid between £9 and £14 per year, depending on their role. Female servants such as cooks and dairy maids received rather less: between £5 and £7.[46]

Farm servants were usually provided with board and lodgings in the farmhouse, at least until the 1830s, since livestock and horses required their regular attention. Comparison of the wages of indoor servants with those paid to married servants living away from the farm suggests that boarding was worth around £13 to £15 a year by the late 18th century. This meant that a skilled farm labourer at this time could expect to earn between £25 and £30. Indeed, monthly paid labourers at Cobham Hall in 1790 were also paid around £25 a year.[47]

Unskilled field labourers received less generous remuneration. Hired for short periods when needs arose, they were usually paid by the task, or at hourly, daily or weekly rates. The Earl of Darnley's estate accounts illustrate the great variety of wage rates paid in the mid-18th century. Work in the garden brought in 1s. 6d. a day, as did ploughing, carting and binding and loading straw. Weeding was clearly considered less onerous, earning only 8d. a day. Other tasks were paid at piece rates: threshing oats was rated at 1s. per quarter, cutting wood at 2s. per cord, and hoeing turnips at 5s. per acre.

Over time this pattern of wages changed, with a greater emphasis on day rates and fewer distinctions drawn between different tasks. By the 1780s most entries in the Cobham accounts simply note the name of the labourer and the number of days worked, with a fairly standard rate of 1s. 6d. a week applied for much of the year, rising to 1s. 8d., and then 2s. in the summer and early autumn when the working day was longer and demand for labour greatest.

On top of their wages labourers were often given beer or allowances to purchase it, particularly during the summer when warmer weather made hard physical exertion thirsty work. At Cobham Adam Wollis was given 1s. 2d. of beer in addition to 13s. 10½d. in cash for threshing 13 quarters 7 bushels of oats in

Figure 17 Bringing in the
harvest, North Halling,
1917. Methods appeared
to have changed little
since the 1790s when it
was estimated that a man
could reap three quarters
of an acre in two days,
and a family of three earn
as much as 40s. to 50s.
from harvest work.

1754, while in 1780 those involved in haymaking, both men and women, were allowed 2d. a day each for beer.[48]

Wages were at their highest during the harvest period in August and September when demand for labour was at its peak. At Cobham in the 1790s labourers could earn 2s. a day at this time of the year. Additionally, high piece-rates were offered for harvest work as crops needed to be gathered speedily once they had ripened before they were 'exposed to all the casualties of weather'.[49]

Rates varied depending on the type of crop and its physical condition: the onset of wet weather would inject extra urgency and provide a boost to payments. Wheat attracted the highest harvest premium: 6s. to 7s. per acre in the 1750s and between 8s. and 12s. in the 1790s. Barley and oats brought in rather less at 1s. 8d. to 2s. 6d. per acre.[50]

Picking hops and fruit also provided lucrative seasonal employment in the Medway valley, which lay on the fringes of the main fruit and hop-growing districts around Maidstone, Faversham and Canterbury. Fruits ripened in sequence, first soft fruit such as raspberries and strawberries, then cherries, plums, apples, pears and filberts, providing sustained employment for women and children over the summer months and into the autumn. By the 1860s earnings ranged from 1s. 4d. to 2s. per day for women, with children receiving around half this amount.[51]

Harvesting hops generated high seasonal labour demand and high piece-rate wages. Picking had to be done quickly as the crop was easily spoiled by prolonged rain or aphid attack rendering it useless to commercial brewers. Daily earnings for hop pickers ranged from 1s. 8d. to 3s. 4d. in the late 18th century, rising to between 3s. 4d. and 5s. 4d. by the 1900s.[52]

Chapter 3

Industry and Manufacturing

The Lower Medway Valley may have been within the Garden of Kent, but by the second half of the 18th century it was also home to a wide range of industrial concerns, some of recent origin, others of longer standing. At Frindsbury there was a thriving shipbuilding industry, with several yards building warships for the Navy under contract. The largest of these, Joseph and Thomas Brindley's yard at Quarry House Farm employed 51 shipwrights and apprentices in the early 1800s. Small paper-mills were to be found at Snodland, and at Cobtree Manor, Pratling Street, Forstal and Millhall on the fringes of Aylesford parish. These were effectively a northern extension of the main papermaking district around Maidstone. Other industries were more directly linked to the river Medway and its role as a conduit for trade. There was barge building in Strood, Frindsbury and Aylesford, and oil seed crushing at Maidstone and Frinsbury, using cotton, rape, hemp and linseed imported from the Baltic and Egypt. Strood had two substantial breweries by the early 19th century, one on the High Street, the other on Frindsbury Road.[53]

THE BEGINNINGS OF INDUSTRIALISATION

In the later 18th century, industry in the valley was still on a relatively small scale. At Frindsbury Gouge's map of 1792 shows two shipyards, each set within a chalk quarry along the south side of the peninsula. Inland from the larger of these yards is Quarry House, an early 17th-century red-brick mansion. Other shipyards lined the opposite side and the rest of the ground is marked as arable, pasture or marshland. Much was to change in the succeeding decades.[54]

Brickmaking and lime burning, industries which were later to dominate the valley, were already much in evidence by the late 18th century. By 1800 there were substantial brick fields in the Manor Farm, Whitewall Creek and Upnor areas of Frindsbury, at Temple Farm in Strood and on the Earl of Darnley's land in Cuxton, with smaller-scale operations scattered along the valley wherever there were deposits of brick earth.[55]

Lime burners were also active in the area, although often from a single kiln with associated chalk pit. A number of larger businesses were operating by the 1820s. Messrs Poynder and Hobson were said to be burning 'a very great quantity' of lime at a site on the

border of Snodland and Halling; further to the north Joliffe and
Banks had a substantial works close to Halling village, while on
the opposite bank of the river William Lee had established works
at Burham Court Farm in 1826. To the south George Fowle of
Cobtree Manor had five lime kilns near Pratling Street in Aylesford
by 1815, and two other lime burners were active in the parish.
Another important works was that of Cutbush, Cutbush and Jarvis
who had been operating from a two-acre site at Whornes Place,
Cuxton since 1799.[56]

These activities, many of them small-scale, were possible
because of the rich natural resources of the area. With deep, slow
flowing waters, a muddy bottom and meandering course the river
Medway offered a number of sheltered anchorages ideally suited
for shipbuilding and repair. One of these developed as the Royal
Dockyards at Chatham, but across the river in Frindsbury the
south side of Chatham Ness also afforded a good natural harbour.

Most of the Frindsbury ship and barge builders had their
building slips here, taking advantage of the tidal range which
allowed grounding of vessels for caulking, scraping and other
repairs. Timber to build the ships was available locally from
woodland on the clay soils of the high Downs. Supplies could also
be transported down-river from the heavily wooded Weald.

Further upstream the river and its tributaries provided power
to a number of mills, some grinding corn, others making paper.
Papermakers chose to locate here, on the sandstone ridge north
of Maidstone, due to the purity of the water. Springs and streams
in the area were generally free from mud, pollution or mineral
content that might have discoloured the paper.[57]

The valley also enjoyed a profusion of mineral resources.
Chalk is known to have been excavated by the Romans at various
locations, as was Kentish ragstone around Maidstone and
Aylesford, while the thick deposits of fuller's earth in Boxley were
exploited from at least the 16th century. Quarrying was particularly
important in Aylesford. We know, for instance, that a company of
potters from Lambeth was renting claypits here by 1775, paying
a royalty of 2s. 6d. per ton. Elsewhere in the parish there were
extensive sand, gravel and stone quarries. The white sand quarried
in the area was highly valued by local brickmakers who mixed it
with gault clay, which was also dug from pits in the vicinity.[58]

Most quarrying in the area was for chalk. The Lower Medway
Valley had particular advantages, which encouraged the
development of the industry: easily accessible chalk on the valley
sides and cheap bulk transport by barge along the river Medway.
As early as the 13th century farmers in areas like Frindsbury were
using chalk to improve the fertility of their acidic sandy soils.

Figure 18 The Lower Medway Valley *c.*1820 showing the distribution of industries across the eight riverside parishes. Although the importance of lime burning is already evident, it is the traditional industries of brewing, shipbuilding and papermaking which still dominate.

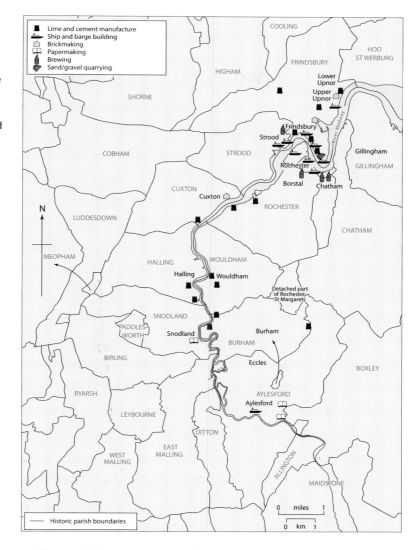

Evidence of their activities can be seen in the substantial number of deneholes that have been identified over the past century. These were deep circular shafts sunk through overlying deposits into the chalk layer, at the bottom of which chambers were excavated in the shape of a double trefoil. Later examples, described as chalkwells, were less skilfully excavated, but remained an important source of chalk for marling (dressing the land to improve soil fertility). A report of 1887 noted that each chalkwell could provide enough to dress eight acres at 800 bushels per acre.[59]

Chalkwells were also dug by lime burners and brickmakers, although much of the quarrying in the valley was conducted at a far larger scale. Philip Boghurst excavated just under 7,000 tons of chalk annually from pits on Chatham Ness between 1756 and 1810. J. and T. Brindley, the shipbuilders, dug a further 52,380 tons between 1810 and 1817. Upstream at Cuxton Thomas Boorman was by 1830 leasing two acres of land from the Earl of Darnley 'with liberty of digging chalk therein'. These larger works were generally located by the riverside, which allowed easy transport of the chalk or lime by barge to distant customers. Edward Jarvis sent consignments of chalk and lime from Whornes Place in Cuxton to Yalding early in the 19th century, while Henry Skinner, a Strood bricklayer, operated a fleet of at least three barges from his quarry at Manor Farm, Frindsbury in 1770.[60]

The main impetus for this expansion of quarrying was the emergence of brick and cement industries in the valley. All the materials needed for the manufacture of bricks and cement – chalk, sand, gravel, brickearth, clay and mud – were found locally in deposits that could be exploited relatively easily. More significantly, these minerals were generally found in close proximity, which minimised transport costs. Cement was made by burning a mixture of chalk and clay at high temperatures and then milling the resulting clinker. At Chatham Ness in Frindsbury chalk was mined from the headland itself, while unlimited supplies of blue Medway mud could be dug from the salt marshes at low tide. Similarly, land at Burham Court Farm was described in 1825 as containing 'an inexhaustible mine of the chalk esteemed the most valuable for making lime', while not far away in Eccles the soil was a 'cold clay'.[61]

Brickmakers were usually able to combine materials excavated at a single location. Many brickfield sites show evidence of chalk quarrying, as yellow London stock bricks were generally produced by adding chalk to clay in order to produce an artificial malm. Henry Everest, who operated the Manor Farm brickfield during the 1830s, dug substantial quantities of chalk from an adjacent field called Chalk Hole Bank, and also leased an area of

Figure 19 A view looking south from Windmill Hill to the Frindsbury Peninsula and Chatham Ness. The photograph clearly shows the dramatic impact on the landscape of mining chalk directly from the headland. In the middle distance, running north to south are the Phoenix, Globe, Bridge, Crown, Quarry and Beaver Cement Works, emphasising the dominance of the Portland cement industry in the valley by the late 19th century.

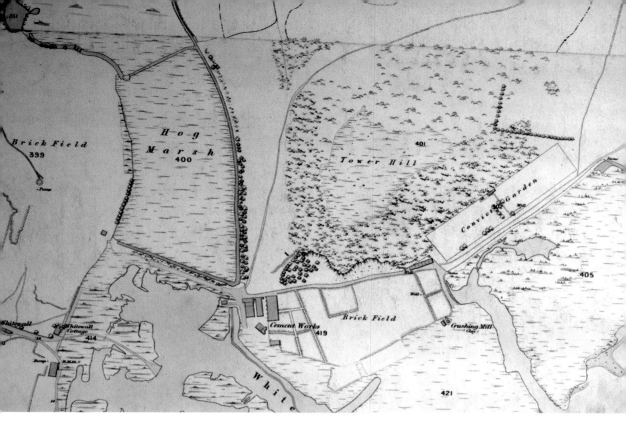

Figure 20 Section of the 1st edition, 25 inch to the mile, Ordnance Survey map of Frindsbury showing part of the Manor Farm brickfield and Whitewall Creek cement works in *c.*1868.

nearby salt marsh to provide mud, which he added to the clay slurry to stop shrinkage during firing. In Aylesford and Burham bricks were made by combining gault clay and sand, and again these were both found locally. When Sittingbourne brickmaker George Smeed leased the Lower Nicopits in Aylesford in 1869, his agreement specified that certain quantities of sand should be provided to brickmakers who, like Smeed, were working on the Earl of Aylesford's land.[62]

Quarrying expanded rapidly from the 1830s with the continued growth of brickmaking and development of important lime and cement industries in the valley. By 1831 there were chalk pits all along the valley from Aylesford to Frindsbury. Those in Snodland employed 26 men over 20 years of age, those in Wouldham 19, and those in Halling more than forty.[63]

INDUSTRY IN THE MID-19TH CENTURY

By the 1850s the pattern of industry in the valley had changed. With the decline of activities such as shipbuilding and papermaking there was now a greater concentration on the manufacture of building materials. In the north of the study area brickmaking continued to prosper in Frindsbury and Strood. Bagshaw's directory of 1847 lists eight brickmakers in

How to make stock bricks

The raw material for brickmaking, the London clays or brick earth, could be found in the Medway and Swale areas in a layer of varying thickness, usually six to 10 feet deep. On the west bank of the Medway suitable deposits for brickmaking existed between Upnor and Cuxton, with occasional deeper pockets which could be exploited as earth holes. The brick earth was won by first stripping the topsoil, which would be stored for eventual replacement. A 'heading' was dug into the clay wide enough to take a cart or narrow track to run side-tipping trucks. The brick earth was hand-dug using forks or spades during the winter months, often by the brickmaking gangs.

On small sites the clay was loaded onto horse drawn carts to be taken to a washmill where it was turned into a slurry and any stones removed. Ground chalk was added if London stock bricks were to be made, with the amount of chalk in the mixture affecting the colour. To get the required shade of yellow for a stock brick the usual mix was something like 85-90% clay and 10-15% chalk.

The mixture was then pumped into washbacks formed by earth banks lined with bricks, or as later at Burham with concrete shuttering. The slurry was left to settle for six to nine months, often over winter, while the excess water ran off and the slurry dried the right amount for brickmaking.

Access to the washback was via a shuttered entrance of thick boards slotted into grooves each side. These were removed and the clay dug from the washback by men using a 'cuckle', a three-pronged fork with a blade across the bottom. Clay was loaded onto a truck and taken to a pug mill, initially horse powered but later powered by a portable steam engine, to prepare it for the brick moulder. Ash containing particles of unburnt coal and coke was added to provide fuel during burning. The ash was obtained by sieving refuse, known as 'rough stuff', brought by barge from London.

The brickmaking season was reckoned to be from the beginning of April until the end of October. Each brick gang consisted of six men led by the moulder.

Figure A   *Brickmaking by hand in 1821.*

Figure B   *Brickmaking gang, 'Clover Lay', Rainham, 1890.*

One man made sure that there was sufficient pugged clay available while the next cut enough clay to make one brick, rolled it in sand to stop the clay sticking in the mould and passed it to the moulder. The moulder pushed the clay into a wooden mould which also had been dusted with sand and struck off excess clay by running a 'striker' across the top of the mould. The third member of the team removed the bricks from the moulding bench. These were then loaded onto a long one-wheeled 'crowding' barrow, and wheeled by the next gang member to the drying hacks. The hacks consisted of covered stands on which the green bricks were left to air dry.

When the bricks had dried a further gang would build a clamp. Rows of bricks would be laid on edge about a brick width apart and the channels formed filled with coke. The clamp was built up to some

12 feet, and the sides and top covered with already burnt bricks. The finished clamp was fired and might take several weeks to burn through, depending on the strength of the wind. Once burnt through a sorting gang would dismantle the clamp, and grade and stack the bricks. The best ones were usually half way into the clamp, and, if even and a good yellow, were used as facing bricks. Bricks from the outside of the clamp were generally less well burnt and classified for use in interior walls. Over burnt bricks of an orange brown hue were used for footings, and those which had fused and vitrified were fit only for use as hardcore or garden walls. Totally under-burnt bricks, often from the edge of the clamp, were discarded. Distribution to markets was mostly by sailing barge, the 'brickies' being the most cost effective means of shifting a high bulk, low value cargo.

the area, and 200 brick workers are recorded in the 1861 census. Larger producers included J. Foord and Sons operating from Ten Gun Field in Upnor and Henry Everest, who had several brickfields around Temple Farm in Strood. Everest produced over 7.7 million bricks here in the 1845 season.[64]

Around Aylesford and Burham the 'good white brick earth' noted in earlier estate surveys was also now being fully exploited. There were at least four substantial brick fields here including the highly mechanised works at Burham, established in 1852 by Thomas Cubitt, the great building contractor, developer of Belgravia and architect of Osborne House, Queen Victoria's home on the Isle of Wight. Another major employer in the area was the 'very extensive brown stone pottery' of Edward Ladd Betts, the owner of Preston Hall, which lay half a mile east of Aylesford church. Lime burning continued to prosper with new works appearing on both sides of the Medway.[65]

During the 1850s many of these works started to manufacture cement, which was increasingly in demand for public works and house building. Early innovators included George Burge on Chatham Ness in Frindsbury, William Lee at Snodland and Boorman, Wild and Co., who had taken over from Cutbush and Jarvis at Whornes Place. There was also a small cement works at Burham alongside Cubitt's brickworks, and two in Wouldham run by Thomas Freen and Co. and William Peters.[66]

Figure 21 A view of the cement works at Burham in 1859. This lay to the south of Cubitt's mechanised brickworks, and grew in importance later in the century. The house in the background, Rose Villa, was occupied by the works' foreman, William Varney.

Figure 22 The Lower Medway Valley *c*.1865 showing the distribution of industries across the eight riverside parishes. By the middle of the 19th century, London's demand for building materials had changed the focus of industrial production along the Medway. Brickmaking and lime and cement manufacture were increasing steadily, while the brewing and shipbuilding industries were in sharp decline.

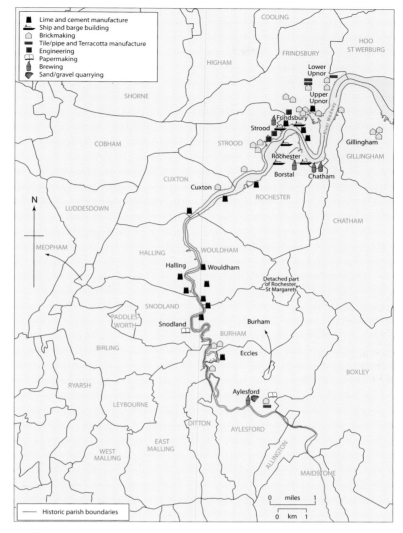

To local observers these changes were a wonder to behold. An 1859 account of the Burham brickworks focused on the revolutionary layout of the site, which made use of tramways to links each stage of production. 'Nothing', the author suggested

strikes the visitor to these works more than the substantial character of everything on the estate … On viewing the whole field, with its various and numerous engines, buildings, tramways, kilns, wharves, etc, one cannot but see that here are what may be justly termed the model brick-works. Here are concentrated the results of near half a century's experience and improvements. Everything is in the right place. Nothing superfluous. Every possible attention has been given to

Figure 23   Quarry House in Frindsbury shortly before its demolition in 1897. This fine Jacobean house was once a sought-after residence offering spectacular views across the Medway to Chatham and Rochester. By the 1890s, however, it was surrounded on all sides by the expanding quarries of the nearby cement works, and soon to be sacrificed for the chalk on which it lay.

economise labour and material, and every advantage taken of the natural position of the estate.[67]

A similar tone can be found in other accounts from this period. Snodland was praised for its 'extensive lime works' which supply 'an immense quantity' to the metropolis, while the 3.5km Higham and Strood tunnel was considered an engineering wonder of its time. Tallis commented that, 'The tunnel is so perfectly straight, that a person placed at one end, may discern a small light entering at the other.'[68]

The example of Frindsbury peninsula illustrates the extent to which the landscape of the valley had been transformed by industry over the preceding half century. Gouge's map of 1792 shows two shipyards, each set within a chalk quarry along the south side of the peninsula. Inland from the larger of these yards is Quarry House, an early 17th-century red-brick mansion, with extensive grounds, known as the Warren, and an associated farm. The rest of the ground is marked as arable, pasture or marshland. By the time of the tithe survey in 1840 industry was more in evidence: a chalk pit had been opened in a field south of the parish church, and, to the west of this, Strood Dock and its associated wharves indicated the presence of the Thames and Medway Canal. Further down the peninsula were the boat building slips of John Curel, and beyond them the ballast wharf and lime works of Edward Cole. An oil mill close to Quarry House, and a row of cottages at Gridiron Wharf were shown, while, east of Manor Farm, Henry Everest had established an extensive brickfield.[69]

The first detailed Ordnance Survey map of the area in 1864 revealed continued industrial development. The lime works and their associated quarry had been extended northwards towards Curel's boatyard, while a cement works, established by I.C. Johnson and George Burge in 1851, occupied the site of the earlier oil seed mill. Development of the area around Strood Dock had continued apace, with a small cement works located on one side and a railway goods yard on the other. The brickfield near Manor Farm had prospered, with a tramway now linking the different parts of the site, while a further brickfield and cement works had been established on the other side of Whitewall Creek. What had been a predominantly rural landscape was now dominated by industry.

THE LATER 19TH CENTURY

Changes to landscape, economy and society accelerated in the later 19th century. By now the Portland cement industry had assumed a dominant position in terms of both output and employment, with more than 25 works spread across the Lower Medway Valley. The

Figure 24 The machine shop at Aveling and Porter's works at Strood in 1907. From 1861 the company manufactured steam locomotives, agricultural machinery, and a range of other products.

greatest concentration were the seven strung out along Limehouse Reach in Frindsbury. By 1898 the industry produced around 15,000 tons of cement a week, paid out £6,000 in wages and provided 'constant employment' for over 300 barges.[70]

Cement manufacturing was not the only growth sector during the second half of the 19th century. The success of the industry created opportunities for a number of related businesses, most notably barge building and engineering. Many barges were built in the Medway towns. Curels had two sites, one adjoining the Railway Tavern in Canal Road, Strood, the other next to the Phoenix cement works in Frindsbury: this had formerly been the Brindleys shipyard until their bankruptcy around 1820. Other barge builders of note included W.B. Little at Lower Upnor and Cheetham, and Gill and Co. in Frindsbury. A number of cement manufacturers also set up their own barge yards including the Burham Brick Lime and Cement Co. at Burham and William Lee and Sons at Halling.[71]

Engineering firms and iron foundries, many specialising in the production of machinery for the brick and cement industries, were found mainly in the Medway towns. The largest was that of Aveling and Porter, who manufactured steam locomotives, agricultural machinery and a range of other products from a large works in Strood from 1861. Another Strood firm, Collis and Stace, specialised in cement grinding mills, while the Eagle Iron Works in Strood and Frindsbury Ironworks of W.R. Curel produced a range of machinery.[72]

Brickmaking remained important, particularly in Frindsbury, Strood and Aylesford, although the industry was in decline by 1900 due to competition from cheaper Fletton bricks produced in the Peterborough area.

All this activity is clear from the second edition of the Ordnance Survey map in 1897. Much of Windmill Hill had been quarried away,

The Development of
the Frindsbury Peninsula

'The English landscape itself, to those who know how to read it aright, is the richest historical record we possess'. In his seminal 1955 volume; *The Making of the English Landscape*, W.G. Hoskins claimed that the landscape around us could be read like a document and that the layers of human occupation could be metaphorically peeled back to understand the landscapes of past generations. But whereas a field archaeologist can literally read the stratigraphic layers exposed during excavations, a landscape archaeologist must rely on the ability to interpret discrete features, separating them from the events which have subsequently altered the historic environment.

For example, while it is possible to discern medieval ridge and furrow within a landscape transformed by Parliamentary Enclosure or identify stretches of Roman road within the modern network, it is not always possible to reconstruct the industrial landscapes of 18th- and 19th-century England. This is often due to the dramatic changes to the landscape and is especially true of the extractive industries, coal mining and quarrying. These destroy the historic landscape and replace it with an artificial one of pits and spoil heaps, accompanied by functional structures or the remnants of them.

The landscape archaeologist has to use a different approach when faced with interpreting a post-industrial landscape. He or she is reliant on maps to help interpret the changes. The first step is to survey the existing landscape, and then relate it to relevant maps, or draw the maps, in a process known as 'map regression'. Landscape features, places and boundaries are identified and located, producing a sequential explanation of landscape development in reverse. Crucial evidence is provided by the first and second editions of the Ordnance Survey. The Ordnance Survey, established in 1791 to undertake a comprehensive survey of England, had by 1855 surveyed the entire United Kingdom at a scale of six inches to the mile, a scale replaced in 1854 by 25 inches to the mile. In 1891 a revision of the maps at both scales was begun, and it is the comparison between first edition and first revision which provide snapshots of the landscape during the middle and end of the 19th century.

The development of the landscape can be traced further back than the Ordnance Survey maps by using tithe maps and estate maps. The Tithe Commutation Act of 1836 which converted the medieval system of tithe payments into a tithe rent charge, resulted in detailed survey of all parishes in England and Wales. A tithe map for each parish showed the boundaries of the tithe district and the constituent parcels of land to be apportioned. Estate maps, on which some tithe maps were based, were produced from the late 16th century as a method of detailing landowners' estates. They generally depicted field or landholding boundaries, with the more detailed examples showing the location of individual buildings.

The four maps opposite show how a map regression has been used to chart the industrial development of the Frindsbury Peninsula during the 19th century. The maps are based on the Frindsbury tithe map of 1842, with early features and field boundaries located using an estate map of 1792. The first edition six inch to the mile Ordnance Survey map, Kent sheet XIX 001, published in 1869 has been compared with the first revision of the same map, Kent sheets XIX north-east and north-west to chart the major developments of the late 19th century.

The first map shows a landscape of c.1800 which is experiencing the early stages of industrial change. The isolated parish church and dispersed farms are joined in the landscape by small scale quarrying, brick manufacture and boat building. By the time of the tithe award in the 1840s, the Manor Brickfield has been dramatically expanded and a limeworks and quarry have replaced the shipyard at Quarry Farm. Frindsbury Peninsula recorded by the Ordnance Survey is a hive of industrial activity. The expansion of the Manor Brickfield has continued, while the first of the peninsula's cement works have also been established. The canal has been replaced by the railway and tramways for transporting materials have begun to appear. By c.1900 the Frinsbury Peninsula is fully industrialised. No fewer than seven cement works line the bank of the Medway as cement manufacture becomes the dominant concern in the area. Tramways criss-cross the landscape connecting the works to piers and quarries and the once dominant Manor Brickfield is now abandoned.

Further Reading

Hoskins, W.G., *The Making of the English Landscape* (1955).
Royal Historical Society Guides and Handbooks, No. 18, *Historians' Guide to Early British Maps* (1994).

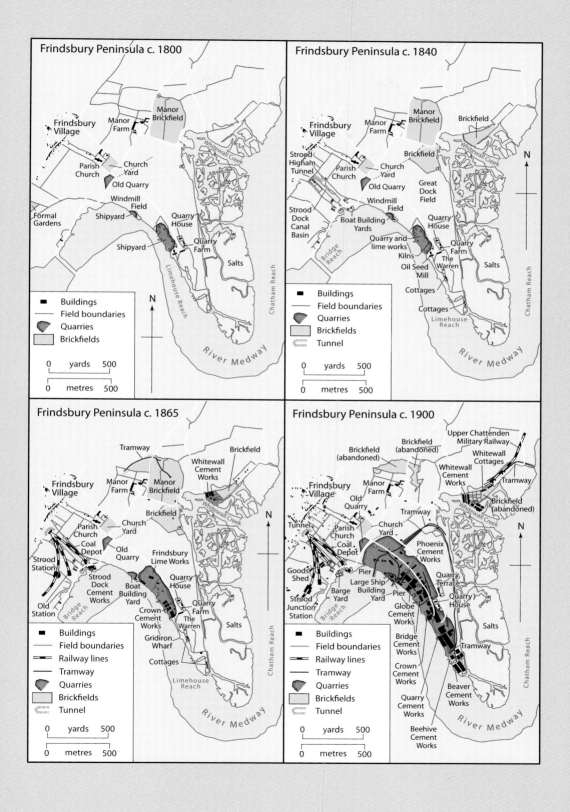

Frindsbury Peninsula c. 1800

Frindsbury Village · Manor Farm · Manor Brickfield · Whitewall Creek · Parish Church · Church Yard · Old Quarry · Windmill Field · Formal Gardens · Shipyard · Quarry House · Quarry Farm · Shipyard · Salts · Limehouse Reach · Chatham Reach · River Medway

Buildings
Field boundaries
Quarries
Brickfields

N

0   yards   500
0   metres   500

Frindsbury Peninsula c. 1840

Frindsbury Village · Manor Farm · Manor Brickfield · Brickfield · Whitewall Creek · Strood Higham Tunnel · Parish Church · Church Yard · Old Quarry · Brickfield · Great Dock Field · Strood Dock Canal Basin · Windmill Field · Boat Building Yards · Quarry and lime works · Quarry House · Quarry Farm · Kilns · The Warren · Oil Seed Mill · Salts · Bridge Reach · Cottages · Cottages · Limehouse Reach · Chatham Reach · River Medway

N

Buildings
Field boundaries
Quarries
Brickfields
Tunnel

0   yards   500
0   metres   500

Frindsbury Peninsula c. 1865

Tramway · Brickfield · Whitewall Cement Works · Frindsbury Village · Manor Farm · Manor Brickfield · Whitewall Creek · Brickfield · Parish Church · Church Yard · Coal Depot · Old Quarry · Strood Station · Strood Dock Cement Works · Boat Building Yard · Frindsbury Lime Works · Quarry House · Old Station · Bridge Reach · Crown Cement Works · Quarry Farm · The Warren · Salts · Gridiron Wharf · Cottages · Limehouse Reach · Chatham Reach · River Medway

N

Buildings
Field boundaries
Railway lines
Tramway
Quarries
Brickfields
Tunnel

0   yards   500
0   metres   500

Frindsbury Peninsula c. 1900

Upper Chattenden Military Railway · Brickfield (abandoned) · Brickfield (abandoned) · Whitewall Cottages · Whitewall Cement Works · Tramway · Brickfield (abandoned) · Frindsbury Village · Manor Farm · Old Quarry · Whitewall Creek · Tramway · Tunnel · Parish Church · Church Yard · Phoenix Cement Works · Coal Depot · Goods Shed · Pier · Quarry Terrace · Large Ship Building Yard · Quarry House · Strood Junction Station · Barge Yard · Pier · Bridge Reach · Globe Cement Works · Salts · Bridge Cement Works · Tramway · Crown Cement Works · Quarry Cement Works · Beaver Cement Works · Beehive Cement Works · Chatham Reach · River Medway

N

Buildings
Field boundaries
Railway lines
Tramway
Quarries
Brickfields
Tunnel

0   yards   500
0   metres   500

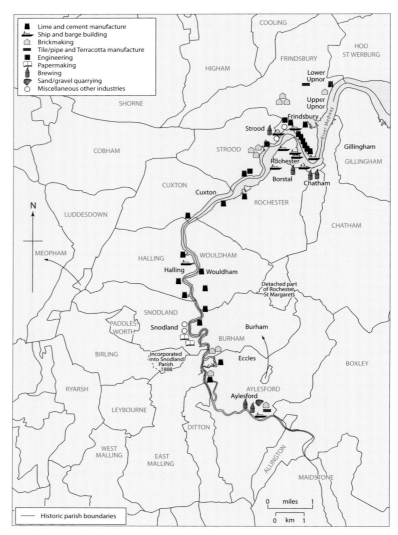

Figure 25　The Lower Medway Valley *c.*1900 showing the distribution of industries across the eight riverside parishes. As the 20th century dawned, cement manufacture had become the main industry in the valley with plants located throughout the study area parishes and especially concentrated in Frindsbury. Also clear from this map is the concentration of papermaking in Snodland by the late 19th century.

and a line of seven cement works occupied most of the shoreline between Curel's boatyard and the tip of the peninsula. The Warren had gone, too, though Quarry House remained, marooned on top of a pedestal of chalk within the quarried area. The map also reveals an elaborate system of tramways linking each works to the quarry, and expansion at Whitewall Creek cement works, although the neighbouring brickfields appear to have been abandoned.

CATALYSTS FOR INDUSTRIAL DEVELOPMENT

How best can we explain what happened in the Lower Medway Valley during these years? The most obvious starting point is to think in terms of proximity to London. The location of the valley relative to London, and the role of the river as a conduit gave the area an advantage over other parts of the country with similar resources. Demand from the capital supported the diverse industrial base in the region. Most of the bricks, cement, paper, and seed oil from the valley were consumed here. Over time, proximity to London also contributed to the growing specialisation in the manufacture of building materials. Water transport was most cost effective for such low value, bulky commodities, leaving the Thames and Medway valleys better placed to serve this vast market than competing producers at inland sites. Bagshaw noted that the metropolis had at one time been supplied with lime principally from Dorking in Surrey, but by the 1840s received 'immense quantities' from Lee's limeworks in Snodland. This continued to be the case even after the advent of the railways because of the lower freight rates.[73]

The Thames and Medway had a virtual monopoly of Portland cement manufacture until the 1870s when a few producers in other parts of the country began to enter the market. Even in 1900 some 80 per cent of cement was produced here, and a significant proportion of the national output of bricks came from north Kent.[74]

The importance of the London market is emphasised by the fact that the fortunes of the brick and cement industries fluctuated in sequence with the London house-building cycle. A building boom during the 1870s coincided with an expansion of the Medway cement industry: new works were established by Messrs Hilton, Anderson and Co. at Halling Manor (1878); and by the West Kent Gault Brick and Cement Co. in Aylesford and Burham (1876), while existing works, such as Whornes Place, expanded. The subsequent depression in the building trades from the late 1880s coincided with a slump in output and a number of bankruptcies, including that of John Adams at the Wickham works in Strood, and the Medway Portland Cement Co. Ltd in nearby Cuxton. This same period also saw the closure of a number of brickfields in Frindsbury, Gillingham and Rainham.[75]

Government Policy

The government played an important role in determining the course of change in the valley, not least because of its massive investment in the dockyards at Chatham. Shipbuilding at Frindsbury developed as a direct result of the Admiralty sub-contracting work under wartime conditions, while the royal dockyards were occupied mainly in maintenance and repairs. Once sub-contracting ended after the defeat of Napoleon in 1815 the industry went into rapid decline, leading to the bankruptcy of several shipbuilders including Joseph and Thomas Brindley in about 1820. By 1841 only seven shipwrights appeared in the census listings for Frindsbury and Strood.

Many brickfields and lime and cement works were also established by government contractors, or owed their success to fulfilling contract work. Brickmaking at Manor Farm, Frindsbury expanded dramatically after Henry Everest contracted to make eight million bricks for a Mr Nicholson, while J. Foord and Sons of Rochester acquired Ten Gun Field in Upnor in order to meet the needs of various government departments with whom they had local maintenance contracts. Similarly, William Lee, who owned limeworks in Burham and then Snodland and Halling, was the son of a Lewisham building contractor, and George Burge, a partner in the first cement works on Limehouse Reach in 1851, had worked as an engineer under Telford during the building of St Katherine's docks.[76]

The development of Roman and then Portland cement was itself driven largely by the need for a reliable waterproof cement for large civil engineering projects such as harbours, tunnels, and lighthouses. The military also played a role in its development, with Lieut-Col Charles Pasley of the Royal Engineers conducting some of the earliest scientific tests on different types of cement to determine their relative cohesiveness and durability.[77]

Government taxation policy also had an impact on the industries of the valley. The high tax on bricks, which amounted to around 20 per cent of their price, acted as a discouragement to brick building until it was lifted in 1850. Similarly, a reduction in customs duties as the country moved towards free trade at the end of the 19th century, provided opportunities to expand into foreign markets: by the 1890s cement from the Medway was being exported not only to Europe, but also to the USA, Argentina, Australia, South Africa and India.[78]

Of course this was a two-way process which also exposed local manufacturers to overseas competition. Writing of cement manufacture in 1895, G.R. Redgrave noted that

> The supremacy we have long enjoyed has undoubtedly been to some extent wrested from us by the products of Continental industry and enterprise, and in the absence of some limited action and intelligent leading, our manufacturers are threatened with a competition they are not adequately armed to encounter.[79]

Technology

Another important driver of change was technology, impacting particularly on the two main industries of the valley, lime and cement manufacture and papermaking. Each industry witnessed substantial improvements in the quality of its products, numerous innovations in production processes took place, and investment in mechanisation reduced labour costs and increased output.

Cement The development of Roman and then Portland cement involved a good deal of experimentation by pioneers such as James Parker, William Aspdin and I.C. Johnson. Subsequently the success of the industry depended on improving the consistency of the product. Portland cement had not initially been widely adopted by building contractors as it varied greatly in quality due to rule of thumb methods used in mixing the slurry and in the amount of fuel used. When plans were made to extend Chatham Dockyard in 1867 'so little confidence was placed in Portland cement that the material was not even mentioned in the contract specifications; grey stone lime, blue lias lime, and pozzalano being specified for all descriptions of mortar and concrete'.[80]

The unreliability of the product almost certainly contributed to the failure of many of the early firms such as Thomas Freen and Co. of Wouldham who filed for bankruptcy in 1855. By the 1860s more rigorous testing was introduced, backed up by scientific research. Much of the early testing was conducted by Mr John Grant for the Metropolitan Board of Works between 1859 and 1871. Cement works recognised the value of having their own testing rooms. The 1901 census lists 20 chemists working in the area. The recognised tests for Portland cement were its weight per bushel, the fineness of the powder, its colour and tensile strength. It was now widely regarded as the most valuable building material with a multitude of uses from foundation work to fireproofing.[81]

Efforts to improve the quality of cement were aided by incremental advances in the production process, with a series of changes to plant and equipment design during the second half of the 19th century. The usual method of making cement in the 1850s was set out by Edwin Harris in his description of the works at Strood Dock:

There were a number of conical shaped kilns in which the cement was baked; these kilns were nearest the mouth of the basin. Beyond these the ground had been dug out in the form of dripping pans, and from the works ran a number of dripping gutters, in an inclined direction towards those dripping pans. The cement, in liquid form ran down these troughs, looking like pure milk. When one of these squares was full, the fluid was diverted to another. This was left for several days until it began to harden; its colour used to change, with dust and soot, until it became a kind of ashen grey. As it dried cracks and fissures were observable on the surface. Then, men, with puddlers' spades, dug out these pans and loaded into wheelbarrows, which were wheeled on planks into the kilns. Fires were lighted, and the cement baked until the fires dried out; it was then taken to the grinding mills and ground into fine powder.[82]

The whole process from mixing the clay and chalk in a wash-mill to packing the cement into barrels for despatch to market took between three to four months, with the firing of the kiln occupying five to six days. Most of the stages of production were done by hand making this a very labour intensive exercise (Panel 5).

Over the following decades innovatory activity was focussed on three key issues: how to speed up production, cut labour costs and reduce fuel consumption. One early development involved passing the slurry through millstones so that it could be pumped straight to drying floors without the need for settling. This effected a saving in both time and labour. Another innovation pioneered by Thomas Sturge at Northfleet during the 1860s was the use of hot gases from the kilns to heat the drying floor. Further improvements were achieved by the introduction of chamber kilns from the 1870s. Technological advances also took place in grinding plant led by Medway firms such as Collis and Stace, and Taylor and Neate.[83]

Revolutionary change, however, came to the industry only in the 1890s with the introduction of the continuous kiln, which used 50 per cent less fuel as the heat loss incurred during cooling and unloading was eliminated. The most successful design was the rotary kiln introduced from the United States of America. Between 1900 and 1905 over £550,000 was invested in the cement industry of the Thames and Medway, with most of this going on the installation of rotary kilns.

Among the works to benefit from this new technology were Martin Earle and Co. of Halling and the Crown works in

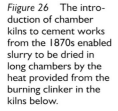

Fiigure 26   The introduction of chamber kilns to cement works from the 1870s enabled slurry to be dried in long chambers by the heat provided from the burning clinker in the kilns below.

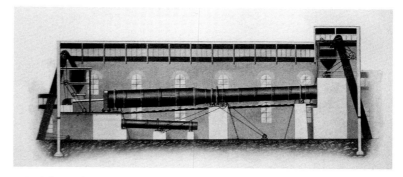

Figure 27 Diagram of a rotary kiln and cooler. This device was essentially an inclined iron cylinder which was lined with fire bricks and rotated slowly. Liquid slurry was pumped into the upper end, heated with powdered coal injected into the cylinder, and the clinker was collected from the opening at the bottom.

Frindsbury, both of which were modern plants, well located with access to large reserves of chalk and clay. The impact of these changes was to consolidate the industry, an essential move in the early 1900s when the Medway producers faced increased competition both at home and abroad.

Modernisation of plant impacted significantly on the structure and organisation of the lime and cement industry. The lime burners of the early 19th century were mostly independent entrepreneurs or small partnerships. Most works employed no more than 20-30 labourers. Similarly the early cement works were small-scale enterprises. Smetham estimates that the output of Burge's pioneer plant at Limehouse Reach was only 50 to 60 tons per week, and that of the Strood Docks works of Larke and White no more than 160 tons per week.[84]

New technology served to increase the scale of production and encourage consolidation. Each development tended to be more costly than the last, requiring ever greater capital investment, which only the more successful manufacturers could afford. Consequently, by the 1880s production was dominated by the larger firms, some of which operated a number of separate plants. The Burham works had an output of 1,000 tons per week from 36 chamber kilns by 1888. Even outdated works were able to survive, and many of the larger works retained outdated beehive kilns and grinding equipment. At Peter's works in Wouldham a row of 17 early beehive kilns dating from the 1860s was still in use around 1900.[85]

The shake-out came after 1900 with the establishment of the Associated Portland Cement Manufacturers combine (APCM) under conditions of growing competition and a depressed market. By 1918, 15 of the 25 cement works in the valley had closed and over 90 per cent of cement production in the Thames and Medway region was in the hands of the combine or its subsidiaries.[86]

Papermaking The other industry to be affected by technological change was papermaking. It had been transformed in the later

Figure 28 The stamping engine at a paper-mill was used to reduce rags to pulped fibres suitable for papermaking. Early examples such as this relied on water power and had often been converted from fulling mills previously used in the Kentish woollen industry.

17th century when skilled Huguenot papermakers introduced improved techniques enabling the manufacture of fine white paper to become established in the Maidstone area. As the technology involved was relatively simple most of the mills remained small. The only substantial piece of equipment needed was a beating or stamping machine to break down the rags from which paper was made until the fibres were separated. Pratling Street mill in Aylesford was typical in having only one of these machines in 1851.[87]

The second period of innovation in papermaking came in the early 19th century when mechanisation transformed the prospects of the industry. The introduction of Foudrinier machines allowed the making of continuous sheets of paper instead of separate sheets in moulds. This cut production time for each sheet from three weeks to three minutes. Across the country mechanisation proceeded relatively slowly due to the costs of installation, but the consequence was clear enough: a reduction in the number of mills along with a significant increase in output.[88]

This concentration of production saw the closure of the smaller mills in the Medway valley during the 1830s and 1840s. Frequent changes of occupier and a number of bankruptcies attest to the difficulties they encountered in trying to compete with larger producers such as William Joynson at St Mary Cray and Balston's Springfield Mill in Maidstone. By mid-century only two mills remained: at Pratling Street where George Mason employed 'many hands in the manufacture of millboard and brown paper, and at Snodland where William Wildes had a workforce of 13 men, 39 women and four boys.[89]

Only Snodland mill continued to prosper into the 20th century due partly to its advantageous position along the banks of the Medway, but also to a constant cycle of modernisation. As early as 1834 the lease taken out by Buckinghamshire papermaker, Reuben Hunt, specified that he was to erect 'with all convenient speed two cast iron rag engines with a steam engine of 10 h.p … also to erect a four feet paper engine with drying cylinders driven by a 4 h.p. steam engine' at a total cost of £1,500. By 1838 there were four rag beaters, one rag cutter, a paper machine and large pair of mill board rollers all powered by steam engines.

By 1840, a new tenant, John Clark, planned further improvements including 'a new high and low pressure steam engine of 20 horse power', four new rag engines and a new paper machine with drying cylinders, but he was declared bankrupt in

Figure 29 Detail from the assignment of the lease of the Snodland papermill by Reuben Hunt to John Clark in July 1838. The lease includes a plan of the mill, detailing the location of the cast iron rag engines, a 10-horse power steam engine and a paper engine that Hunt had been charged with installing when he took the lease in 1834.

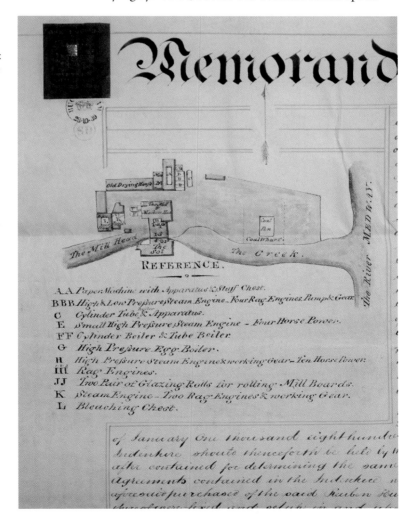

September that year, emphasising the precarious nature of the business. The mill was operative again shortly afterwards, and in 1851 was managed by William Wildes, aged only 26, who employed 13 men, 39 women, and four boys.[90]

The period of greatest expansion came after 1854 when Charles Townsend Hook took over the business. Hook updated the machinery, and sought to make improvements to the production process. Conscious of the growing shortage of rags he experimented with a variety of new raw materials including reeds, straw and esparto grass, applying for a series of patents for his inventions. Straw proved the most successful and Hook set up a straw boiling plant at the works. By the time of his death in 1877 there were three paper machines, and in 1882 output stood at more than 90 tons of paper per week.[91]

Progress during this period is reflected in the increasing numbers of hands employed: a total of 100 in 1861 (66 men, 18 women and 16 boys), 120 in 1867 and 200 in 1874. Hook's death did little to slow growth; under a capable new manager, Lt.-Col. T.J. Holland, employee numbers rose to 250 in 1878, and 350 in 1882. Thereafter the number of employees levelled off, but production continued to expand.[92]

Structure and Organisation

One final factor that helped steer the course of industrial development in the Medway valley was the structure and organisation of the industries themselves. Around 1800 most brickmakers were small operators with maybe a handful of workmen, yet by mid-century some of the larger firms had over 300 employees: the Burham Brick and Cement Company employed 577 people and had an output of half a million bricks per week. Evidence from the census suggests that average business size across the whole range of industries rose from eight to 12 employees between 1861 and 1881. Larger firms were more able to invest in new premises or machinery, and had better access to lucrative contract work and to distant markets through building up business contacts and brand recognition.[93]

In the cement industry Martin Earle's 'Rhinoceros' brand and Trechmann, Weekes & Co's 'Goliath' brand were two of the most highly regarded, while the brands of oil produced at Stewart Brothers and Spencer's large seed crushing mill in Strood were 'known throughout Britain and in various foreign markets for their sterling character and uniformly reliable quality'. Additionally the more successful firms usually had a London office to deal with potential customers, and were often early adopters of new

Figure 30 Badge of the 'Goliath' brand of Portland cement produced by Trechmann, Weekes & Co.

communications technology such as the telegraph and telephone. From the mid-19th century many also organised themselves as limited companies with shareholders.[94]

Mergers and takeovers were commonplace amongst all the leading industries in the valley, furthering the cause of consolidation. In the brewing trade there were 14 businesses operating in 1840, but only five by the 1890s, as the coming of the railways opened the Medway valley up to competition from the big industrial brewers such as Guinness and Bass.[95]

In brickmaking growing pressure from cheaper Fletton bricks led to consolidation of the Medway industry during the 1880s, with five leading firms including Butcher's of Frindsbury merging under the Eastwoods banner.[96]

The most systematic consolidation was in the cement industry. Already by the 1880s there were a number of key firms operating from several sites in the area. Hilton, Anderson and Brooks had works at Upnor, Halling, Faversham and Grays in Essex, while John Bazley White and Brothers had expanded from their original base in Swanscombe to Greenhithe, Frindsbury and Gillingham.[97]

By the 1890s severe competitive pressures in the industry led to efforts to amalgamate all manufacturers in the Thames and Medway region, co-ordinated by the financier Henry Osborne O'Hagan. This resulted in the establishment of Associated Portland Cement Manufacturers (APCM) in 1900, incorporating 27 companies.

Further consolidation occurred in 1911 with the creation of British Portland Cement Manufacturers (BPCM) as a subsidiary of APCM, bringing in many of the firms who had chosen to remain outside the original combine. The two companies controlled between them 75 per cent of the UK cement industry.[98]

Another structural feature which particularly benefited the more substantial businesses in the Lower Medway Valley was agglomeration, the process of clustering together related firms. The valley contained not only a large concentration of brick and cement works, but many related businesses supplying them with equipment and services. The most important of these were barge building and engineering.

Both prospered in the Medway valley because of the business that the brick and cement works generated for them. By 1881 there were over 1000 vessels of under 50 tons registered at Rochester, most of which would have been barges engaged in the building material trade. Many of these were built in the Lower Medway Valley, often by the brickmakers or cement manufacturers themselves.

Various different designs of barge were produced, each adapted to a particular task: stumpies, which worked the cement trade,

had short masts to contend with the numerous bridges on the
higher reaches of the river Thames; muddies had low sides to allow
loading of mud from the Medway marshes and brickies had large
holds which could accommodate 40-45,000 bricks.[99]

Engineering firms relied heavily on business from the brick and
cement industries during the 19th century, although they later
diversified into road vehicles, aviation and consumer products.
Advertisements from the period make the close association between
the two sectors clear. The Eagle Iron Works, for instance, described
their engines as being 'suitable for cement manufacturers, millers,
brewers, agriculturalists, and for pumping and sawing'.[100]

The benefits of having these related industries in close proximity
were considerable. It helped generate networks between customers
and suppliers, facilitated the sharing of knowledge and expertise,
created a fertile environment for innovation and provided the area
with a pool of skilled labour. Engineers were able to work with
brickmakers to develop new machinery or modify existing designs
to suit local conditions.

EMPLOYMENT

Earnings in industry were generally higher than those in
agriculture. Farm wages rarely exceeded 14s. per week before the
late 19th century, whereas a young man could earn as much as 25s.
to 30s. a week as a labourer in the brickfields by the 1860s. Wages
were also higher in craft occupations and the building trades.
Philip Skinner, for instance, received 8s. a week plus board and
lodging when hired by an Aylesford wheelwright and blacksmith

in 1800. Similarly, in his settlement examination James Goldsmith recalled that as a young man in the 1820s he had worked for a Boxley bricklayer for 'a guinea a week and garden stuff and lodging', later living out for a weekly wage of 24s. In 1836 William Morgan, a Maidstone builder, was paying his bricklayers 5s., and his labourers 3s. a day.[101]

Wage differentials between agriculture and industry became important from the mid-19th century as industry expanded. Wages in brickmaking and cement ranged from 24s. to 36s. per week by the 1880s, and even better money could be had in the paper-mills around Maidstone, and the shipyards and engineering workshops of the Medway towns. At the steam engine builders, Aveling and Porter, a skilled pattern-maker could earn as much as 40s. per week, while ordinary labourers in the dockyards received 12s. to 15s. per week. Faced with these real alternatives to agricultural employment, many labourers left the land in the final decades of the century producing acute labour shortages. It was this shortage of manpower that encouraged farmers to invest so heavily in mechanisation at the close of our period.[102]

Some industries had a clear hierarchy of skilled, semi-skilled and unskilled workers. This could lead to rather complex pay scales and job demarcations. In papermaking there were three different categories of worker: the skilled and semi-skilled men responsible for the main production process; women engaged in rag-cutting and sorting; and children employed in sundry tasks about the mill. Within each of these broad categories were further gradations. From a document drawn up at a meeting of Kentish mill owners in 1803 we know that skilled workers such as vatmen and couchers were paid different rates depending on the type and size of paper

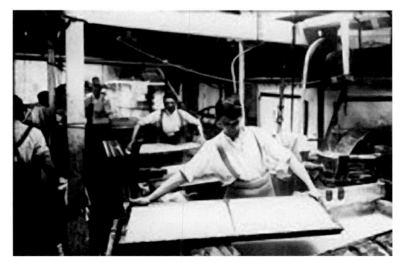

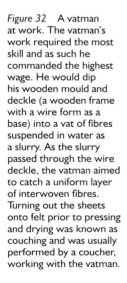

Figure 32 A vatman at work. The vatman's work required the most skill and as such he commanded the highest wage. He would dip his wooden mould and deckle (a wooden frame with a wire form as a base) into a vat of fibres suspended in water as a slurry. As the slurry passed through the wire deckle, the vatman aimed to catch a uniform layer of interwoven fibres. Turning out the sheets onto felt prior to pressing and drying was known as couching and was usually performed by a coucher, working with the vatman.

they produced. Beer was also provided or 1s. per week allowed instead, and overtime was paid at full rates. For a vatman in class I this could mean a weekly wage of 38s. 8d. in 1840 and 44s. in 1865 at a time when agricultural labourers were earning little more than 17s. a week. These wage levels reflected both the skills of the papermakers and the strength of their trade union, the Original Society of Papermakers.[103]

Rag cutters were paid by the piece, with children from 11 to 13 earning about 4s. per week and young women 8s. Children working elsewhere in the mill generally earned between 3s. and 5s., although boys of 15 or more, who assisted the papermaker, could make as much as 10s. a week.[104]

Brickmaking and cement manufacture had a small nucleus of skilled workers, with a larger body of unskilled labourers. In the brickfields, the moulders, who shaped the bricks, earned a good wage: 50s. to 60s. a week in the summer and 18s. to 26s. during the rest of the year. Each moulder employed a gang of assistants, many of them children or adolescents, to prepare the clay and carry off finished bricks. These jobs required less skill but were still well paid by 19th-century standards: boys of 14 could earn 10s. a week, plus overtime, while men got 20s. to 30s. Gangs usually consisted of seven people including the moulder, although where bricks were made by machine, as in Aylesford, they could number as many as twelve. Other men dug out clay and loaded bricks into the clamp or kiln.[105]

In the cement industry a small army of unskilled labourers worked in the chalk pits, or as 'muddies' in the Medway estuary, often managed by a single foreman. Skilled workers such as engine drivers, kiln stokers, cement burners and millers were outnumbered by the many men and boys employed as general 'cement labourers'.

Wages were good, even for unskilled labourers, but employment in the brickfields and cement works remained highly seasonal for much of the 19th century. Most activity was concentrated into the summer months when slurry in the washbacks could dry more easily. The Aylesford and Burham Brick Works, for instance, employed 291 people during the summer of 1867, but only a third that number over the winter.[106]

Since so many activities were highly seasonal, few people in the Medway valley relied for their earnings on a single occupation. Most combined several jobs over the course of the year. In Strood and Frindsbury many households were involved in both fishing and agriculture. Similarly, agricultural labourers, used to heavy spade work, were often employed to dig clay in the brick-fields of Frindsbury, Cuxton and Aylesford. When Thomas Cubitt established his extensive brick works at Burham he recruited most of his workforce locally from among the agricultural labourers of the surrounding parishes. Other farm labourers worked as navvies on the Medway Canal, and later the railways during the 1840s and 1850s. Harvest time saw industrial workers lured into the fields by high seasonal wages. A typical labourer in the Medway valley in the mid-19th century might spend the winter working on the farm, before heading for the brickfield or chalk quarry in the spring where wages were higher, only to return to the fields for haymaking and then the harvest in August and September.[107]

By the later 19th century multiple occupations were less commonplace. Employment in the valley was now concentrated in industrial and service occupations, with relatively few working full-time in agriculture. Even so, many households still kept a pig or a few chickens, or grew vegetables on an allotment, and there continued to be an exodus to the fields for fruit picking and the hop harvest.

THE LANDSCAPE TRANSFORMED

The changes to the economy and society of the Lower Medway Valley brought about by industrialisation impacted on the character of the area. By the end of the 19th century the landscape had been transformed both physically and culturally: something that generated mixed feelings locally. Industry had brought prosperity to the valley but at a substantial cost. As early as 1862 residents of Wouldham brought an action against a local cement manufacturer complaining of the nuisance caused by noxious gases from his works. In a similar vein, Thomas Sturge of Northfleet reported to a government committee that gases from a nearby cement works had killed a number of trees on his premises and affected the health of the local inhabitants.[108]

Figure 33 Fishing boats moored near Strood pier in the early 20th century.

The river was becoming polluted with sewage and the toxic effluvia from paper-mills, brickfields and cement backs, contributing to the decline of the local fishing industry. Hasted noted that 'The inhabitants consist in great measure of seafaring men, fishermen, and of oyster dredgers, the latter being conducted by a Company of free Dredgers, established by prescription' but subject to the authority of Rochester. Until the 1860s over 200 boats operated on the Medway, and the oyster fishery alone was said to employ 400 people. By 1914 only five or six boats and 20 dredgermen remained, and the fishery was finally closed in 1936 under the Public Health (Shellfish) Regulations of 1834.[109]

Descriptions of the valley from the later 19th century place a clear emphasis on the transformation of the landscape, something which must have been starkly apparent to many locals as it had happened within living memory. Bevan commented that the valley had been 'utilised for chalk quarrying and lime burning to such an extent, that it has almost the appearance of a northern manufacturing district.' Only in the last decade of the century did industry come to be seen in a generally negative light. Black's *Guide* of 1901, for instance, commented that:

> Since Mr Pickwick's day, the view from the bridge down the river has been blocked out by a hideous railway viaduct, while up-river the scene is greatly marred by the intrusion of groups of tall, unsightly chimneys, connected with the cement industry.[110]

By the 1930s the emphasis turned to decay, reflecting the visible decline of the brick and cement industries throughout the Medway region: a mood epitomised by the 'ruined kilns and tottering chimneys' described by Donald Maxwell.

These changing narratives matched the changing fortunes of industry on the ground. As the impact of industry became increasingly visible, nostalgia for a simpler rural past grew more attractive. This is reflected in the critical tone of many accounts from the latter part of the century. The cement industry was depicted as looming large over the valley, whether in the form of towering chimneys, gaping quarries or all-pervading dust. Now that most of this industry has gone it too is being sentimentalised.

What we also see in the late 19th- and early 20th-century accounts is a preoccupation with the antiquities of the area; with links back to an ancient past before the valley was 'despoiled' by industry. Descriptions of Aylesford focused not on the brick and pottery works and paper-mill which provided employment to many of the parishioners, but on Kits Coty House and the Countless Stones, two Neolithic chambered long barrows in the north of the parish on Blue Bell Hill. This prehistoric landscape is often given mythical significance through the identification of the barrows as the resting place of Catigern and Horsa, believed to have been killed in battle between the Britons and Saxons nearby. Other landscape features picked out consistently by writers throughout the 19th century include the parish church, the Friars, formerly a Carmelite Priory, and old Aylesford bridge. All are ancient structures with a long and varied history.[111]

This preoccupation with ancient things reflects a longstanding tradition of antiquarianism that, in Kent, can be traced back to Lambarde, Pepys and Stukeley. But it also reveals an aversion to modernity with which the landscape historian, W.G. Hoskins would have concurred. He wrote in *The Making of the English Landscape*: 'Barbaric England of the scientist, the military men, and the politicians: let us turn away and contemplate the past before all is lost to the vandals'. This was a sentiment which was probably shared by many of those viewing the industrial landscape of the Medway at the turn of the 20th century: a landscape that had been transformed out of all recognition within living memory.[112]

Of course, not all commentators viewed the valley in the same way. There was a clear distinction between the attitudes of residents and visitors. Travel writers, the compilers of gazetteers and directories, and those visiting the Medway valley, portrayed the area in conventional ways, focusing on the more obvious landmarks, usually discussed in aesthetic terms. Bagshaw describes the view across the Medway from Frindsbury churchyard:

> The scenery from this eminence is most picturesque and beautiful: on the opposite side of the river is the venerable cathedral, and ancient castle of Rochester; a little more to the east the dock-yard and barracks at Chatham, and still further down the meanderings of the Medway may be seen as far as Sheerness.[113]

Often there are attempts to seek out ancient relics (long barrows, or the sites of Roman villas), and the picturesque (Aylesford bridge); elements of the landscape with which a wider readership might identify.

Where industry appears in these scenes it is usually as a blot on the landscape: something to be regretted. Donald Maxwell provides a neat characterisation of these attitudes in *Unknown Kent*:

> Marred by intruding commerce and stained by sordid manufacture, a lovely valley has become, they say, a valley of desolation – its villages black with the smoke of the furnaces and its fair hills devoured by the encroaching works.[114]

Often industry is simply excised from the text. A reader of Black's 1885 guide to Kent would, for instance, be unaware that there were brick and cement works in the Medway valley as neither was given a single mention.[115]

Accounts by local people provide us with a more nuanced view of the valley. They acknowledge the destructive force of industry, but also recognised its benefits in the form of jobs and prosperity. Canon Colson, the Rector at Cuxton, commented in the Church Magazine in 1898:

> cement making just now seems to be prosperous; for all around us new factories are being built, and old ones largely added to. Who would have thought, 60 years ago, that such a trade would have sprung up? Unhappily cement can't be made without smoke and dust; so our river and the country on its banks are fast losing the beauty they used to be famous for; but this can't be helped.[116]

Colson clearly regretted the predations of industry in the valley, but saw this as a necessary evil.

In a similar vein Edwin Harris wrote in 1897:

> Here we shall not fail to notice the number of cement works as we proceed up the stream, which, while whitening the banks of the river, and casting a smoky atmosphere over the sky, does not fail to bring wealth and commerce to the adjoining towns and gives employment to hundreds of men.[117]

Other writers even came to see beauty in the juxtaposition of industry and nature. Donald Maxwell perhaps expressed this most eloquently, reflecting an attachment to the 'land of cement' that could only come from familiarity:

> To those, however, who know this country intimately there is another side. The Medway, even here, has an indescribable charm. The association of tidal water and marshland with high wooded country on both sides gives it a unique character. The great chalk cliffs add ruggedness and the smoking furnaces grimness, so that the effect of the whole is singularly impressive.[118]

Elsewhere he notes 'the Dantesque effects of lurid light' at night in Halling 'when the stokers throw open the furnace doors and chequered lights appear on the drifting smoke'; describes the 'romantic and Eastern' imagery of beehive kilns on Bluebell Hill, and likens the scenery around Wouldham to a strange and magical 'lunar landscape'.[119] Maxwell, a trained artist, found that it was industry which made the Medway valley interesting. He recognised the possibilities of this landscape of contrasts; its rich texture and ethereal light.

The writings of Maxwell encapsulate the changes that had taken place in the Lower Medway Valley during the 19th century: the transformation of landscape, economy and society. Industrial expansion had changed the way of life in the valley out of all recognition. Many of those working in the quarries, claypits and sand holes were former agricultural labourers, or in many cases combined this activity with farm work. By the end of the 19th century agriculture no longer played the dominant role in terms of employment and income generation, even if the majority of the land was still devoted to cultivation of some sort. Nowhere is this clearer than in Frindsbury where the proportion of the adult male population employed in agriculture fell rapidly from around 1830 to 1881. Any visitor to the parish would have recognised these changes as they watched the quarries and brickfields steadily encroaching on the market gardens and other farmland.

Chapter 4 Landowners and Industrialists

Edward Hasted, the Kent local historian, writing towards the end of the 18th century, was in no doubt as to who the most important people were in any parish in Kent, and his account of the Lower Medway Valley is no exception. He focused on the landowning families, their illustrious pedigrees and the extent of their landed property. The principal aristocratic and gentry houses were also a prominent feature of the detailed maps that accompanied his text. His account of the lower Medway focuses on three major landowners: the Earl of Aylesford who owned land in Aylesford and Burham, Lord Darnley who had holdings in Frindsbury and Cuxton, into which his Cobham Park estate extended, and Lord Romney who had estates in Cuxton, Halling and Strood.

LANDOWNERSHIP

In an area characterised by relatively small estates, this aristocratic presence at the end of the 18th century is perhaps surprising, but despite the changes in the valley over the decades that followed, an underlying continuity of land ownership and occupation can be detected. In the 1840s the Darnleys held over 5,500 acres of land in six parishes, Aylesford had over 2,500 acres, also in six parishes, and Romney just over 2,000 acres spread over four parishes. Each parish also had one or two long established gentry families. In Snodland, the Mays bought the Court Lodge estate in 1732 and three generations of the family lived at Holloway Court in Holborough, enjoying the proceeds of the paper-mill they set up in 1744. By the third generation the Mays were occupying a 'handsome new-built house', suggesting that they had invested some of the profits in raising their profile in the county.[120]

Similarly in Aylesford the Milners, 'descended of a good gentleman's family' in Yorkshire, had come into possession of the Preston Hall estate by marriage into the Colepeper family in 1734. The estate covered most of the southern half of the parish, and it was probably during the Milner period that purchases began to be made north of the Medway, including properties and land within the village itself. Charles Milner junior, who inherited in 1836 and died a decade later, improved the estate, but by the last year of his life he was running into financial difficulties. In June 1846 he raised £10,000 on the security of several farms. Nevertheless, by the 1840s

Figure 34 The only known portrait of John May of Snodland (1734-1805). Born in neighbouring Birling, the son of a wealthy yeoman farmer, he had amassed a considerable fortune by the late 1770s, with land in Birling, Luddesdown, Wrotham, Boughton Monchelsea, Halling and Rochester as well as Snodland.

Figure 35 The Lower
Medway Valley showing
the location of the major
gentry houses from
the late 18th century in
relation to historic parish
boundaries.

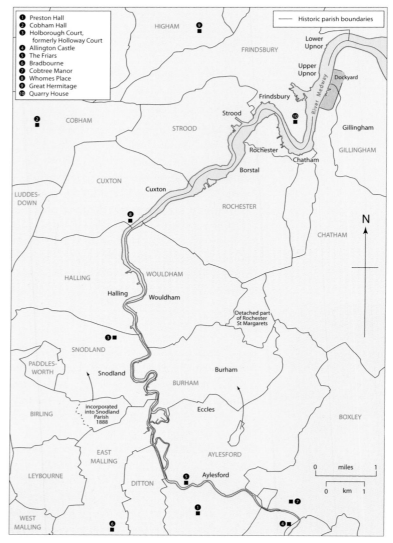

Figure 36 John Bligh,
4th Earl of Darnley
(1767-1831), from an
1810 pencil drawing by
Thomas Phillips. The
Darnleys were major
landowners in the lower
Medway and resided at
Cobham Hall to the west
of Cuxton parish.

Milner owned more land in the area than Lord Romney and was
the largest landowner in Aylesford.[121]

Some of the tenant farming families who held land from aristocratic owners were also relatively permanent representatives of the
local social elite. William Pye moved into Court Lodge and Brick
House farms in Cuxton in 1808 and the family continued to live
and farm in the village until 1916. In the mid-19th century the Pyes
were the largest tenant farmers in Cuxton, working over 750 acres of
Lord Darnley's land, mostly as arable and pasture. The Pye family's
empire extended beyond the boundaries of the parish, as they also
farmed land in Wouldham (478 acres), Strood (100 acres) and
Halling (72 acres). On a smaller scale, the Tiesdell family farmed

land in Cuxton, at Bush Farm and later Whorne's Place from 1745 until the early 19th century, and the family remained in the village until 1895.[122]

Almost inevitably, the arrival of industry brought with it industrialists who hankered after a country estate, and the first half of the 19th century saw changes in the ownership of many of the gentry estates. When landowners died without heirs to succeed them, ambitious industrialists were ready to purchase the houses and estates that came on the market as a sign that they had earned the wealth to support an elite lifestyle. In 1819 John May's executors sold part of the Holborough Court estate in Snodland to Thomas Poynder and William Hobson, the partners in a London firm of limeburners. They established limeworks at Halling, and by 1823 Thomas Poynder was in residence at Holloway Court. Poynder's son and his new partner Edward Medlicott sold the business in 1846 but the family retained substantial landholdings in Snodland, including land near All Saints church. W.H. Poynder gave land to enlarge the churchyard in 1867. Successive Poynders were described as lords of the manor of Snodland.[123]

Newcomers did not remain in the valley for generations as their predecessors had done. Both the Preston Hall and Holloway Court estates changed hands twice within 20 years. Edward Ladd Betts bought Preston Hall estate in 1848. The son of a Dover land surveyor, he had made his fortune in the railway boom of the 1830s and 1840s and bought Preston Hall at the height of his success. Brought down by the banking crisis of 1866

Figure 37 Holborough Court, Snodland was built in 1884-6 for Colonel William Henry Roberts and replaced Holloway Court, constructed for local landowner John May in the late 18th century. This lavish 'Queen Anne'-style house was itself demolished in 1928 when the estate was sold to Associated Portland Cement Manufacturers.

Betts filed for bankruptcy, and sold the property a year later to Henry Arthur Brassey, son of the outstandingly successful railway magnate, Thomas Brassey. The Holborough estate passed from Poynder to William Lee, the son of a Lewisham building contractor, who had moved to the Medway area in the 1820s, becoming manager of a cement works in Burham. By 1851 he had transferred his operations to Poynder and Medlicott's works at Halling and was living at Holloway Court, the house built for John May.

SOCIAL ACCEPTANCE

Having bought a house and estate the next step was for the new owner to stamp his mark on the property by carrying out extensive renovations. Preston Hall underwent two such remodellings in less than a hundred years. Despite the fact that Joseph Milner had modernised and rebuilt the house in the late 18th century, on taking up ownership Edward Betts demolished it and built a new mansion on a more elevated site. Today the building is used as hospital premises.

William Lee's Holborough estate came to his son-in-law, Colonel William Henry Roberts of Birling, in 1881. Roberts demolished the existing house, Holloway Court, and erected a new mansion, Holborough Court, in a more advantageous position and in enlarged landscaped grounds. Built in 1884-6 by the Maidstone architect Hubert Bensted, this was a flamboyant affair in the fashionable 'Queen Anne' style of the day, of red brick with dressings of red concrete and moulded bricks. It cost £30,000.[124]

An estate and a country house were physical manifestations of success, but new owners craved local acceptance. Edward Ladd Betts, owner of the Preston Hall estate, and the local brickworks and pottery, was lord of the manor and principal landowner in Aylesford by the 1860s. We know of his activities from a slim volume entitled *A Handy Book for the Villagers of Aylesford*, printed locally during this period. In the book Betts is repeatedly described as 'Our Squire', and the many initiatives in which he had a hand are described. He was said to have 'greatly improved the village by the substitution of modern and comfortable dwellings for the decayed structures which formerly disfigured it'; he was patron of and largest subscriber to the Garden Society; he funded the erection of reading rooms in 1860, and allowed the village fete to be held in the grounds of Preston Hall.

In the style of a true aristocrat, Betts took particular care to celebrate the coming of age of his son, Edward Peto Betts. All his tenants, employees of two years' standing and their wives and

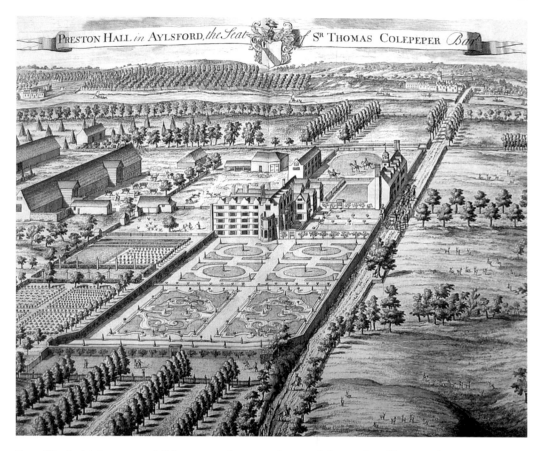

Figure 38 Aerial view of Preston Hall from John Harris' *History of Kent* (1719) showing the Tudor house surrounded by formal gardens and parkland. At the time of this engraving the estate was owned by Sir Thomas Colepeper. The house was demolished by Edward Ladd Betts in 1848 and a new mansion built a short distance away, though the large barn to the left of the picture survived until the early 20th century.

children over the age of 14 and the main village tradesmen were transported in a 31-carriage train to Crystal Palace where they were wined and dined, grateful speeches were made, and many toasts were given in honour of Betts. According to the author of the account 'arrived all home safely to their homes, full of good feeling and gratitude to the giver of the feast'. Perhaps tellingly, Betts and his family did not attend the festivities, and his subsequent bankruptcy in 1866 revealed just how fragile this newly acquired wealth and status could be.[125]

William Lee's cement business may have provided him with the money to buy the Holborough estate in Snodland, but for the rest of his life he worked tirelessly to build and maintain a prominent and respected position in local society. He worked with his fellow industrialists to found the Medway Conservancy Board and became a Bridge Warden, a magistrate and MP for Maidstone.

Lee also served as churchwarden in Snodland, and his Anglican allegiance is indicated by his having been a 'staunch and generous supporter' of the National School in Brook Street. His

Figure 39 Early photograph of William Lee, seated on the left, his daughter Sarah and her husband Alfred Smith. The child is their son, Samuel Lee Smith, who later went into partnership with his grandfather.

principal benefaction to the village was the Workmen's Institute in Holborough Road, opened in January 1877 at a cost of nearly £3,000. Stone built, it contained reading and billiard rooms, library and concert hall. It has since been demolished.[126]

At the same time Lee prepared subsequent generations to follow in his footsteps. Both his sons died young, but Lee's daughters made marriages which embedded the Lee family all the more firmly into the local elite and provided grandsons to carry on the family business. His daughter Sarah married Alfred Smith, brother of the Recorder of Margate. Their son Samuel Lee Smith joined his grandfather in the business in 1875 and took his cousin William Lee Roberts into partnership after the death of William Lee senior aged 80 in 1881. Samuel Lee Smith not only took on the business he also pursued the political ambitions of the family. Educated at public school, he took his grandfather's place on the Medway Conservancy Board in 1881, at the age of 25 its youngest member. In 1889 he became one of the first County Councillors for Kent, and he was also a magistrate and President of the Medway Rowing Club.[127]

The industrialists who bought or leased houses and estates, and adopted the lifestyle of the landed gentry, sometimes found themselves uncomfortably close to the industry that had brought them wealth and status, and looked to move on. Quarry House in Frindsbury, a 17th-century mansion and estate owned by the Rochester bridge wardens, was leased by a series of local manufacturers. Among them were George Burge, an early cement manufacturer, and the shipbuilder Joseph Brindley. William Tingey and Son, cement manufacturers, took over the lease in 1884 and the house was demolished in 1897 to extend their business. Holborough Court, built in 1884 to replace Holloway Court, the May family's old mansion in Holborough, was itself demolished in 1928 when the estate was sold to the cement combine Associated Portland Cement Manufacturers (APCM). Now part of BCI-Lafarge Cement, this company continues to own land on both sides of the valley, although many acres have been sold off in recent years for house building.[128]

SOCIAL LIFE

The newcomers were keen to adopt the social and leisure pursuits of the established aristocracy. This meant immersing themselves in the local social circuit, much of which centred on the county town of Maidstone. From the late 17th century Maidstone cultivated an image as a smart urbane centre offering a wide range of fashionable entertainments to the well-to-do inhabitants of mid-

Figure 40 Cobham Hall, ancestral home of the Earls of Darnley. Aristocrats such as Lord Darnley were key figures in the county community and would have been in Maidstone for important events such as the Assizes.

and West Kent. Regular assemblies for cards and dancing were on offer from the 1720s and assembly rooms were established in one of the leading inns by mid-century. By 1770 there was a purpose-built theatre, and a Society for Promoting Useful Knowledge was active from around 1768. There were also several circulating libraries, a book club, regular concerts and an array of specialist shops selling fashionable luxury goods. Each year the arrival of the county gentry in town for the summer assizes prompted an intense burst of social activity, with a week of assemblies, concerts, theatrical performances and sporting events. Indeed, by the later 18th century there was a sustained 'season' of fashionable entertainment on the London model which lasted from March until May.[129]

Rochester with its cathedral was also an important social centre. Here the visitor could find assembly rooms, a theatre and several circulating libraries by the 1830s, while the High Street constituted an agreeable promenade after an Improvement Act of 1769, as did the elevated grounds of the Norman castle. There was also a literary society, the Rochester Book Club 'for the cultivation of useful knowledge'. Founded in 1797, from the outset this attracted members from the outlying parishes. The first president was James Hulkes, a Strood landowner, and other early members included George Fowle, of Cobtree Manor, who had lime kilns at Aylesford and John Nicholson, the Frindsbury shipbuilder. By 1866 society members included 'many of the best tradesmen and business people of the City'. They were joined by industrialists, professional men and traders from the neighbouring communities. Thomas Aveling of Aveling and Porter and four of the Strood Trustees of 1898 – Owen Ball, George Robinson, Rei Fry and Charles Levy

Figure 41 Maidstone. The theatre at the bottom of High Street, erected by 1770 and shown here as rebuilt in 1798.

– were all members. The society offered not only the intellectual stimulation of the regular weekly meetings but also an annual excursion. In 1882 this entertainment took the form of a barge trip down the Medway with 37 men sharing a lunch of 1,000 oysters followed by a lavish dinner.[130]

The Medway also had a rowing club from around 1865, although the Royal Engineers had been holding regattas on the river since the 1840s. The Club's annual regatta became a key date in the social calendar attracting spectators and crews from a wide area. The Medway Yacht Club was founded in 1880 by W.S. Nicholson together with a group of local industrialists and members of the Royal Engineers Yacht Club, though it also attracted members from amongst the aristocracy, including the Earl of Cavendish and Lord Beresford. Also inaugurated in 1880 was the Medway Barge Match, a competitive race for sailing barges organised by the leading barge owners on the river such as the brickmakers, Eastwoods, and cement manufacturers APCM Ltd.

At a parish level, newcomers slotted into an established social hierarchy. Most were keen to play an important role in local affairs. The *Handy Book for the Villagers of Aylesford*, printed locally in 1866, offers a snapshot of community life in one mid-century Medway valley village. Scattered among the details of who won the fruit and vegetable growing competitions, and the latest additions to the lending library, were lists of the membership of every committee in the village: the Horticultural Society, the Penny Bank savings club, the Reading Room, the Rifle Corps, the Cricket Club, the Trinity Hospital, the Parochial Club and the only group for women, the Dorcas club.[131]

The same names appeared again and again on these lists. The men and women who ran the clubs and societies came from several different walks of life. Membership ranged from the local schoolmaster and his children, to the largest landowner in the village through the professions, the army, the church and the more substantial tenant farmers. The trustees of Trinity Hospital, the local almshouses, were the local vicar, Archdeacon Grant, Edward Betts of Preston Hall, Captain Cheere, RN, resident at the Cedars, John Monson Shaw, tenant farmer at Roe Place and Edward Wood, tenant of Tottington farm, Henry Simmonds, merchant and hop planter, tenant of the Earl of Aylesford at the Friary, Joseph Bateman, grocer, and Henry French, coal merchant. These same men were all on the committee of the reading rooms, joined by 20 other local worthies.

The women's club, the Dorcas Society, met to make clothes to sell at reduced rates to the village poor. In this group there was a social division between those who supported the good work that they did by donations and those who ran the club. The list of subscribers was headed by Mrs Betts of Preston Hall, contributing one guinea (£1 1s.), closely followed in generosity by the vicar's wife and the wives and daughters of professional men and tenant farmers. However, the work of organising the charitable activities of the club was shouldered only by the wives of the professional men and tradesmen. Mrs Hammond, the accountant's wife, and Miss Wagon, the schoolmaster's daughter, were secretary and treasurer respectively.

SOCIAL RESPONSIBILITY

Though there were changes in the families who led local society in the Lower Medway Valley between 1750 and 1900, the responsibilities that went with social leadership remained much the same. Throughout this period the actions of the men and women at the head of local communities show that they felt a sense of duty to oversee many aspects of community life.

Education

Providing a basic education for local children was a responsibility they clearly took seriously. In 1785 Charles Milner of Preston Hall left instructions in his will that his nephew and heir Joseph should set up a trust of £20 a year for the appointment of a schoolmaster. Similarly in 1800 John May of Snodland bequeathed £20 per year to allow 20 children from Snodland, ten from Halling and ten from Birling to be taught reading, writing and arithmetic. Half a century later Edward Ladd Betts built a pretty Tudor-style infants' school and teacher's house at Aylesford for the children of his estate workers, while his successor at Preston Hall, Henry Arthur Brassey, established a schoolroom at his Pratling Street pottery in the 1880s.[132]

Figure 42 Aylesford Infants' School, 2008. Built of Kentish ragstone with gault brick dressings in a Tudor style, it stands 200 yards south of the bridge, on the edge of Preston Hall Park and was designed to complement Preston Hall, rebuilt between 1849 and 1857 by Edward Ladd Betts.

The local elite were also supportive of the national schemes for providing schooling in the early 19th century. The gentry of Halling met with the National Society in 1813 to begin discussions about setting up a Church of England school in the village. In Aylesford, Brassey contributed generously to the rebuilding of the National School in 1872, while the British School in Snodland received significant financial support from the Hook family, owners of the local paper-mill. From 1870 they paid all the expenses of the school, over and above the government grant of £90.[133]

The British School had been founded in 1857 beside the Congregationalist Providence Chapel on Holborough Road by papermaker William Joynson of St Mary Cray, a former owner of Snodland's paper-mill. The school was purchased in around 1867

Figure 43 Halling
School, *c*.1910. In 1876
the board of governors
consisted of three cement
manufacturers – John
Anderson, Thomas
Weekes and William
Lee – a farmer, Edward
Norman, and the vicar,
the Revd J. Nailson.

by Charles Townsend Hook to save it from closure and thrived
under his generous superintendence. Following Hook's death in
1877 his sisters, Edith, Maude and Agnes, continued to offer strong
support. In 1887 they bought the neighbouring Providence Chapel
for 1,000 guineas to provide classrooms for an infant department.
The same year, in celebration of Queen Victoria's Golden Jubilee,
they gave a silver brooch to every mother who had children
attending the school and made a generous contribution to the
costs of the celebratory feast. In 1893 the sisters made provision
for some secondary education for the more capable boys at the
School by establishing a Manual Training Classroom in the High
Street to the west of Mulberry Cottages, only the second of its type
in the country.[134]

Nor was such generous support limited to Snodland. In June
1865, 98 pupils of the Cuxton National School enjoyed their annual
school treat 'through the liberality of the Rector'. The event was
'greatly enlivened by the presence of many influential ladies and
gentlemen' and the children received gifts of clothing made by the
rector's wife and other ladies in the village.[135]

When Board schools were set up in response to legislation
in 1870, local industrialists were prominent on their governing
bodies. The school log books at Halling show that the governors,
who included cement manufacturers John Anderson, Thomas
Weekes and William Lee, took a hands-on role, visiting the
school regularly, dealing with complaints and problems, and
offering prizes.[136]

Figure 44 The Hospital of the Holy Trinity, almshouses founded in 1607 under the terms of the will of Sir John Sedley.

Charity

The social elite of the valley also followed the time-honoured tradition of charitable giving to the poor. John May designated £20 of the annual rent from his property Gassons in Snodland to buying warm coats for the poor of Halling. Responsibility for this charity appears to have been shouldered by subsequent owners of the Holborough Court estate, as in 1893 the vicar mentioned that William Lee and Colonel Roberts had made the annual payments.[137]

Not all charitable funds were so easily collected. In Aylesford, Trinity Hospital almshouses, established in the early 1600s to house four men and two women, had been more or less abandoned by the late 18th century. It was not until 1827 that the Quaker Thomas Robson took up the cause of re-opening and the charity was eventually re-established in 1842. In 1866 Edward Betts was one of eight local men acting as trustees when the decision was taken to stop the annual distribution of bread and coals to the poor. The money saved, which came from bequests made in the previous century, was to be used to create a new place in the almshouse and to provide the chosen inmate with 6s. a week. The almshouses received a further boost in 1892 when, thanks to the generosity of Anna Brassey of Preston Hall, four new rooms were added.[138]

New charities were also established. In Snodland in 1893 Charles Townsend Hook's sisters had three new almshouses built in memory of their brother Eustace. One house was reserved for a member of the New Jerusalem Church, another for a member of the Church of England, to be nominated by the Rector, and the third for a member of the nonconformist congregation. A further four apartments were added later by Agnes Hook in memory of Amelia Drummond, the Hook family governess.[139]

Figure 45 The Eustace Hook Almshouses on Waghorn Road, Snodland were erected in 1893 by local Snodland builder, Joshua Wilford, for £830 to a design of George R. Cobham, though they have now been substantially altered.

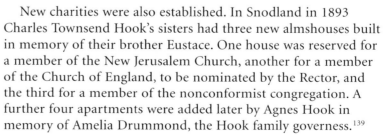

On a less grand scale, the Parish Officers of Aylesford, who met monthly to consult ratepayers on parochial business, imposed a fine of one shilling on members who arrived late. In 1865 the fines amounted to £6 14s. of which £6 4s. was 'disposed of to the poor, sick, widows and infirm'.[140]

Recreation

On the estates themselves, servants and employees were treated to parties and outings, both on a regular basis and to celebrate specific events. The *Maidstone Telegraph* of 24 January 1863 reported that the servants at Preston Hall were 'a merry party' at the annual ball provided for them by their master. Dancing took place in the servants hall which had been decorated for the occasion, and 'an excellent supper' was provided for the 40 guests. Local industrialists also provided fetes for their workers. The Halling school log book entry for 24 May 1877 noted that 'No school on Friday afternoon in consequence of the room being required for the purpose of giving a dinner to the workmen of Messrs Hilton and Anderson's Lime and Cement Works'.

The Pye family regularly arranged entertainment for the whole village of Cuxton. In 1887 they organised a concert in their barn, attracting an audience of around 300 people. And village memories of the early 20th century include the Pyes' annual garden party to which the whole village was invited. Small acts of generosity were remembered. 'Every day Mr Pye always gave the farm workers skimmed milk free of charge. When the milk was ready for collection a white card was placed in the kitchen window by the cook and Mrs Ablett and the local children used to run down and collect it.'[141]

For day-to-day recreation Edward Betts built a Reading Room and Library at Aylesford for the use of 'the workingmen and lads of our Village'. His generosity also extended to paying for gas lighting, the wages of an attendant and the daily newspapers. In 1865 he added 46 books and seven series of magazines and periodicals to the library shelves. Betts' stated motive in providing this facility had been 'that after a man had done his day's work he might find a comfortable place where he might pass an hour or two with advantage to himself…'. The hidden agenda may have been to keep men out of the local pubs. This was certainly the overt intention of Miss Maude Hook, 'an ardent advocate of the temperance cause', in building and furnishing a Temperance Coffee Tavern in May Street, Snodland in 1881 for the benefit of workers at the paper-mill. Charles Townsend Hook, perhaps showing a little more realism, had provided a Beer Hall for the workforce.[142]

Figure 46 Edward Ladd Betts funded the erection of reading rooms in 1860 adjacent to Aylesford Infants' School. Betts also paid to light and staff the reading rooms and for the provision of daily newspapers.

On occasion the elite themselves were the entertainment, offering the villagers a glimpse of a more glamorous lifestyle. The presence of 'fashionable company' at the Cuxton Cottage Gardener's tenth annual show in 1885 attracted the attention of the local paper, at pains to mention the presence of the Earl and Countess of Darnley, and a long list of local worthies. When Henry Brassey and his new bride Lady Violet returned to Aylesford from their honeymoon the occasion was marked by an extravagant welcome:

Much time and labour had been expended in preparing for the homecoming, and the decorations were of the most elaborate description. The station had had special attention bestowed upon it, and the workers engaged thereon must have felt the greatest satisfaction at the result of their labours. A large marquee was erected for the presentation of addresses and the whole of the route from the station to Preston Hall, a distance of about a mile, was lined with Venetian masts, while at intervals were erected triumphal arches.[143]

Having achieved ownership of a country house and an elite lifestyle, newcomers to the valley were well placed to take part in the political life of the area. Local administrative office was often the first rung of the political ladder. For many this involved taking on parish duties. Both Edward Betts and Charles Townsend Hook demonstrated their commitment to local affairs by serving on the parish council in their respective communities.

By the mid-19th century successful manufacturers who had bought into the country house lifestyle had joined the local landowners in the ranks of the Wardens of Rochester Bridge. Thomas Poynder, William Lee, Edward Betts, and two generations of Brassey's enjoyed this honour. Another frequently held local office which signalled membership of the elite was Justice of the Peace. Two generations of Brasseys, William Lee, Samuel Lee Smith and Thomas Aveling were amongst those who served in this capacity.[144]

In 1881 the formation of the Medway Conservancy Board provided a further opportunity for the elite to hold local administrative office while protecting their manufacturing interests on the river. All the early elected members were drawn from the lime and cement manufacturers: William Lee, Samuel Lee Smith, Henry Peters, William Porter, J. Anderson and A. Robertson were the first to serve.[145]

From the 1890s there were also opportunities to serve as county councillors, an honour enjoyed by Samuel Lee Smith and Henry Peters, both cement manufacturers. The next rung on the ladder was to hold office at county level as Sheriff or Lord Lieutenant of

Figure 47 Bridge Chambers, headquarters of the Rochester Bridge Trust, situated on the corner of the Esplanade and Castle Hill, Rochester, at what was once the east end of the medieval Rochester bridge. The chambers, which originally had a classical façade, were rebuilt in 1879. Adjacent to them is the Bridge Chapel, a medieval chantry chapel built by Sir John de Cobham in the late 14th century, seen here prior to its renovation by the Bridge Wardens in 1937.

Kent. The Brassey and Lee families and Edward Betts were amongst those who held such offices. Edward Betts was Sheriff of Kent in 1850, as was Henry Brassey in 1890.

The most successful went on to stand for parliament. William Lee was Liberal MP for Maidstone from 1852-7 and 1859-70. His election in 1859 was celebrated in grand style by the people of Snodland and Burham.

Flags were hoisted in front of his residence and guns were placed on the lawn. The labour of the day ceased on the arrival of the intelligence, and groups of villagers might be seen standing and discussing the event. Great numbers of the workmen and inhabitants of the neighbouring cottages were collected together awaiting the arrival of the 7.50 train, which was not too long in making its appearance when a volley was fired instantaneously from the guns, followed by loud cheers and the waving of hats and flags, which was returned by the occupants of the train…. Later in the evening there was a display of fireworks. Refreshments were provided in abundance for all present, and the merriment was continued till a late hour.[146]

The idea that a man with Lee's background might be greeted so effusively as a social leader would have been unthinkable a century earlier – the valley had been socially as well as industrially transformed.

Chapter 5

House, Home and Community

The population growth in the lower Medway parishes had a profound effect on the villages in terms of their physical fabric and social makeup. Terraces of workers' cottages were grafted onto existing village cores, and in some places entirely new settlements of workers' housing were established close to the cement works and brickfields. In Strood and Frindsbury large areas of new housing were erected, effectively joining the two places together. In Halling and Wouldham terraced housing spread along the main thoroughfares. Life was also different for their occupants, most of whom were not, as had traditionally been the case, earning their living from agricultural work. What did this mean for everyday life in the valley?

HOUSING

Farmers in the valley in 1750 had roomy, well-built houses. They were often medieval in origin but had usually been modernised by the introduction of brick chimney stacks and enclosed hearths in the place of a central open fire.

Houses built after 1600 increasingly adopted a two-part plan, with a central chimney stack, and an entry lobby providing access to the ground-floor rooms. Once brick came into widespread use more flexible layouts were possible. Chimneys could be built into the external wall, so the lobby could be extended to form a vestibule giving access to all ground-floor rooms and to a staircase leading to the upper floors. The basic layout of two ground-floor rooms, with chambers and garrets above, and ancillary service rooms at the rear, remained the same. By 1750 variants of this design were common, and included Anchor and Cowleaze Farms in Aylesford, the Old Parsonage in Strood, and the old farmhouse in Paddlesworth.[147]

Farmers in the valley were quick to adopt new consumer goods, at least by comparison with rural households elsewhere in the country. By the 1760s china, tea ware, cane and mahogany furniture, window curtain and ornamental looking glasses were relatively commonplace. William Charlton of Lodge Farm, Aylesford, who died in 1761, had the standard three-part arrangement of kitchen, parlour and washhouse on the ground floor, with a chamber above each, and further service rooms

Figure 48 The old farmhouse, Paddlesworth. Dating from the mid-18th century, the old farmhouse is an interesting example of house with a lobby entrance, which was widely adopted in Kent in the 17th and 18th centuries.

behind. The kitchen was used for both cooking and eating. It contained cooking utensils, two tables, 14 chairs and four joint stools. The parlour was the main public room, used for business and entertaining. It was furnished with four tables, nine chairs, a looking glass and corner cupboard. Charlton kept the family silver and china ware in a glass-fronted bureau. The three chambers on the upper floor, which formed the family's private space, each contained a bed, chest of drawers, looking glass and window curtains. The servants slept in garrets in the roof space which were rather more sparsely furnished.[148]

Luxury items and fashionable modern furnishings were more common in the houses of Strood testators than of those living in the more rural parts of the area. The front parlour of Thomas Taylor's house in 1777 contained, among other items, a 'pier glass in a painted frame', two mahogany pillar claw tables, one square the other round, a wainscot desk, a bookcase with a drawer, six pairs of crown glass, 12 flowered wine glasses, and an assortment of china and chimney ornaments. Elsewhere in the house he had an alabaster figure, numerous framed prints, a japanned tea table, two clocks, walnut dressing tables and more than two dozen cane and mahogany chairs. Another Strood resident, Edmund Pearson, who died in 1730, had an entry lobby decorated with 'twenty pictures and six china cups and saucers'.[149]

Cottages

Agricultural labourers did not enjoy such finery. Most lived in fairly
basic cottages of two or three rooms, with a thatched roof, mud or
'cob' walls and an earth or cobble floor. They would have had few
possessions other than a bed, table, chairs, basic cooking utensils
and their working tools. This did not mean that the accommodation
was necessarily inadequate. In 1813 John Boys thought the cottages
of the county 'in general comfortable habitations for farming
labourers', although he found evidence of poor sanitation, lack of
proper ventilation and overcrowding. Many Kent labourers living
in cottages built from clay, with chimneys fashioned from poles
daubed inside and out with the same material.[150]

Cottages were provided either by landowners, who built on
land they leased to tenant farmers, or by speculative builders.
Unfortunately the low agricultural wages of the early 19th century
meant that few labourers could afford an economic rent, so
builders had little incentive to erect cottages in rural parishes.[151]

This put the onus on landowners to provide accommodation
for labourers as an act of paternalistic benevolence. Some had a
remarkable record in this respect. Edward Betts' efforts in Aylesford
are clear from sale particulars of 1867, which show the superior
quality of many of the dwellings he provided. Lower Tottington
Farm was to be sold with two brick and tile cottages, each of four
rooms, with a small garden, while the bailiff's cottage on the Home
Farm was of brick, board and tile, containing five rooms, plus a
pantry and woodhouse. Other landowners were less interested,
and paid little attention to cottage building. The Earl of Romney
voiced a commonly held view when he argued that the provision
of cottages should be left to market forces. He preferred to see a
man receive 'fair remuneration for his labour and pay fair rent for
his cottage than be underpaid for his labour in consideration of his
being under rented'.[152]

Attitudes such as this ensured that cottage accommodation did
not expand quickly enough to meet the requirements of a growing
population and the growing practice amongst tenant farmers of
'boarding-out' labourers, rather than providing accommodation
on the farm, only made matters worse. The seriousness of the
situation by the 1850s and 1860s is clearly illustrated by the large
numbers of households which included lodgers, and by the long
journeys to work endured by many workers in the newly opened
brick and lime works.

The model cottage movement emerged as a response to
this overcrowding and the wretched conditions in which
many labourers were forced to live. Across the country cottage
improvement societies were established, including the Maidstone

Cottage Improvement Company, which by 1868 had built 54 cottages and accumulated capital of £4,200. These societies aimed to provide accommodation at modest cost which provided adequate space for living, cooking, sleeping and storage, and allowed separate space for children and adults. Designs were often picturesque, as at Aylesford, and produced by some of the leading architects of the day. In reality such philanthropic bodies played only a small part in tackling the rural housing problem, but the ideals they espoused influenced the designs of houses built for workers in the Lower Medway Valley later in the century.[153]

In the end the impetus for house building in the Medway valley came not from philanthropic landowners, but from industrialisation and the higher wages paid to industrial workers which generated a rash of speculative cottage building from the 1850s. Whereas farm cottages across Kent rarely rented for more than 2s. 6d. per week, E.L. Betts was able to lease out five cottages in the industrial hamlet of Pratling Street for around 3s. 2d. apiece. Manufacturers, keen to have their workforce close at hand, became involved with the provision of housing, although some of this was initially of poor quality, often located next to the brickfields or chalk pits.[154]

Even so, the shortage of cottages in the industrialising parishes of the Medway valley continued to generate real social problems. In the 1860s many of the labourers, quarrymen and brickmakers working in Burham and Aylesford had to live four miles away in Maidstone due to a shortage of accommodation. Even in the county town they were hardly living in luxury: in 1868 a Maidstone resident complained that 'cottages in this part are generally bad and insufficient in number'. Others noted poor construction, lack of repair, overcrowding, and poor sanitation. The Reverend S. Hornibrook, curate of St Faith's Mission District in Maidstone, commented that many cottages had no back yards or separate water-closets, and many were occupied by two families, or let out as single rooms to an entire family.[155]

The Terraced Cottage From the 1850s one type of housing came to predominate: the brick-built terrace. These were relatively cheap to build through increasing standardisation of layout and the building process itself. Cheap building materials were locally available with the development of the brick, lime and cement industries. As early as 1852 the Wouldham lime burners Thomas Freen and Co. were advertising a range of products including tiles, chimney-pots, plaster, hair and 'welsh goods' as well as 'grey and chalk lime'.[156]

The terraced cottage had a very simple layout: two floors with two rooms on each. Access was either via a long and narrow corridor to one side of the house, or directly into the front room

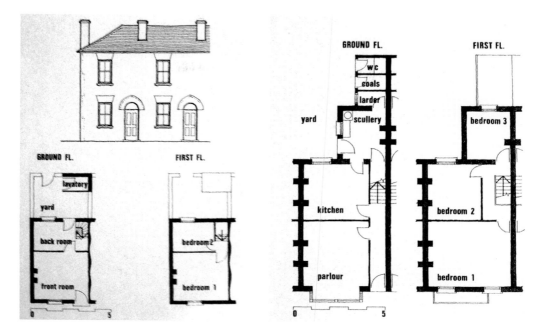

Figure 49 Diagrams showing the internal layout of the two-up, two-down terraced cottage which became widespread in the Medway valley in the second half of the 19th century. The design on the right includes a back extension, which allowed the addition of a scullery or larder and third bedroom.

from the street. Both these layouts were limiting, but they did allow far greater differentiation of function than was possible in older farm cottages. This sat well with the Victorians' preference for order and privacy. Generally the upstairs rooms were used as bedrooms, with those downstairs providing the living space. The front room, usually described as the 'parlour' or 'sitting room' was reserved for best, while the back room, usually the 'kitchen', was for cooking and eating. Beyond the kitchen many houses had a small scullery used for dirty work such as washing up and cleaning meat and vegetables. If extra space were needed it could be provided by the addition of an attic storey, as in Eccles Row in Aylesford, or through a back extension.

Back extensions grew in size and importance through time. By the 1870s most terraces built in the valley had them, usually two-storeyed and containing a kitchen-cum-scullery on the ground floor with a small bedroom above. Perhaps typical was 7 Prentice Street, Strood, a six-room brick-built house with a slate roof. This consisted of two living rooms, both with fitted stoves and cupboards, and accessed off a passage. Behind them in the back extension was a kitchen fitted with sink and copper. Upstairs were three bedrooms and below a substantial cellar. Outside was a toilet and small garden.[157]

One significant area of improvement that terraces brought was in sanitation. Whereas country cottages had traditionally relied on a privy or midden, from the mid-19th century terraces

Figure 50 Formby Terrace, Rochester Road, Halling in *c.*1910. The *Kent Messenger* said of Halling in 1892: 'Its cottages are models of comfort and cleanliness, and with their ample and neatly-kept front gardens present a picture of cosy domesticity'.[158]

were generally built with flushing toilets in the back yard. Sales particulars for six cottages in Millhall make specific reference to 'outside closets'. Inside toilets were definitely a sign of higher status, and in the valley were rarely found in workers' cottages built before 1900. Most houses were also provided with piped water by the 1880s, and many with gas lighting. Their tenants generally looked after them.

The relative uniformity of these new workers' cottages contrasted sharply with the earlier buildings characterised by vernacular features such as the use of ragstone, rubbed bricks, thatch and weatherboarding. They gave places such as Halling and Snodland a quasi-urban feel, that to many seemed just as much an alien intrusion into the landscape as the cement works and quarries in which their residents worked. Donald Maxwell described them in the 1920s as 'hideous yellow-brick boxes, sometimes cement-faced, and of the most dingy appearance'. In his view they were 'a blot on the landscape'.[159]

In villages such as Wouldham and Halling it is easy to spot where rows of workers' cottages have been grafted onto an existing village centre. Often they form ribbon-like extensions along the roads to the works, as at Holborough Road in Snodland and New Town in Halling. Elsewhere terraces occur in splendid isolation, marking the location of former works. Ravens Knowle south-east of Wouldham and Scarborough Cottages, a mile north of Burham, are good examples of this. Only in Strood and Frindsbury is the late 19th-century housing more varied in style, reflecting the more diverse economies of these parishes, although they, too, had their fair share of workers' terraces, particularly in the area north and west of Strood station.

Industrialisation also brought an expansion of villas and terraces on the outskirts of the towns and villages housing the emerging middle classes – the tradesmen, professionals and manufacturers who had benefited most from the expanding economy of the valley. Wealthy residents of the Medway towns spread into surrounding rural parishes, leading to the development of rural areas of Strood and Frindsbury, and later Cuxton. Some villa-type development took place on the outskirts of the cement villages, too, away from the dust and dirt of the industrial processes. These houses were designed to reflect the wealth, status and culture of the occupants. Families had freedom of choice over location so it was important for the builder to sell the property to them, hence an emphasis on the use of ornamentation, and the employment of fashionable architectural styles.

Unlike workers' cottages the layout of middle-class villas was designed to provide a series of specialised spaces for different activities, and often to provide space for servants whose daily lives had to be kept separate from those of the family. Seven semi-detached villas offered for sale in Borstal Road, Rochester in 1890 had the benefit of a drawing room, dining room, breakfast room, kitchen, scullery, larder, coal cellar, four bedrooms and a bathroom, and most importantly side entrances giving servants separate access.[160]

HOUSEHOLD ECONOMIES

In the 18th century men and women worked side by side in the fields, although men were traditionally paid rather more than their wives or children. Dame Luck received only 5s. for a week's haymaking at Cobham in 1780, while her husband was paid 10s. In his evidence to a government enquiry in 1868, Charles Whitehead noted that in the agricultural districts around Maidstone women's earnings were 'a great help to a working family, especially in summer; hop picking is looked forward to pay off old debts and rents, and the woman here is the chief contributor'. Relieving officers were instructed to calculate money earned by children or rent paid by lodgers when assessing whether an applicant was deserving of poor relief.[161]

Women and children were fully involved in both agricultural and industrial work, particularly in tasks that were repetitive or required manual dexterity. In farming areas work was available throughout the year. Much of the weeding on the Darnley estate was done by women or young girls, while boys were given duties such as picking stones, scaring off birds, and leading the horse for the plough team. Often the family worked together as a unit. At harvest time corn was cut by the man, then collected by his wife and laid on bands prepared by the children. The man then bound the sheaves on his way back while his wife carried the scythe. Working as a team in this way it was reckoned that a family could reap around one and a half acres in two days, earning them around 6s. to 9s. per day in the late 18th century. In this case family members assisted the head of household without receiving a separate remuneration.[162]

Similar arrangements were often made for industrial occupations. In paper-mills women and girls were employed in cutting and sorting rags, while both boys and girls worked in the glazing room. In the brickfields children were given tasks such as carrying and turning bricks, raking ash from the kilns, and turning points on the tramways. Employers dealt only with the brick moulders, whose 'gang' was often composed mainly of family members. Those who were not part of a family were usually

Henry Wraight: from farm to cement works, a life shaped by industrial change

To understand fully the history of the Lower Medway Valley in the 19th century we need to look at the human stories that lie behind the process of industrialisation. To do this, we can look at the research of family historians. Their work tells us about labour mobility, household structures, welfare and family relationships. It brings colour to what would otherwise be rather lifeless official statistics and distribution patterns. Outlined below is the story of just one family, the Wraights, and their journey from farm to factory; a journey that epitomised the changes taking place in the Lower Medway Valley during the 19th century. The family themselves were unremarkable, but the story that unfolds encapsulates what it must have felt like to experience rapid industrialisation first-hand.

Henry Wraight was born in about 1791, the son of a labourer, within the small agrarian community of Kennington, Kent. He was married at All Saints Church, Maidstone on 14 October 1811 to Thomasine Bolton. The couple's first child, Jane, was baptised in the nearby parish of Aylesford in 1812. Ten further children were to follow, all of them christened in Burham, just to the north of Aylesford.

Census returns are useful for piecing together the history of a family, but parish records can provide additional clues. The 1841 census lists Henry as a farmer at Burham Hill, an area enclosed by the Earl of Aylesford in 1815. Living with him was his wife and four sons: John, Henry, George and Edward. The tithe award compiled a year later provides more details about the Wraight's farm: a house, garden and three acres of pasture rented from J.H. Hooper and some pasture, arable and woodland amounting to more than 11 acres leased from P. Seaton.

Figure A   *Burham Hill Farm, Common Road, Bluebell Hill. The original farmhouse burnt down in 1977 and was attached to the end of the barn, pictured. A new farmhouse has since been built.*

Figure B   *Prentice Street, Strood, now demolished. The north side of Prentice Street, in the vicinity of number 16, the 1861 residence of Henry Wraight..*

By 1851 Henry is listed as a farmer of 20 acres living at 55 Old Bell House. All of his sons still worked in agriculture apart from Henry, now a chalk labourer in Frindsbury. Thomasine died of cancer in 1852 and Henry remarried the following year. His second wife, Mary Hassam, née Tye, born 1803, had moved to Strood from Eye in Suffolk sometime after 1851. She is described in the census as a washerwoman and widow. By 1861 Strood was a bustling industrial centre, thronging with migrants from surrounding rural areas: only 1,321 of the 3,795 inhabitants were born there. Amongst these migrants were Mary's sons, William and Charles, who are listed as resident in Temple Street, Strood. Both were 'coke burners to the South Eastern Company', probably the South Eastern Railway which had installed coke ovens at the canal basin after 1847 to supply their locomotive engines. A third son, John, a cement works labourer, lived in Prentice Street.

Following their marriage, Henry and Mary returned to Burham. The Church Rates of 1856 show Henry paying rent of £1 1s. 3d. for land at Burham Hill. The 1861 census lists Henry as a farmer employing one man and a boy. He was living on the Maidstone Road with his wife, and young grandson, William Stoller.

By the end of the 1860s Henry had given up work through old age and relinquished his holding. By now all but one of his surviving children had abandoned farming for the cement works or related industries, and Henry and Mary went to Strood to live with Mary's son John

Hassam and his family in Prentice Street. Construction had begun here in 1854 following the sale of land by a Mr Lines to the builder Kennett Spicer. The western end of Prentice Street faced the entrance to the North Aylesford Union Workhouse, and it was here, at number 16, that the Wraights resided.

Strood was a very different environment from rural Burham, and in 1872 Mary died of exhaustion, brought on by erysipelas, an itchy bacterial infection of the skin. Following Mary's death, Henry moved again to Wouldham, where, according to the 1881 census, he lived 'on charity'. He shared a rented house in the High Street with grandsons John Clifford, a chalk labourer, and Henry Wraight, a bricklayer's labourer. Now blind, Henry remained here until his death in 1885 of 'a fracture to his leg' aged 94. He is buried in an unmarked grave at All Saints' Church, Wouldham.

Figure C   *Wouldham High Street, July 2007. Henry Wraight lived here in 1881 and died here four years later.*

Figure D   *All Saints' Church and graveyard, Wouldham, July 2007.*

provided with board and lodgings by the moulder, rendering them effectively part of the household.[163]

Given the importance of children's earnings to family income, it is not surprising that many parents objected to compulsory schooling. Children were often withdrawn from classes when work was available, particularly at harvest time, and few stayed in education beyond the age of 10 or 11 even as late as the 1880s. Levels of attendance rose significantly following the Education Acts of 1870 and 1876, which made schooling until the age of 11 compulsory. Absenteeism remained high among the children of agricultural labourers. The school log book for Halling records children absent from school to go pea picking and gleaning during the 1880s. One schoolmaster complained in 1867 that 'out of the 414 times when the school has been open, no child has attended more than 202'. By the 1890s most children helped only with hay-making and the harvest, and in 1911 just eight per cent were in gainful employment across Kent as a whole.[164]

In the brickfields children were said to be 'born with a brick in their mouths'. Many started working at seven or eight, after which they attended classes only during the winter when work was unavailable. A similar situation prevailed in cement-producing areas where work was also concentrated into the summer months.[165]

Unemployment, Poor Relief and the Economy of the Poor

Few households could make ends meet through paid work alone. The old, sick and disabled required permanent support, but many more families lived on the margins of subsistence. Survival for these families depended on piecing together a living from a variety of sources: a patchwork of support sometimes characterised as an economy of makeshifts. Often they turned first to family or friends for support. Sarah Woolven, for instance, asked her mother in Maidstone to look after an illegitimate child so that she could return to London in search of work. Similarly, in 1881 George Kirk, a Snodland labourer, earned on average only 5s. a week due to a damaged hip, but could also draw on 15s. in 'board and lodgings' from his two eldest sons.[166]

Common resources could also be a useful supplement to paid work. The woodland on the slopes of the North Downs provided access to some grazing and fire wood, and there were common meadows along the banks of the Medway. Charity was an alternative means of support. All of the eight parishes had charitable endowments, many dedicated to providing bread or other assistance to the poor. Frindsbury was particularly fortunate, with four charities providing a combined sum of £42 2s. in 1837, whereas in Burham the two charities identified by the Charity Commissioners contributed only around £13. Charity funds were not available to all poor parishioners, as bequests often came with strings attached: Watson's endowment was for the use of the 12 poorest people in Frindsbury, while Dyer's Charity provided only 'flannel, or any other necessary article of clothing' for the poor of Halling.[167]

Payments were often limited to certain days of the year, rather than providing a regular source of income. In Aylesford money from Sedley's and Savidge's charities was distributed on 6 January each year. There were 73 recipients in 1791, with payments ranging from 1s. to 4s. according to the number of people in the family. By the 1830s payments were with half-quartern loaves, purchased by the parish authorities and handed out to all poor households irrespective of whether they were receiving relief. We know from a surviving set of accounts that 228¾ gallons of bread were distributed in 1861, plus a shilling's worth of tea and sugar.[168]

Poor relief was clearly a significant element of the 'makeshift economy' of many households. It provided a valuable safety net when other avenues of support had been exhausted. Those most in need – the elderly, disabled and widows with dependent children – received parish pensions, regular weekly or monthly payments which were often their primary means of support. In Aylesford there were 26 parish pensioners in 1750, 21 of them women or children. Some parishes, including Strood and Aylesford, erected workhouses to house paupers. In 1723, the inmates at Strood were 15 parish orphans who were set to work spinning jersey for stockings. In Halling parts of the old Bishop's Palace were pressed into use as a workhouse in 1749, which was shared with neighbouring Birling, Luddesdown and Snodland.[169]

The majority of needy households continued to receive outdoor payments. Many drew on parish resources only occasionally, at times of crisis or to meet a particular need. Payments could be in cash or kind; the 1750 overseers' accounts for Aylesford record amongst other payments, £1 14s. for buying and setting up a bed for Dame Hayward, 1s. 6d. for 'making of a gown for Ann Peters', 15s. 2d. to pay John Thornton's rent for 13 weeks, 5s. given to Richard Summers while sick and 10s. 6d. 'for nursing and for necessaries for a sick man that died in Mr Stevens barn'. Some of the most common payments were to cover the costs of rent and fuel for poor families. The Aylesford overseers gave Widow Balding 1s. 6d. to buy wood in 1760 and paid rent for several paupers including Sarah Scotchford, Benjamin Brand and Widow Baldwin.[170]

Poor Law

The Poor Law Amendment Act (1834), better known as the New Poor Law, was designed to cut the cost of relief. Kent was divided into more than 20 'unions', groups of parishes whose poor went to a common workhouse. The eight Lower Medway Valley parishes were divided between two Unions. Strood, Frindsbury, Cuxton and Halling were in North Aylesford Union, which had its workhouse in Strood, while Aylesford, Snodland, Burham and Wouldham were in Malling Union, with the workhouse in East Malling.

Expenditure on poor relief fell dramatically in all the parishes once the new Unions were established in 1836. In theory, outdoor relief was no longer available for the 'able-bodied', those deemed capable of working. In practice, it never entirely disappeared. In Malling Union 481 unemployed paupers received out-relief payments in the first quarter of 1836, by the following quarter this had fallen to 213, and by the end of the year to 64.[a] In later years the inadequacy of the New Poor Law for dealing with short-term industrial fluctuations became apparent.

Figure B   *Strood infirmary block from the south-east, 2001. Erected in 1869, this is now the only surviving building from the complex and is used as a doctor's surgery.*

Notes

a   NA MH12/5226.

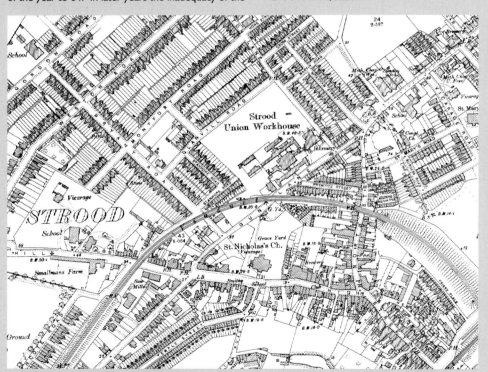

Figure A   *North Aylesford Union workhouse was erected in 1837 on the north side of Gunn Lane in Strood. The design of this workhouse represented a move away from the radial layouts which were proposed in a series of model plans published by the Poor Law Commissioners in 1835 and 1836 and which were designed to ensure segregation and supervision of the inmates. The layout of the North Aylesford Union workhouse has more in common with corridor plan workhouses, popular from the 1840s. The Aylesford workhouse is depicted here on an Ordnance Survey map of 1896 which shows later alterations to the plan.*

In Aylesford and Snodland dependence on poor relief is
clear from a steep rise in relief expenditure during the 1790s.
Most of this extra money was for cash payments to supplement
inadequate wages and cover for seasonal bouts of unemployment.
From 1814 agricultural depression following the French wars
intensified the problem, with widespread unemployment and
falling wages throughout Kent. By 1820 the list of disbursements
in Aylesford's overseers' accounts runs to 17 pages, and most of
the recipients were men. Individual labourers received monthly
payments of up to 40s., constituting possibly 40-60 per cent of
their yearly income.[171]

Outdoor relief, which entailed the assistance of the poor in the
form of money, food, clothing or goods without the requirement
that they enter an institution, was effectively curtailed by the Poor
Law Amendment Act of 1834, though it never entirely disappeared.
Outdoor payments continued, for many of the aged and infirm,
and for those suffering from short-term sickness or injury, so that
expenditure on out-relief still exceeded that on in-maintenance in
most of the parishes in the 1850s.[172]

The introduction of the New Poor Law in 1834 had implications
for the survival strategies of poor households. Evidence in the
out-relief books for Strood Union following the 1834 Act suggests
that for the poor the workhouse was just another element, albeit
an unpalatable one, to be taken into account in making ends meet.
James Langridge, an amputee labourer from Frindsbury, came to
the attention of the guardians on 51 occasions between April 1848
and June 1852. Over this period he and his family received £3 15s.
in cash, plus 131 loaves of bread and £2 3s. 9d. to cover medical
bills. He was also sent to the workhouse on six occasions when out
of work, often remaining there for little more than a week. Men
such as Langridge moved seamlessly from work, onto outdoor
relief, or a spell in the workhouse, then back into work again. They
were in contact with the poor law authorities for most of their
adult lives, yet never became institutionalised. The workhouse
simply provided a period of respite when work was hard to come
by, although Langridge's life may have been particularly difficult
because he had lost a leg.

Over time the welfare needs of the population changed.
The growth of industrial employment reduced the impact of
seasonality in agricultural work, but left the workforce prone
to periodic trade slumps and unemployment during the winter
months. Many labourers in the brickfields were laid off when the
'season' ended in late October. The dependence of the valley on
brickmaking and cement also made it particularly vulnerable to
the fluctuations of the building cycle. There was a slump in trade

around 1870, followed by further downturns in 1886-95 and the
mid-1900s, with several large firms going bankrupt during each of
these episodes.

The effect on the brick workers was often severe. Villages such
as Eccles suffered particularly badly: during the winter of 1870
many men found themselves out of work and a soup kitchen was
opened here and in nearby Aylesford. Similarly, in February 1895
the *Chatham Observer* noted that nearly 400 men in Strood were
out of work and their families 'little less than starving' due to the
depressed state of trade. The Beehive cement works had recently
closed with the loss of 45 jobs, while 'the dullness of trade at the
Globe and Quarry works' meant that another 150 to 200 men were
forced 'to eke out a bare existence on a few shillings a week'. Messrs
Tingey's were considering a 10 per cent wage reduction.[173]

The poor relief system was not well suited to dealing with
sudden influxes of unemployed workers. In 1858 Malling Union
was forced to give out relief of flour and bread to a number of able-
bodied paupers against the poor law regulations 'in consequence of
the Workhouse being too full for their reception'. Likewise, during
the crisis of 1895 the people of Strood turned to the Strood and
Frindsbury Relief Committee, who quickly distributed tickets for
food and coal to the needy.[174]

For those in work membership of a self-help body such as
a trade union or friendly society could provide an additional
means of support. These organisations provided people with
insurance against sickness, and gave payments to widows at the
death of a member, in return for a small monthly subscription.
By 1877 at least 19 friendly societies had been established in the
eight parishes of the valley, many of them affiliated to national
organisations such as the Ancient Orders of Foresters and Druids.
Their combined membership stood at over 2,000 people. Typical
of friendly society members was Francis Lanes, a cement worker
of Stone near Dartford, who died around 1835. In her settlement
examination, his widow Elizabeth noted that she used to carry
money to a benefit club in Aylesford on his behalf once a quarter.
One of the best supported societies was the Court Anchor of
Aylesford, which had 172 members in 1870, and had paid out
1,130 weeks and five days' worth of sick pay over the preceding
five years.[175]

Income from a benefit society could form a vital part of the
patchwork of resources available to poor households at times of
urgent need. In 1881 William Broomfield, a 44-year-old Aylesford
labourer, supplemented his 14s. a week earnings during a period of
illness with 2s. 6d. from 'his club' in addition to 12s. from his son,
William and 6s. in poor relief.[176]

For much of the 19th century trade unions offered their members similar benefits. The Original Society of Papermakers was particularly influential, with branches across the United Kingdom. Journeymen were provided with relief when out of work, and allowances paid to widows or children of deceased members. In the 1820s monthly contributions were usually 5s. or 6s., but could rise significantly when trade was depressed.[177]

Trade unions for skilled workers continued to offer generous benefit packages in the late 19th century: the United Brotherhood of Papermakers, based in Maidstone, gave its members out-of-work benefits of 14s. a week for the first 12 weeks and 6s. for a further 36 weeks, while the larger national Union of Paper Mill Workers offered between 5s. and 10s. a week depending on the size of a member's contribution. Although viewed by some with suspicion, membership of friendly societies and trade unions was generally welcomed by employers and parish authorities as an example of working families making provision for their own future welfare needs.[178]

Figure 51 Snodland Fountain of Friendship banner. The Fountain of Friendship was a lodge of the Ancient Order of Foresters, a Friendly Society offering mutual support to those not in a trade union. They provided benefits to members who fell on hard times and a regular programme of social events.

Less welcome were illegal activities that formed an element of some households' survival strategies. For much of the 19th century poaching was rife in the valley. Between 1857 and 1862 there were 59 prosecutions under the game laws in the eight parishes, including 22 in Halling alone. Those caught and prosecuted suffered the indignity of being named and shamed in the local press. Stephen Wilson was caught in possession of a hare and two rabbits on Mr Peters' land at Wouldham in August 1881, while William Ruck was convicted of 'trespassing … in search of game' on the Reverend Formby's land at Halling.[179]

For some, petty pilfering was a means to make ends meet. Local newspapers record the theft of sacks of oats, loaves of bread, and even 29 turnips. Others, such as Eliza Harris

Figure 52 Page from the Poor Law Commissioners correspondence with the Poor Law Unions, kept at The National Archives. This entry details the emigration to Australia of George Stedman, a 37-year-old agricultural labourer from Aylesford. In 1841 he left for Sydney, with his wife and four children. The parish officers allowed him £12 for subsistence, plus £1 for travelling expenses.

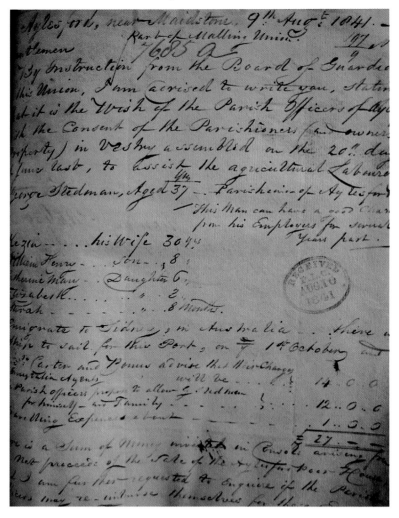

of Aylesford, turned to prostitution. What these examples reveal is the harsh reality of everyday life for many families. Industrialisation brought benefits to the valley, but many still struggled on the margins of subsistence.[180]

A common response to destitution, available largely to single people, was to go 'tramping' whereby they were supported, usually by a union until they reached the next place that they could find work. Edward Grice chose this course in the 1830s after completing his apprenticeship to an Aylesford shoemaker as his master had no work.[181]

A more radical option was emigration. Over the period 1801-31 Kent lost some 15,000 people to migration, many heading to North America, and in 1832 alone 200 emigrants left from Rochester and district. Downturns in the brick and cement industry prompted further bursts of emigration later in the century. Thomas Buss, who moved to Eccles at the age of six, left the village for America in the autumn of 1870 with four friends. He stayed six years in Boston, but subsequently returned to Eccles. A further 90 people from old Eccles Row emigrated to New Zealand in 1872, about a fifth of the resident population.[182]

POPULAR CULTURE

Towns were the location of a wide range of entertainment. Maidstone and the Medway towns were both within easy walking distance, and access was made easier with the coming of the railways. Writing in 1883, Canon Colson commented that people in Cuxton generally enjoyed their weekly entertainment on Saturday evenings at the Corn Exchange in Rochester, before catching the late train home.[183]

Fairs and Celebrations

Popular activities were associated particularly with the various fairs which punctuated the calendar. Although primarily trading events, these developed a recreational dimension from an early date. Numerous fairs took place across the Lower Medway Valley, among them the three-day fair in Strood from 26-28 August. This annual event drew large crowds from across north-west Kent. Based on marshy ground between Grange Road and Station Road, stalls often overflowed into the High Street, and local tradesmen kept their shops open late into the evening.[184]

A sense of the atmosphere of the fair can be gleaned from a poem written by the vicar of Allhallows, the Reverend Thomas Austin in 1756:

Here nuts and almonds in whole heaps are spread;
Here children, gaping, squall for gingerbread.
Here some with copper halfpence try their luck,
And others urge th' advent'rous chance of chuck.
Here ribbons, ear-rings, grace a lady's stall;
There other fancies do the eyes enthral.
Here Jews, with pencils, seals, and gaudy rings,
Convert your money into needless things.
But would you have the quintessence of all?
Then step you to the oyster-wench's stall;
There crabs and shrimps (both stinking) new you'll buy,
Your palate teasing till you come to try.
The noise thus made alarms each gaping fool,
With much proverbial cry, but little wool.

The fair also meant dancing, theatre booths, street musicians and travelling menageries. Robert Pocock recorded in 1812 that he went to Strood fair 'to see Mr Pettito's wild beasts and birds'.[185]

Sports and Games

Towns were also the venue for boisterous and often unsavoury entertainments such as cock fighting, bull baiting and low-brow theatrical performances. Prize fights were frequently held on the lonely marshes of the Medway during the 19th century, with spectators travelling by boat from Strood pier. On one occasion so many spectators tried to board a boat that it sank leaving its occupants struggling in the water. Onlookers were apparently kept amused by 'the number of "top" hats that went floating away on the tide'. In Maidstone there were bare knuckle fights and foot races sponsored by local publicans, and each Whitsuntide was marked by sports on Penenden Heath including donkey and wheelbarrow races.[186]

Many of these activities crossed the social divide. Cock fighting was a favourite pastime of the gentry, with county matches held in Maidstone during Assize week attracting large audiences. The cockpit and race course were among the few places where lord and labourer could rub shoulders.

For most working people leisure time was limited, their social life centred in the local community, and fitted into the rhythms of the farming year. Harvest was a particular time for merrymaking. Once the crops had been gathered the farmer would by custom treat the harvesters to a Harvest Supper. In Cuxton money for the supper was provided by passers-by and local tradesmen.[187]

The hop picking season was also associated with merrymaking. In the 1970s Harry Ablett, a long-time resident of Cuxton recalled

that in his youth the pickers had gathered on Bush Green after
the last day of the harvest in their Sunday Best: 'Here bread from
the Bush Bakery and beer from the off-licence were distributed
together with lemonade for the children and while people sat
around in little groups, with their backs to the garden fences, a
fiddler played and some of the pickers danced on the little patch of
grass in the middle'.[188]

The custom of beating the bounds continued in some places,
including Frindsbury, offering another opportunity for revelry,
especially as beer was provided for everyone taking part. In Halling
the practice was revived in 1881 with the children of the parish let
off school for the afternoon to attend.[189]

Most free time was spent in informal activities such as gaming,
drinking and playing 'street' sports. Indeed, the local inn or
alehouse was often the hub of community life. The 'Five Bells' was
not only the oldest local hostelry in Halling, it was also a venue
for inquests, village meetings and concerts, and a base for the local
friendly society. According to Thomas Buss, in his recollections
of Eccles, the brickmakers 'earned good wages, and spent a lot of
money at the end of the week on brandy and gin'. This may explain
why in the early 1860s the village was able to support two public
houses, but only one shop. For the men of Halling, 'A gamble or bet
or wager was a way of life … and often a wager would be made at
work or whilst drinking in the local'. Of course, not all socialising
revolved around the alehouse. Buss noted that on Saturday
evenings 'the men and women would gather in groups, and dance
and sing till 12 o'clock at night'.[190]

By the second half of the 19th century, the more enlightened
manufacturers of the Lower Medway Valley were already offering
leave and leisure facilities to their workforce. The *South Eastern
Gazette* reported in 1867 that Mr J. Wagon, the Aylesford sand
contractor, had given his 30 workmen a half-holiday. They had
'amused themselves at cricket' in the afternoon, and been treated to
a meal at the *George Inn* in the evening.[191]

By the 1880s works outings had become annual events,
eagerly anticipated by labourers and their families. Employees of
Trechmann, Weekes & Co. of Whornes Place went each year by
brake to Sutton Valence, where they had refreshments at the *Queen's
Head Hotel* before playing cricket at the local recreation ground.
In 1900 a party of more than one hundred attended, stopping
on the way back in Maidstone for tea and further refreshments.
Improvements to transport with the development of the railways
made trips to seaside towns like Margate, Hastings and Whitstable
more straightforward. These treats were intended, in the words
of T. Woolmer, a senior employee at Trechmann, Weekes & Co., to

ensure that 'good feeling may always exist between the Company and its employees seeing that their interests were mutual'.[192]

Employers also looked to cater for the physical and moral improvement of their workforce by providing schools, and by setting up mutual improvement societies, or contributing to the erection of public buildings. Henry Brassey funded a schoolroom at Pratling Street for the children of employees at his pottery works.[193]

Sporting activities were also well catered for. Many of the cement works had their own cricket or football teams, which often played in local leagues. Edward Butler, manager of the Burham works was president of Eccles football club for many years. At Halling, Hilton, Anderson, Brooks and Co. made one of their reservoirs available as a public swimming baths. Such acts frequently drew favourable media coverage. In September 1898 the *Chatham Observer* reported that, since taking over the Wouldham Cement Company's works earlier that year, Col. Joseph Gaskell and Mr J.S. Gaskell had 'taken a deep interest in the social welfare of their employees. Already an athletic club has been formed and a scheme is on foot for the provision of a Workmen's Club and Institute'.[194]

Figure 53 Ashby's Wagonette outside the Halling Institute. The cement manufacturer Messrs Hilton, Anderson and Company provided the £1,600 to build the Institute, opened in 1889.

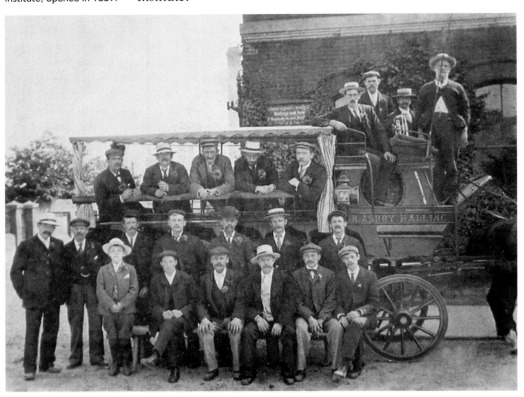

Some manufacturers were driven to take a genuine interest in their employees as a result of their religious convictions. Charles Townsend Hook's Swedenborg faith informed all his actions as an employer and leading member of the community in Snodland. His sense of duty extended not just to the provision of adequate accommodation for his workforce, and schooling for their children, but he also sought to provide spiritual and moral guidance through his position as main benefactor to and Secretary of the New Church Society.

Many of the social activities that Hook supported were organised through the New Church. There were outings for the children at the Sunday school, and a series of entertainments called 'Evenings for the People', set up to rival the 'Penny Readings' put on by the Anglican church. These evening events, held in a 'lecture hall' near to the parish church, included a concert of vocal and instrumental music on 12 January 1884, and an account by Col. Holland of his visit to Ninevah the following week.[195]

Other activities were centred on the mill itself. For instance, friendly games of cricket were often played among the workmen, including one in September 1871 between married and single employees, and there was an annual works outing. Local newspapers reported trips to Brighton in 1877, and to Ramsgate and Margate in 1878. Workers were given money to cover expenses incurred during these visits, enjoying themselves 'in the way they thought best until the evening when the special train conveyed them back to Snodland'.[196]

After Hook's death in 1877 his sisters carried on their brother's work. They established a Temperance Coffee Tavern in May Street in 1881 in place of the public house built by their brother for the use of mill workers, and in 1895 opened the Devonshire Rooms, which were to act as the main venue for village meetings and social events as well as housing the expanding Sunday School.[197]

The local parson was often prominent in promoting clubs and societies, particularly those dedicated to learning. The vicar of Aylesford, Archdeacon Grant, was patron of the village's Literary Institute, while in Cuxton the annual exhibition of the Cottage Gardeners' Society was hosted by the vicar, Canon Colson, who was himself a keen gardener. In the parish newsletter of 1876 he mused that 'few things add more to the temporal comforts and well being of a labouring man's family than his taking pride in his garden. It may help to lead him to better things – certainly keep him from worse'.[198]

Workers were increasingly involved in organising their own recreational activities through organisations such as trade unions, friendly societies and co-operatives. Friendly societies offered

Figure 54 The *Walnut Tree* public house, Bull Lane, Eccles. Like its namesake in Burham, it was the base for a thriving Friendly Society and was a centre of community activities.

members the conviviality of the club room in the local inn, and the celebration of the annual 'club day'. The sense of belonging fostered by the societies may have been important in helping migrant workers integrate themselves into the local community. The festivities which accompanied the third anniversary of the Ancient Order of Druids' Burham lodge in 1868 were typical. Members met at the lodge house, the Walnut Tree, before noon 'arrayed in the insignia of their order, and headed by the band of the RHA'. After parading around the parish, they 'returned about two to a hot dinner, which was spread in a marquee, erected in a meadow behind the lodge house'. The afternoon was spent playing various outdoor sports. The cost of such entertainments usually came out of society funds though this was officially frowned upon. The rules of the Amicable Society of Aylesford (established 1792) included provision for an annual dinner on the first Monday in June to be paid for 'out of common stock'. Other societies encouraged conviviality by specifying in their rules that members should pay three pence towards the cost of refreshments at each meeting.[199]

In Eccles, the 'People's Hall' was the centre of the community's social life, and also doubled as a Methodist chapel. In 1897 a large two-storey Workmen's Hall was erected on Bull Lane, by Abel Burren, founder of the family firm active locally in the first half of the 20th century. The hall, which subsequently became a social club, burnt down in 2001.

Working people also took responsibility for developing sporting activities. Most towns and villages in the Lower Medway Valley had football teams by the 1870s, with players and club officials drawn mainly from the labouring population. By the close of the century the sport was becoming increasingly popular and received wide coverage in the local newspapers, not all of it positive. The *Kent Messenger* reported on crowd trouble at a match between Eccles and West End in January 1897. After the referee had dismissed an Eccles player, 'Six-foot' Hayman, for using bad language, he was pelted with turf by the spectators forcing him to abandon the game. The game between Halling and Snodland in December 1892 drew a crowd of 300, and significantly was played during the evening under artificial lights lent by Mr Anderson of the cement works; possibly one of the earliest examples of floodlighting.[200]

Other popular sports included cycle racing and athletics. The *Rochester and Chatham Journal* reported on an abortive lamplight parade organised by the Strood Cycling Club in November 1891. Because of bad weather the group of 'some 70 wheelmen' retired to the *Bridge Hotel* for a 'highly successful "smoker"'. Those involved were some of the leading tradesmen of the town, including Henry Smetham and Charles Woollett who were both Town Trustees.[201]

Both cycling and rambling were popular activities among the working classes by the 1890s. The Halling Sports Meeting of September 1909 attracted competitors from all over Kent, and involved track races for local athletes, cycle races over a mile, two miles and three miles including handicaps and novice events, and a horse race known locally as the Halling Derby.[202]

Figure 55 The Grand Picture Palace, Holborough Road, Snodland. Constructed in 1912, the cinema is Snodland's last pre-war public building. No longer used as a cinema, the building survives in 2009 as a Roman Catholic Church.

For the less energetic there were the delights of the music halls in Chatham and Maidstone, or the newly established cinema: Strood had one by 1910 and Snodland by 1912. Local inns laid on dances and music nights, and offered bar games such as quoits and skittles. There was, in short, no lack of entertainment for the residents of the valley, which may be why so few of them appear to have been regular churchgoers.[203]

Chapter 6

Church, Chapel and People

Kent was a predominantly Anglican county in the mid-18th century, and within the Lower Medway Valley the parish church remained at the heart of each local community. Nor had the position changed greatly a century later. Around two-thirds of those attending a place of worship in 1851 belonged to the Established Church, although there were pockets of nonconformity in the more industrial parishes. The Anglican Church was most strongly supported in Cuxton, where the parish church was the only recorded place of worship, and in Wouldham, where its only rival was a small congregation of Primitive Methodists established three years earlier.

Aylesford, with its resident landowner Edward Ladd Betts, also had a strong Anglican presence. The vicar of St Peter's, the Revd Edward Marsh, estimated the average attendance to be 280 in the morning and 360 for the afternoon service. The Betts family clearly expected attendance: in 1852 Mrs Betts presented the church with a clock salvaged from the renovation of Preston Hall and made worship in the church more comfortable by providing stoves. Henry Brassey, who followed them at Preston Hall, provided three new church bells and paid for extensive renovations, notably to the church tower and the chancel, between 1878 and 1891. He also provided land to enlarge the churchyard.[204]

Nonconformity flourished in the Medway towns, including Strood, and in parishes with a maritime tradition like Frindsbury. Here there were four chapels, two occupied by Wesleyan Methodists, the others by Primitive Methodists and Baptists. In Snodland the Independent chapel had 50 attendees at the afternoon service on census Sunday in 1851, and 91 people at the evening service. In his submission to the enumerators the Revd Henry Dampier-Phelps, rector of Snodland, tellingly remarked that 'The great Body of the Inhabitants are Lime Burners – a fluctuating people – religious only by fits and starts – sometimes at Church, sometimes at a preaching house – never fixed long together at anything, or any place'.[205]

Perhaps most significant of all, around 65 per cent of the population of the Lower Medway Valley attended neither a church nor a chapel on census Sunday. Some local commentators sought to link this lack of religious observance with lax morals and dissolute behaviour. The Revd Spencer Phillips of Aylesford

thought that the morality of young women in the neighbouring
brickfields was 'decidedly lower than that of females of the same
age in an ordinary agricultural village'. Workers in these industries
were highly mobile, and this set them beyond the reach of the
Established Church. Mr Phillips complained that in one nearby
brickfield 'there are scarcely two families now employed who were
working there last year'.[206]

Industrial workers also harboured strong anti-establishment
attitudes, particularly in regard to the Church of England which
was seen as too closely allied to the ruling elite, a view clearly
articulated by Thomas Buss in his recollections of Eccles. New
evangelical churches willing to reach out to the industrial
labouring classes were able to thrive in the Lower Medway Valley,
and they posed a serious challenge to Anglican hegemony.

THE ANGLICAN CHURCH

The most pressing challenge facing the Established Church in
the valley was how to accommodate the growing population of
industrial workers. The existing Anglican churches in the valley
were too small to accommodate newcomers, and often too cold
and dark to compete effectively with new, brightly lit, and heated
nonconformist chapels which proliferated in the valley. At Halling
Church in 1848 it was noted that 'the interior of the church and
chancel in many parts requires restoration and cleaning'. This
work was eventually undertaken in 1853, but the church was still
too small. The vicar, F. Goldsmith, highlighted the issue in a letter
to the local paper in 1886. He pointed out that the population of
Halling had risen from 800 in 1871 to around 2,100, but that there
had been no additional provision for worship in the parish church
other than the building of a Mission Room in Upper Halling,
funded by Colonel Roberts. Plans had been drawn up to improve
the church and just over half of the £2,000 needed to execute the
expansion had already been raised. In his plea for more financial
support Goldsmith noted that 'Our cement manufacturers have
come forward most liberally'. The work was undertaken in 1889.[207]

All the existing medieval churches were either enlarged or
restored both to increase seating accommodation and to make the
buildings more 'fit for purpose'. At Burham the old church was in
an inconvenient position close to the banks of the Medway, and
in 1851 it was recorded that 'in bad weather few can attend'. This,
combined with competition from a Wesleyan Chapel built in the
village centre in 1847, encouraged a local movement to call for the
erection of a more convenient new church and in 1880 this was
planned in a village centre location, the medieval church being

Figure 56 Interior of St John the Baptist, Halling, looking towards the chancel. The church dates from the 12th century. Enlarged in the 13th century, and aisled in the 14th century, it was restored in 1889 by H. Bensted. This major restoration was part-funded by local cement manufacturers.

more or less abandoned after its erection. George Cubitt MP gave the site for the new church and a donation of £100 was received from Henry Brassey.[208]

Strood church was rebuilt in 1812 to designs by the architect Sir Robert Smirke to seat 750 people. This work had been co-ordinated by a body of Trustees, appointed by Act of Parliament, and comprising many of the leading citizens of the town. Funding was provided by a loan of £4,400 raised against an additional church rate levied on all property in the parish. This proved insufficient in a parish where the population rose threefold in less than 50 years, so in 1868 St Mary's was built as an additional Anglican church.[209]

The restoration of Cuxton church between 1863 and 1868 was partly financed by Lord Darnley, who added a south aisle to increase accommodation. While there was no place of nonconformist worship recorded in the parish in 1851 total seating capacity of the church, at 125, was not considered sufficient for a population of 374. Several landowners contributed towards the work including Lord Calthorpe, Lord Caernarvon and Lord Romney, none of whom seems to have had a direct link with the parish. In Snodland the restoration of the parish church, undertaken in 1869-70, benefited from the munificence of the Roberts and Lee families, although on completion of the work there was still a deficit in funds amounting to £70.[210]

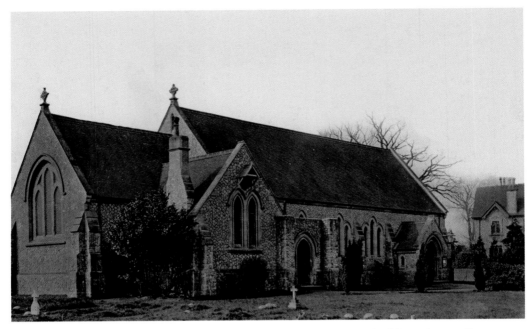

Figure 57 Christ Church, Lower Birling on Malling Road, Snodland. One of a number of new Anglican churches built during the second half of the 19th century to cater for the growing industrial population of the Lower Medway Valley.

At Frindsbury, where the church rate had been 'generally opposed by dissenters', the unusually long incumbency (1826-81) of the Reverend James Formby, seems to have been the reason for the relatively late and uncoordinated restoration of 1883 undertaken by his successor. A new church had also been built in 1878 for outlying parishioners at Upnor through the generosity of Captain and Mrs Savage of Goddington Manor.[211]

The largest medieval church in the area was Aylesford which had 520 seats in 1851. High pew rents charged at the parish church may well have meant that people travelled elsewhere to worship. We know that earlier in the century some Aylesford residents shared their allegiances when it came to places of worship. In her diary covering the years 1814-35 Rosamund Spong noted that her attendance alternated between church and chapel.[212]

Some entirely new Anglican churches were built to provide accommodation for industrial workers, including Upnor (1878), St Mark's, Eccles (1887) and Christ Church, Lower Birling (1893). Christ Church served the residents of new housing built along the Malling road south of Snodland and the expanding industrial hamlet of Ham Hill to the south in Birling parish. St Mark's served the expanding village of Eccles, close to Burham cement works. It was brick-built in a lancet style, on a site at the west end of Alma Road in the village. The architect was Thomas Day, the contractor J. Fullman of Birling, and the cost of construction and furnishing amounted to just under £1,500. A curate with responsibility for

Eccles had been appointed by Aylesford parish in January 1886, but the detached curate's house south-west of the church was not built until *c*.1892. St Mark's has now been demolished.[213]

THE GROWTH OF NONCONFORMITY

In the early 19th century only Strood, Frindsbury and Snodland had a significant nonconformist presence. In Strood this reflected a general and longstanding concentration of old dissent in the Medway towns – the Compton Census of 1676 recorded 300 dissenters in Chatham and 104 in the parish of Rochester St Nicholas. In Snodland, dissent was linked to the influx of papermakers, many of whom had nonconformist leanings. The Compton Census recorded 40 dissenters in Snodland in 1676.

Strood's first place of nonconformist worship opened in 1785, when a Church of Christ was formed, meeting in the 'Strood Tabernacle', a converted house on the south side of the High Street close to Rochester Bridge. In 1796 these premises were pulled down and rebuilt as the Zoar Independent Chapel, an unpretentious brick building set back from the street, at a cost of £142. By 1851 the chapel was regularly attracting over 300 worshippers to its morning and afternoon services, many of whom had to stand as the building seated only 236. The minister, Charles Dycear Gawthry, noted that attendance tended to fluctuate with the weather, as many of the congregation came from some distance. Evidence from the baptism registers and minute books suggests that just over a third of members came from Strood, with many more travelling from Frindsbury, Chatham and Rochester, and a few from as far afield as Maidstone, Sittingbourne and Dartford.[214]

Although dissent had been strong in Snodland in 1676, the first clear evidence of later nonconformity in the parish dates from 1822 when agents of the Chatham Itinerant Society began preaching in the area. At first worship was conducted in the cottage of Thomas Kidwell, a local papermaker. By 1836, however, a chapel capable of accommodating 200 people had been erected and fitted up, chiefly at the expense of William Joynson, manager of the paper-mill. The *Church Book of the Independents* reveals the pivotal role of Joynson, noting that he 'was not only the honoured instrument of providing a chapel without any charge for rent, but also of inducing many to attend'.[215]

Joynson later moved to St Mary Cray where he built up an extremely successful papermaking business employing 630 people by 1865. But he retained an interest in Snodland and its Independent Church, providing funding towards a new Providence chapel and school on Holborough Road in 1855 and acting as a trustee alongside his son Edmund. Succeeding papermaker masters also espoused the Independent faith, as did many of the workers who accompanied them, ensuring the chapel continued to thrive. John Clark, who leased the mill from 1834 to 1842, was a member of the Independent Church in Buckinghamshire, an important centre of the papermaking industry.[216]

In 1854 the business passed into the hands of Charles Townsend Hook, originally from Gloucestershire, whose family introduced a new form of nonconformist worship to Snodland. The family were adherents of the Church of the New Jerusalem, created in 1787 by English followers of the Swedish mystic Emmanuel Swedenborg (1688-1772). The English Swedenborgians were in the Wesleyan tradition, but the Hooks were sympathetic to all nonconformists. Early meetings of the New Church Society led by Hook were held in the house of Joseph Privett, a carpenter in Brook Street who was originally from Gloucestershire. Initially 12-15 people attended the services, but from 1864 the meetings were held in a purpose-built chapel attached to the Hook's family home 'Veles'. This chapel seating 70 was decorated at considerable expense with walnut, crimson velvet cloth and stained-glass windows, and was described as 'one of the most elegant little structures to be found in the New Church'.[217]

By 1880 expansion of the Society under the enthusiastic ministry of the Revd Thomas Marsden prompted discussions about the foundation of a larger church. At the annual meeting in 1881 of the New Church Society, 'it was resolved to erect a handsome edifice as a church, capable of meeting the increased requirements of the Society in Snodland and its neighbourhood'. The foundation stone was laid in November and the impressive new church opened in July 1882 on a site in the High Street. The cost of the new building (c.£5,000) was shared between the Hook family and Colonel Holland, manager of the paper-mill. What the papers omitted to mention was the support of the local community through the gift of 'a handsome brass lectern' as 'a unanimous token of good will from all in their employ at the paper works, Snodland.'[218]

The building, cruciform in plan and with a north-west tower, could easily have been mistaken for an Anglican church. Indeed, the *Illustrated London News* pointedly noted that it was 'somewhat similar in form and about the size of the present church at Snodland, except that the tower and the nave are more lofty'. There was seating for 300. The cost was at first reported as 'over £2000', but was later widely stated to have been £5,000. Now it stands empty, neglected and forlorn. At the rear of the church, Holland built himself a large house, today the headquarters of the Mid-Kent Water Company.[219]

Figure 58 The Church of the New Jerusalem, Snodland. Designed by Henry Bridge of Maidstone and built by Messrs J.W. Walker and Sons in 1882. Built of Kentish ragstone in an Early English style, the church bears a close resemblance to Snodland's 12th-century parish church, 400 yards further to the east.

Figure 59 Snodland
Congregational Chapel,
High Street. It was built in
1888 by Joshua Wilford,
whose name is inscribed
on a tablet on the vestry
block at the back. It
replaced an earlier chapel
on the Holborough Road,
built in 1855.

The new Swedenborg Church was built at a time of major
nonconformist chapel building in Snodland, which reflected the
rapid expansion of local congregations. The Independents outgrew
their accommodation at the Providence Chapel on Holborough
Road, which was sold for 1,000 guineas to allow the extension
of the British School founded in 1835. A new Congregational
Church was erected in its place in the High Street and opened on
28 November 1888. The Congregationalists also built a large room
specifically for their Sunday School.[220]

Methodism was also active by this period, with the Primitive
Methodist Church one of the first structures to be built on the old
Bull Fields. The memorial stone was laid in 1872 by an ex-Mayor of
Rochester. The Baptists, according to Woolmer, used the Concert
Room of the Snodland Institute until an iron room with a porch
was built in Church Fields in 1898.[221]

Developments in Snodland were matched elsewhere in the
valley with nonconformity prospering as industrial development
took root, and a wide range of denominations establishing a
presence in the area. Many of the new chapels recorded in the 1851
religious census were linked to the various branches of Methodism,
a movement which had a particular commitment to industrial
workers beyond the reach of the parish clergy. Early Methodist
preachers often had a background in the new industries of the

Figure 60 Wesleyan Chapel, Rochester Road, Aylesford. Built in 1851 on land given by local landowner Edward Ladd Betts, it replaced an earlier building which could no longer accommodate the expanding congregation. The simple Gothic chapel erected in 1851 to a pattern-book design is constructed of polygonal random ragstone. A schoolroom was added in 1864.

valley. Mr J. Lilley, who brought Methodism to Frindsbury when he opened his Bill Street home to worshippers, was manager to Mr Joseph Brindley, a local shipbuilder.[222]

By the 1850s the Methodist Connexion had split into various factions. Within the valley the Primitive Methodists had chapels in Wouldham and Upnor, and the Wesleyans in Aylesford, Burham and Frindsbury. Many worshippers seem to have switched their allegiance from the Established Church to Methodism, as congregations often soon outgrew their original premises. The Wesleyans in Aylesford, opened a new chapel on Rochester Road in 1851 seating 220, an increase of 90 on their previous home. In 1859 the Frindsbury Wesleyans moved to larger premises in North Street, Strood, adding a schoolroom in 1861 at a cost of £240. This soon proved too small with the congregation moving again to a site on Frindsbury Road in 1889, where an impressive brick-built church with a lofty nave and spire, and seating for 850 was erected at a cost of £5,700. In Eccles Methodists worshipped for many years in the People's Hall, though a purpose-built chapel was erected in 1931-2 at a cost of £1800 to the design of Harry H. Stroud of Ramsgate.[223]

Other denominations also prospered. The Congregationalists established a chapel in Cuxton in 1897 with financial support from Rochester. Alderman F. Smith provided money for the building and Alderman Elvy came up from the town to lead services for many years. In Halling a small Baptist chapel was erected in 1898, and in Strood the Salvation Army took over the former Methodist chapel in North Street.[224]

The success of nonconformity in the areas of brick and cement manufacture forced the local Anglicans to redouble their efforts, and prominent churchmen in the valley supported the building of mission chapels aimed specifically at industrial workers. Henry Brassey allowed the Pottery Schoolroom in Pratling Street to be used for public worship on a Sunday, while Lieut. Col. W.H. Roberts of Holborough Hall erected a corrugated iron Mission Church for the workers in North Halling.[225]

By 1900 the religious landscape of the Lower Medway Valley had been transformed just as the physical and economic landscape of the valley had been. The rise of nonconformity mirrored the expansion of industry and commerce in the valley. Ultimately industrialisation sowed the seeds of religious decline by speeding the introduction of a secular administrative regime, but the full effects of this were not felt until the 20th century. During the 19th century the ongoing struggle between church and chapel ensured religion continued to have a prominent public role and social significance.[226]

Chapter 7

Aylesford, Eccles and Snodland

This chapter is by John Newman.

So far we have looked at the Lower Medway Valley as a whole, but what was it like to live in any of the individual villages during the 18th and 19th centuries? In this chapter we focus on the transformation of the built environment in three of the villages, Aylesford, Eccles and Snodland.

Each village had a quite distinctive experience of industrialisation. Aylesford was an ancient settlement and a crossing point over the river Medway which grew only slowly as a result of the control exercised over development by the two main landowning families. Eccles was a new settlement which emerged in the north of Aylesford parish as a speculative venture to house workers in a nearby brick and cement works. Snodland was an established community which grew rapidly through the support of two resident industrialists, and by the late 19th century had acquired many of the trappings of urban status.

Figure 61 Phased map showing the physical development of Aylesford and the building campaigns promoted by major local landowners.

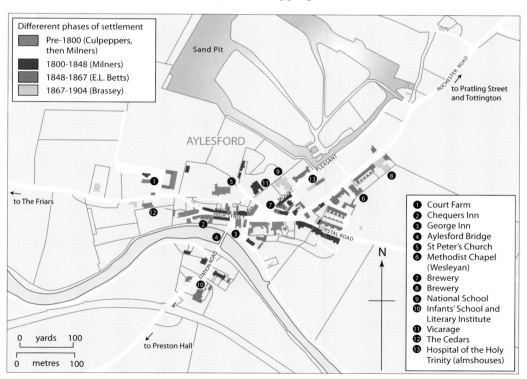

Differerent phases of settlement

- Pre-1800 (Culpeppers, then Milners)
- 1800-1848 (Milners)
- 1848-1867 (E.L. Betts)
- 1867-1904 (Brassey)

Sand Pit

ROCHESTER ROAD

to Pratling Street and Tottington

AYLESFORD

MOUNT PLEASANT

to The Friars

HIGH STREET

FORSTAL ROAD

STATION ROAD

N

to Preston Hall

| | 0 yards 100 |
| 0 metres 100 |

1. Court Farm
2. Chequers Inn
3. George Inn
4. Aylesford Bridge
5. St Peter's Church
6. Methodist Chapel (Wesleyan)
7. Brewery
8. Brewery
9. National School
10. Infants' School and Literary Institute
11. Vicarage
12. The Cedars
13. Hospital of the Holy Trinity (almshouses)

In 1851 the population of Snodland was 625, and that of
Aylesford 1,487. Over the ensuing half-century Aylesford's
population almost doubled, most of the increase taking place in
new settlements related to industrial development, at Pratling
Street, Forstal, and in Eccles, while some new housing was built
alongside the existing industry at Millhall. In the same period
Snodland's population grew almost seven-fold, almost all of it
accommodated in the steadily expanding core settlement. At first
new housing was erected by the owners of the cement works
and paper-mill for the benefit of their employees, but from the
mid-1870s population growth and hence settlement expansion
gathered its own momentum. By 1901, while the population of
Aylesford parish, including Eccles, stood at 2,678, Snodland's had
reached 4,136. It continued to rise steadily for a further decade.

AYLESFORD

*Figure 62 Aylesford.
Photographed from the
14th-century stone bridge
that crosses the Medway,
Aylesford's linear layout
along the north bank of
the river is emphasised,
together with the
concentration of housing
between the bridge and
the church.*

The village grew up on the north bank of the river Medway
where a steep-sided knoll provided a strategic site for a church
and the river Medway narrowed sufficiently for the construction
of a stone-built bridge in the 14th century, immediately south of
the church. Housing developed on the north bank of the river,
its nucleus between church and bridge. There were two principal
medieval estates in the parish. In 1240 a Carmelite priory had
been established a quarter of a mile west of the church, close

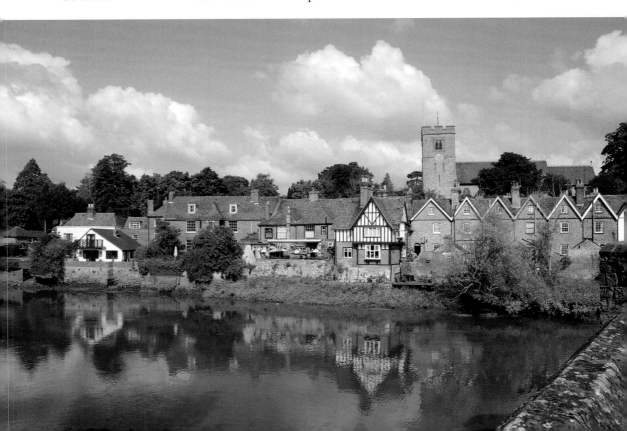

Figure 63 George Inn.
Constructed in the mid-
16th century as a house,
this jettyed timber-frame
building later became
the George Inn, one of
Aylesford's three main
hostelries. In the late
20th century it reverted
to domestic use.

to the north bank of the Medway. The buildings and lands of
the Carmelites formed the post-Dissolution estate known as
The Friars, owned from the later 16th century by the Sedley
family, and in 1657 acquired by Caleb Banks of Maidstone. Sir
John Banks, Caleb's son, amassed great wealth as a merchant in
London. His eldest daughter married Heneage Finch, son of the
Earl of Nottingham. Finch inherited The Friars estate and was
in 1714 created Earl of Aylesford. Successive earls continued to
hold The Friars and lands in the northern half of the parish until
1882, but they never lived in Aylesford.[227]

A map of 1700 by Abraham Walter of Larkfield, showing The
Friars estate at the time of Sir John's death, includes the whole
village except the Hospital of the Holy Trinity, the almshouse
founded under the terms of the will of Sir John Sedley in the
early 17th century on its eastern edge. The map is a copy of the
original, shows one large timber-framed house, Court Farm, to
the west of the church, and another, the vicarage, to the east.
Court Farm survives, but the vicarage was rebuilt in the early
19th century. Among the continuous sequence of riverside
buildings shown in more summary fashion on Walter's map, two
still stand out. The Chequers, at the west end, is an imposing
piece of early 17th-century timber-framing, three-storeyed with
gables. The George, in the centre of the village, is earlier, mid-
16th-century in origin, with continuous jetties towards the road
and towards the bridge. The Little Gem, further east, though also
timber-framed, is much humbler, as the whole eastern half of the
riverside development seems to have been.[228]

During the 18th century several eye-catching red-brick houses
were built at different locations in the village. 'Riverside', west

Figure 64   Church
Walk, Aylesford. This
four-storeyed house at
the foot of Church Walk
bears the date 1767. It
was subdivided soon after
it was built to create a
pair of very tall semi-
detached cottages.

of The Chequers, fronts The Quay and the river rather than the
road. Further east the two riverside houses, numbers 11-13 and
27 High Street, with twin three-sided full-height window bays,
must also belong to the last quarter of the century.

In the century and a half after 1700 the Earls of Aylesford
made piecemeal sales of properties in and around the village
and by the early 19th century their interest was focused
primarily at the western end, closest to The Friars. Here, on the
recommendation of the fifth earl's agent, R. K. Summerfield, The
Cedars, a freestanding house set back from the river, was leased
in 1824 to a new tenant on condition that £600 was spent on
repairs. In the event the tenant spent much more than that, so
that it became the 'very substantial and elegant residence' which
it still is today.[229]

Summerfield's other initiative was of greater significance
for the village as a whole. In 1816 he ordered the replacement
of two dilapidated cottages on the north side of the High
Street by a terrace of 'five respectable Houses suitable to small
tradesmen', at a cost of around £1,000. This terrace can be
identified as numbers 54-62 (even) High Street. Each cottage
frontage shows one window down, one up, with the doorway
over to one side. This pattern, in Aylesford as elsewhere,
remained standard for workers' housing until nearly the end
of the 19th century, with rubbed brick detail normal until the
1850s. Habitable roofspace was soon abandoned. Instead, the
back extension was developed.[230]

There are two other early terraces of workers' cottages in
Aylesford village, both shown on the 1840 tithe map. Numbers
24-36 (even) Forstal Road, though greatly altered, can be
recognised as something unusual in that the lower storey is of
brick, the upper rendered (originally tile-hung), and the plan is
uncharacteristically deep. The adjoining terrace, numbers 14-22
(even) Forstal Road, of yellow gault brick with yellow rubbed
brick voussoirs, follows the pattern of the terrace built in 1816.
Both belonged to small property owners in the village: in 1849
the former was owned by John Sampson and the latter by a
Mr Mayuss, but by *c*.1855 both had been acquired by Joseph
Bateman.[231]

The Preston Hall Estate

Aylesford's second large estate, centred on Preston Hall, was
from 1734 the seat of a Yorkshire family, the Milners. The estate
covered most of the southern half of the parish, and it was
probably during the Milner period that purchases began to be
made north of the Medway, including properties and land within

Figure 65 Terraced houses on the north side of Aylesford High Street. Built of stock brick, the façades of these houses are enlivened by red rubbed brick for the voussoirs of the flat window heads and semi-circular door heads, although this example has been painted. A tiled mansard roof with dormer windows provides habitable attics.

the village itself. Charles Milner junior, who inherited in 1836 and died a decade later, improved the estate, but by the last year of his life was running into financial difficulties, and in June 1846 raised £10,000 on the security of several farms.[232]

Charles Milner was actively engaged in building activities during the 1830s and '40s. From 1833 until 1839, he was a major customer of the widely employed local builder Joseph Poolley, running up bills totalling about £1,000. Several buildings which appear on both the tithe map of 1840 and the 1849 maps of the Preston Hall estate can be attributed to Milner. The most conspicuous of these is the terrace of eight cottages on the south

Figure 66 Terraced cottages on the south side of the High Street dating from 1840. Their picturesque character is shared by other cottages built for the Milner family in the first half of the 19th century.

side of the High Street. Their sawtooth gables form a memorable feature of any view of church and bridge.[233]

On the tithe map the terrace is shown half built, confirming its traditional date of 1840. The story that it was constructed of second-hand bricks taken from the parish workhouse demolished in 1837 is supported by the roughness and the mixed red and pink hues of the brickwork. The style, almost medieval with false arrow-loops in the end gables facing the bridge, and pointed arcading in the glazing bars of the sash windows, is a development of that used in the gabled, cruciform cottage pair (Bridge Cottage and Rose Cottage) close to the south end of the bridge. The pair had been completed by 1838, and are listed together as a shop on the tithe survey – the original south-facing shop window survives. Their first occupant was George Perrin, another Aylesford builder, who in partnership with William Page was responsible for much of the house-building in the village during this period. Park Row, an H-plan gabled terrace of stock brick, across the road from the shop, is also shown on the tithe map. It is in a similar, but slightly simpler style. In these two terraces Milner provided comparable accommodation with habitable roofspace to Summerfield's terrace of 1816.

In the mid-1840s Milner moved on to something more sophisticated. At the Royal Academy exhibition in 1846 John Whichcord, Maidstone's leading architect and Surveyor to the County of Kent, showed designs for 'half-timbered houses for Charles Milner' at Aylesford. Milner died in September that year without, it seems, putting any of Whichcord's designs into practice.[234]

Milner was a bachelor and he died intestate, so his estate was divided under the local custom of gavelkind between his two brothers, John and Henry Robert. John died within a month, but not without having added a codicil to his will bequeathing his half of the estate to his surviving brother. Henry Robert Milner was thus able to sell the whole estate, which he did in August 1848 to Edward Ladd Betts.[235]

Edward Ladd Betts

Betts's first concern was to rebuild Preston Hall. Since 1844 his business partner Sir Samuel Morton Peto had been enlarging his Suffolk seat, Somerleyton Park, in a Jacobean style, to the designs of John Thomas, Prince Albert's favourite sculptor and an occasional architect. Betts also turned to Thomas, who between 1849 and 1857 supervised the erection of the new Hall a little to the south of the old mansion 'upon a more elevated site'. Like Somerleyton it is Jacobean in style, of ragstone with lavish Caen stone dressings, mullioned windows and tall chimney stacks. This is a style mirrored in all the estate's outbuildings, and a number of other non-estate buildings on the south side of the river, notably Aylesford station, the Infants' School in Station road, and level-crossing keepers' cottages at Aylesford and Millhall. In each case the main building material is Kentish ragstone, in contrast to the brick used elsewhere in the village. This seems to represent a conscious effort to impose a unity of design on the built environment fringing the estate. The mansion survives, shorn of skyline trimmings and lacking its huge domed orangery and most of Thomas's overblown interiors. Lodges, a home farm and

Figure 67 Aylesford, the Corner House. An example of the ornamental style employed by Edward Ladd Betts. The house commanded the view westward along the High Street, and also had stone-faced outbuildings behind and a fully equipped butcher's shop, occupied by Benjamin Caryer until at least 1891.

stables (built in the mid-1860s to the design of Banks & Barry) also remain standing.[236]

Betts rebuilt several cottages and shops in the village centre and erected a new public house and several terraces of workers' cottages. Two styles were employed for his village buildings: one ornamental and the other practical. The ornamental buildings include all those in key positions as seen from the bridge or along the High Street, as well as on the crest of Mount Pleasant. They

Figure 68 Aylesford Mount Pleasant. These Tudor-style gabled cottages at the top of Mount Pleasant were erected for E.L. Betts in the mid-1850s. They are wider than earlier workers' cottages and have gardens in front.

employ ragstone for the ground storey, dressed with Caen stone or brick, with the upper storey timber-framed, roughcast and given spindly applied decorative timbers. The roofs are tiled, with barge-boarded gables, the window lattice-glazed. In this style are the two shops in the High Street at the northern end of the bridge, No. 44, the Joy family's saddlery and No. 46, a grocery, and the waterside cottage behind the west end of Charles Milner's many-gabled terrace. At the top of Mount Pleasant Betts erected a picturesque terrace of gabled cottages set back and forth in bold alternation. All these seem to have been completed by the mid-1850s.[237]

On the eastern edge of the village he erected to standard designs, in yellow gault brick with plain slated roofs, numbers 2-20 (even) Bush Row and numbers 19-27 (odd) Rochester Road, together with the gabled *Bush Inn* between them. The terrace, numbers 9-21 (odd) Forstal Road, is also of gault brick, but is

Figure 69 Pratling Street, Aylesford, photographed in 2008. This terrace of 14 cottages in simplified picturesque style was erected to accommodate workers at E.L. Betts' Aylesford Pottery works, which lay a short distance to the south.

gabled on a back-and-forth plan. It was a late development by
Betts, first appearing on the Ordnance Survey map surveyed in
1865. In the industrial hamlets Betts also built a few workers'
cottages. At Forstal they are of gault brick, but the gabled terrace
of 14 at Pratling Street, stone trimmed with brick, is a simplified
version of the picturesque style. A few similar cottages at Millhall
must also have been put up by him. Significantly, many of these
cottages are not only ornamental but are obviously more roomy
than the earlier terraces in the village.

In the mid-1850s, as contractor for the South Eastern Railway's
new line from Maidstone to Strood, Betts had no qualms about
allowing the line to pass through his park, even though it required
the demolition of several cottages and effectively isolated Preston
Hall from the village. Aylesford station and the two crossing
keepers' cottages were built in 1856 in a demonstrative Tudor style.
They were clearly intended to harmonise with, or even outdo,
Betts's ornamental buildings nearby, though they stood too far
west to be seen as picturesque objects from park or village, having
been sited primarily for the convenience of the industrial works at
Millhall. They were probably designed by William Tress, the South
Eastern Railway's in-house architect.

Figure 70 Aylesford. The
South Eastern Railway's
station was built in 1856
of ragstone, dressed with
Caen stone. The station
was designed to match
in style and materials the
nearby Infants' School and
outbuildings of Preston
Hall.

Betts's most important new industrial establishment was the
pottery at Pratling Street, already in business by 1850-1. Products
appear to have included common bricks, hollow bricks, pipes,
roofing tiles, terracotta and pottery. Although sited north-east of
the village on an outlying part of the estate, the pottery provided
employment for many residents of the village.[238]

Betts is credited with having supplied water to the village, from a spring at Tottington, north of Pratling Street, and gas lighting from his private gas works at Preston Hall. In 1865 he erected a stone and half-timber range at the south end of the infants' school to serve as a Literary Institute. It reputedly cost him £3,000. After his bankruptcy in 1866 and the sale of the estate the following year, the villagers and estate workers acknowledged his benefactions by erecting in 1868 a fountain in the infants' school playground. An inscription commemorated his 'many acts of kindness conferred on this parish and neighbourhood . . . by whom this school was erected and the village supplied with pure water.'[239]

Henry Brassey and the end of paternalism

Henry Brassey, the owner of Preston Hall from 1867, continued a paternalistic concern for the village, directed primarily towards the interests of the Established Church. Church Steps Cottage, at the foot of the steps linking the High Street with the churchyard (and on the site of the village lock-up) must have been rebuilt by him. When the National School on Mount Pleasant, built in 1833, was partially rebuilt in 1872 to the design of the Maidstone architect E.W. Stephens, Brassey contributed generously. In 1887 he paid for the completion of Stephens's design as a symmetrical composition, so that girls were as well accommodated as boys. At the Pratling Street pottery he built a school which could also be used for public worship on Sundays. The enlargement of the Sedley almshouses in 1892 was paid for by Brassey's widow and children in his memory.[240]

The death of Mrs Brassey in 1897 brought Aylesford's era of paternalism to an end. Her son and heir, H. L. C. Brassey, prepared in 1900 to sell freehold building plots both along the road from the village to The Friars and in Station Road. His target appears to have been middle-class commuters to London. For some reason the sale was abortive, and the tile-hung and rendered houses in Station Road were not erected until the 1920s. In 1904 Brassey sold the entire Preston Hall estate and moved to a genuine Jacobean mansion, Apethorpe in Northamptonshire. Preston Hall itself became a sanatorium, and is today in use as a hospital.[241]

Aylesford village remained remarkably unaltered for many years. An elderly resident at the start of the 21st century recalled that just before the Second World War it was:

> just a village surrounded by green fields and farms. In 1938 there were three pubs, two schools, a working bakery and shop, a butcher's shop, a post office, two sweet shops, a boot repairer, a blacksmith's yard, a cycle shop, three grocery and general provision stores, a builder and undertaker, a men's barber shop,

a newsagent, a fish shop and a dairy. All overlooked by the lovely old Church of St Peter and St Paul standing on the high ground rising sharply behind the high street.[242]

Today one of the pubs and most of the shops have gone. The fabric of the village remains little changed, having grown only along the Rochester Road. It is an oasis hemmed in by modern industry at Pratling Street, Millhall, New Hythe, and Ditton, by the M20 motorway and by spreading housing estates a few fields away to the east, west and south.

ECCLES

Eccles was a new settlement, which was eventually to house several hundred industrial workers. The driving force in its development was Thomas Cubitt. In 1851-3 he set up a new, mechanised brickworks at Burham on the east bank of the

Figure 71 Phased map showing the development of settlement in Eccles.

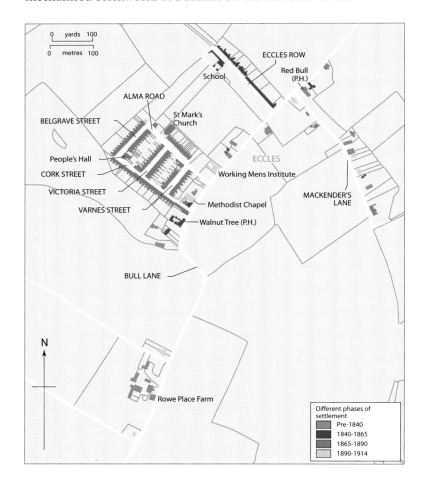

Medway. He also acquired several parcels of land in the area: five acres from G.F. Furnival in 1851, and another 12 acres in 1853, part of Rowe Place (or Eccles) farm, from the Earl of Aylesford. He opened negotiations for a further nine acres on the east side of the Aylesford to Rochester road, but the purchase had still to be completed in 1860, five years after his death.[243]

Cubitt had several objectives: to replace his exhausted Caledonian Road brickfield in east London, to capitalise on the lifting of brick duty in 1849, and to produce a range of brick types including moulded bricks which would render obsolete the traditional time-consuming use of cut and rubbed brickwork. He also established a small cement works at the site, to exploit the easily accessible supplies of chalk and clay in the vicinity. Close to the works Cubitt built Rose Villa for the works manager, William Varney, and nearby Rose Cottage for the works foreman. He also looked to house key workers brought to Burham from his London brickfields, but believed in employing mostly unskilled agricultural labourers from the locality, who could be appropriately trained on the job.[244]

The origin of Eccles, which came to house many of Cubitt's workers, was due not to Cubitt, but to the enterprise of a local farmer, Thomas Abbott of Rowe Place Farm. He developed a site which lay some 200 yards beyond the north-east corner of Rowe Place Farm and must have formed part of one of the plots acquired by Cubitt and leased to Abbott by the Burham Brick Lime and Cement Company for building purposes. Abbott erected a terrace of 22 cottages, subsequently known as Eccles Row. They were brick built and one bay wide, similar to the terraces of cottages in Aylesford village and elsewhere. Each house had a round-headed doorway and straight-headed sash windows. The roofspaces were habitable, lit by attic windows. However, the cottages were narrow of frontage and lacked back extensions for sculleries.[245]

During the 1860s Eccles Row was extended westwards with two semi-detached pairs of considerably larger houses and a further terrace of five, of intermediate size. Facing these last was a terrace of three similar cottages and by 1865 a school. In 1881 these are all referred to as Company Cottages, so it is probable that the Burham Brick Lime and Cement Company itself was responsible for building them. The first pair of larger houses (numbers 23 and 24) were inhabited by foremen at the works. One of these, Thomas Hart, was an engineer from the north of England who arrived in the area about 1860 and was 'a good friend to all the men under him'. Thomas Buss says that he became a substantial property owner in Eccles.[246]

This first phase of development (all demolished c.1980) created a community of over 30 households. Even in 1861, when only the first 22 cottages had been built, no fewer than 184 people lived or

Burham Cement Works

Figure A   *This watercolour of the Burham brick and cement works in 1885 shows how complex and extensive these manufactories could be.*

Thomas Cubitt established a fully mechanised brickworks here in 1852 as his main brickfield at Caledonian Road was reaching the end of its useful life. At the time it was the most modern in the industry, using modified Ainslie brickmaking machines which mixed and kneaded the clay, moulded it into shape, and fired the bricks in a system of kilns and drying rooms. Clay and bricks were also moved around the site on a network of tramways reducing the need for manual labour. By 1859 the works employed between 600 and 700 men and boys and could produce 25-30 million bricks per year.

Cubitt's four-storey pottery and engine house with its immense square chimney stack can be seen in the background centre left (1). This housed a 220-horse power engine by Maudslay and Field, which worked all the brick machines via a 520ft shaft. Drain pipes, ornamental flower and chimney pots and tiles were also manufactured in this building, and dried using waste heat from the boilers and kilns. On either side of the engine house there were extensive drying hacks: rows of wooden sheds in which the bricks were laid out to dry prior to firing. Shortly before Cubitt's death in

1855 a small cement works was added, and this side of the business expanded substantially over the following 30 years. The manufacture of cement required large quantities of chalk and clay. At Burham the chalk came from quarries at Culard to the north, the clay from a large pit visible behind the works building in the centre of the picture. The chalk was ground to a powder using burr stones, then mixed with clay in a horse-powered wash mill. The resulting slurry was the run off into slurry blocks where the water ran off and the mixture dried. Once dried the slurry was dug up and burnt in a kiln at a sufficient temperature to fuse into a clinker. This was then ground into a powder and packed for distribution. The earliest cement kilns were of 'beehive' or 'bottle' form and constructed of brick. The kiln was loaded from ports in the side wall with alternate layers of coke and slurry, and then fired from below using faggots as kindling.

The problem of drying slurry was overcome by the introduction of chamber kilns in the 1870s. These were built in blocks of three, with flues from the rear running under covered drying floors and the smoke exhausted via a common chimney. Both designs can be seen in the view of Burham works. In the centre and to the far right

are banks of chamber kilns, clearly distinguishable by the line of tall slender chimneys venting hot gases.

In front of the kilns is the wharf, where Cubitt built massive river walls to stabilise the banks and dredged the channel to provide a suitable anchorage. The cranes that line it were used to load and unload the barges bringing in supplies of coke and transporting the bricks and cement to market. Most of the output of the works went to London, though the company also supplied provincial and overseas markets.

On the right of the picture is the substantial house built for the first works manager, William Varney, who had been in Cubitt's employ for upwards of 40 years. In 1885 this house, Rose Villa (2), was occupied by Edmund Butler and his family. Nearby was Rose Cottage, a more modest residence, where site foreman Daniel Sharp lived.

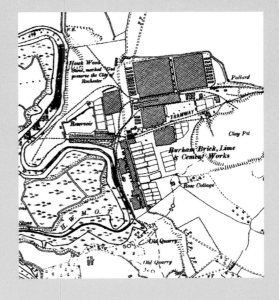

Figure B *Slurry backs, located behind the main buildings of the cement works, can clearly be identified on the 1898 Ordnance Survey map.*

lodged in them. Buss, looking back in 1908, wrote nostalgically of that period: 'I cannot help thinking of the old days of Eccles, 50 years ago, when men, women and girls, and the young men, would all get together on Saturday nights and dance on the green in front of the old row.'[247]

The main body of Eccles village developed south of this 'green', largely on a rectangular strip of land owned by William Varney, manager of the Works. First to be laid out, from 1861 according to Buss, was Cork Street, parallel with Eccles Row but behind the *Walnut Tree Inn* in Bull Lane (the Aylesford to Rochester road), built in the same year. Houses were built only on the south side of the street. The first eight houses, according to Buss, were built by George Cork, who gave his name to the street. They can be identified as numbers 11-25 (odd): the census of 1871 shows George Cork, then a 38-year-old labourer in the brickfield, resident at number 11. Numbers 1-3 were a shop, also built by Cork, and numbers 5-9 three individually built cottages, all inhabited by 1871. Only four further houses are known to have been built by this date.[248]

Expansion and Development

This hesitant beginning to the expansion of the settlement must have been linked to the slump in brick production of the early 1870s. It led to mass lay-offs at the works and the emigration in 1870-2 of many residents of Eccles Row, including Buss, to the United States, New Zealand and Australia. When Buss returned to Eccles from the United States in 1876 he found that by then 'the place seemed to be improving fast', although building in Cork Street appears to have proceeded haltingly, with blocks of four or occasionally eight extending the street to its eventual length of 45 cottages.

The cottages in Cork Street match those in Eccles Row in being only one bay wide, with the same standard arrangement of door and windows, but some minimal decoration. The earliest block of eight is built hard against the pavement, like Eccles Row, and so are the 14 at the farther end; but the cottages in the middle, though aligned with the rest, have railed front gardens a couple of feet deep. In another significant improvement over Eccles Row, all the cottages in Cork Street were given paired back extensions, although there were no habitable attics.

The decoration of the façades shows much variety from block to block. Most openings have (or had) flat heads, many with raised keystones, or doorhoods on brackets, a feature not found elsewhere in Eccles.

The three parallel north-south streets – from east to west Varnes Street, Victoria Street and Belgrave Street – have much greater uniformity. The cottages are of stock brick with segmental

Figure 72   51-7 Cork Street, Eccles. These cottages have exposed stock brick walls, in contrast with the rendered front walls found elsewhere in the street. Doorheads and window heads are segmental, formed of terracotta blocks with incised decoration, and the continuous mid-height stringcourse is also of decorative terracotta.

terracotta heads to doors and windows, and in Varnes Street and Victoria Street there are continuous terracotta stringcourses, though this feature is absent from houses in Belgrave Street.

In Varnes Street discontinuities in eaves-lines and the irregular provision of front gardens suggest that although the design was uniform, construction was piecemeal in pairs and groups of four. The individually designed and dated cottages at the north end of the west side of the street must be additions: numbers 21 and 23 bear a plaque inscribed Lawn Cottages 1879 with the initials G.F.; No. 29 is named Bay Cottage, dated 1879 with the initials A.J.; the corner house, probably built as a shop, has the same date and the full surname of A. Joy (presumably a member of the prominent Joy family of Aylesford).

The west side of Victoria Street was built in two blocks, one of six cottages, the other of 14; but the east side is a unity, 22 cottages named on a central plaque as Alexandra Terrace, 1880, with the initials E.S. Only the large shop and post office at the south end was built to a different design. Belgrave Street represented the most ambitious project in construction, as the 17 cottages on the east side and the 30 on the west side were each built as unified terraces. The census shows that this was the last of the three streets to be built, confirming that the builders' ambition increased as work proceeded from east to west.[249]

With the completion of Belgrave Street the Varney land was fully developed. However, a further piece of land soon became available. Private legislation following the Settled Land Act of 1882 authorised the Earl of Aylesford to dispose of all his Kentish landholdings. The consequent sale in 1884 included a cottage and two small pieces of pasture land, all with frontages onto Bull Lane and in the tenancy of William Hawkes, former farm manager at Rowe Place Farm and now grocer at No. 1, Eccles Row. Thomas Buss tells us that Hawkes bought one of the pastures which formed a long thin strip extending from Bull Lane along the north side of the north-south streets as far as the west side of Victoria Street. He paid £450, and sold the site at the west end in 1886 to Aylesford vestry for £100 to build St Mark's Church. He sold the rest for house building. On most of this strip of land Alma Road was built, a single south-facing terrace.[250]

Early photographs show the impressive uniformity of both Eccles Row and Alma Road as first constructed, and the three north-south streets, with their terraces facing each other, were clearly just as consistent. Cork Street, by contrast, must always have presented a bitty appearance. The reason for the uniformity of Eccles Row has already been explained. The character of the north-south streets must have been due to the involvement of William Varney and thus

Figure 73 Alma Road, Eccles, was built as a terrace of 20 cottages behind narrow front gardens. Their stock brick walls and decorative terracotta window and doorheads correspond with Belgrave Street, but each cottage has one conspicuous extra amenity, a central bay window for the front parlour.

Figure 74 Medina Cottage was added in 1899 to the west side of Belgrave Street so that it commanded the vista down Alma Road. It is not known for whom it was built although George Dewey was living in the house in 1901. By 1903 Albert Greenfield, the leading Methodist in Eccles, lived there.

of the Burham Brick Lime and Cement Company. The erection of uniform workers' housing in brick and terracotta would have been a good advertisement for the Company's products. A flyer, datable after May 1868, proclaimed, 'A great variety of designs are prepared for diapered surfaces, string courses, circular columns, window heads, &c. to be seen at their London Depot.'[251]

The houses have been much altered in recent years. Painting, render and pebbledash have obscured the brickwork of a majority of cottages, and PVC windows and doors are ubiquitous. Concrete tiles have replaced slates on most roofs. As a result, the original uniformity of the streets has now been lost.

SNODLAND

Snodland originated as a riverside settlement beside an early crossing point on the river Medway: church and mill are both mentioned in the Domesday survey. The medieval village developed inland from them; the High Street extended westwards, and Brook Street turned sharply southwards to give access to The Brook, a hundred acres of marshy common land in a bow of the river. The meandering continuation of High Street led to Birling, the next village, while a turning to the north made its way to Holborough, the secondary settlement in the parish. Brook Street was cleared in 1979 to make way for the construction of the inner by-pass.[252]

The only eloquent survivor of Snodland's medieval houses is Mulberry Cottages in High Street, a much-restored 15th-century Wealden hall house. Prospect Cottage in Holborough Road is also timber-framed, perhaps medieval in part, with a large addition built some time between 1758 and 1781, the best example of Georgian brickwork in the village. The *Bull Inn*, at the junction of High Street and Holborough Road, is the successor to a medieval house, an inn by the early 18th century and rebuilt in 1775. It was rebuilt again a century later. The Lodge, upper High Street, is Regency in character though built in 1841, for Snodland's most famous son, Thomas Fletcher Waghorn, a postal pioneer who developed a new overland route from Great Britain to India.[253]

Through traffic from Strood to West Malling had traditionally come from Holborough to the Bull and then turned west along the road to Birling and Ham Hill, skirting Snodland village altogether. In 1825-6 a toll road was constructed from Strood to Malling which took traffic directly south from the *Bull* to Ham Hill. Snodland village was not at first affected, but its potential for growth was much increased by this direct link to the wider world.

Figure 75 Phased map showing the physical development of Snodland and Holborough.

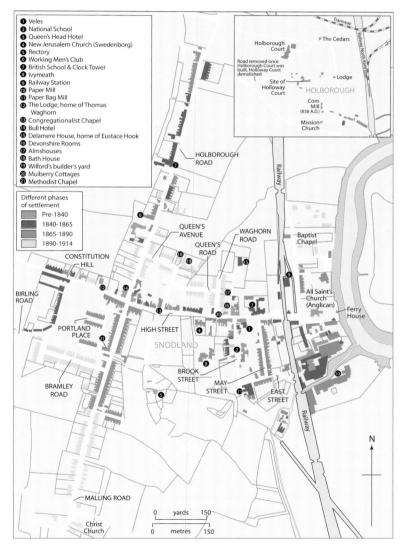

Key:
1 Veles
2 National School
3 Queen's Head Hotel
4 New Jerusalem Church (Swedenborg)
5 Rectory
6 Working Men's Club
7 British School & Clock Tower
8 Ivymeath
9 Railway Station
10 Paper Mill
11 Paper Bag Mill
12 The Lodge, home of Thomas Waghorn
13 Congregationalist Chapel
14 Bull Hotel
15 Delamere House, home of Eustace Hook
16 Devonshire Rooms
17 Almshouses
18 Bath House
19 Wilford's builder's yard
20 Mulberry Cottages
21 Methodist Chapel

Different phases of settlement
Pre-1840
1840-1865
1865-1890
1890-1914

The arrival of the railway in 1856, with a station immediately west of the church, had a much greater impact.[254]

By the later 18th century Snodland parish was almost entirely in the hands of three landowners, John May of Holborough, the Earl of Romney, whose estate was centred in Cuxton further north, and the Bishop of Rochester, who leased his lands to the Dalison family of Hamptons, West Peckham. In the first decade of the 19th century the two main estates fragmented. The Earl of Romney's six farms were sold off separately in 1808. May's estates, which included Snodland paper-mill, the Court Lodge farm and other land close to the heart of the village, were divided at his death in 1805 between four executors. Each of them was given discretion to dispose of the land as they saw fit. It took nearly half a century before two new figures emerged to become dominant in the parish: William Lee, the owner of the lime works from 1846, and Charles Townsend Hook, the owner of the paper-mill from 1854.[255]

The lime works had been established after one of John May's executors, Edward Wickham, in 1819 transferred the Holborough Court estate to two partners, Thomas Poynder and William Hobson. They were subsequently referred to as 'limeburners'. Chalk workings here are indicated on a map of 1823. Major expansion, and diversification into cement-making, took place under William Lee, a resident of Rochester, who since the mid-1820s had been manager of a limeworks at Burham. By 1851 Lee was living at Holloway Court, the house built for John May on the Holborough estate. When his son and heir, Samuel, died the following year, he acquired a vault outside the north wall of the chancel of the parish church and erected a large tombchest over it, as a family monument. This was a significant action, staking a claim that he was the new principal landowner in the parish. The claim was clearly credible, as Kelly's Directory of 1855 lists only two gentry, Lee and the rector, the Reverend H.D. Phelps. Lee later served as churchwarden, and his Anglican allegiance is further indicated by his having been a 'staunch and generous supporter' of the National School in Brook Street.[256]

Lee served as a magistrate and MP for Maidstone. After his death in 1881 at the age of 80 his son-in-law, Colonel William Henry Roberts of Birling, inherited the Holborough estate. Roberts demolished Holloway Court and erected a new mansion, Holborough Court, in a more advantageous position and in enlarged landscaped grounds. Built in 1884-6 by the Maidstone architect Hubert Bensted, this was a flamboyant affair in the fashionable 'Queen Anne' style of the day and cost no less than £30,000.[257]

Figure 76 Veles,
Snodland. Home of
Charles Townsend Hook
and his family from 1854.
Hook rebuilt the house
in classical style and a
decade later added a
substantial chapel at the
rear, used for services
of the New Jerusalem
church until a new church
was erected in 1882.

Figure 77 Clocktower,
Holborough Road,
Snodland. After Charles
Townsend Hook's death
in 1877, his mother and
sisters erected a clock
tower in front of the
school in his memory,
designed by W. Freeman
of Sevenoaks. Its red and
white brick banding and
the idiosyncratic profile
of its crowning clock-
stage catch the eye. Its
positioning, so as to be
visible from afar up and
down the toll road, make
it appear, misleadingly,
as the focal point of the
village, to which it lends
an almost urban status.

The mill by the church is first documented as making paper in 1743, a decade after it had come, as part of the Snodland Court Lodge estate, into the hands of John May senior. Thereafter the names of various papermakers are known, operating as lessees of the Mays until John May junior's death in 1805, and then of one of his executors, Mary Simpson. In 1807 she sold the mill to John Spong of Aylesford, coal merchant, proprietor of the business at Millhall there. He transferred the mill in 1810 to his son William, who entered into a partnership with a papermaker master, Isaac Wenman. In 1818 the property was described as a 'Paper Mill, Six Cottages and about eight acres of Land'. The paper-mill was enlarged and modernised in the late 1830s, but further plans for development fell through when the mill manager went bankrupt in 1840.[258]

In 1854 the business passed to Charles Townsend Hook, who moved his whole family to Snodland: his father Samuel, his mother, his brother Eustace and three sisters, Edith, Maude and Agnes. They took up residence in the mill manager's house, Acacia Cottage in the High Street close to the junction with Brook Street. The family soon rebuilt the house on a larger scale, but on the same site, hard up against the street. The new house was in a severe classical style with heavily channelled walls; but the main concession to its enhanced status was a change of name, to 'Veles', the traditional name of Snodland manor. 'Veles' was demolished shortly after 1930 and its site is now where the inner by-pass runs.[259]

During their time in the village the Hooks were responsible for the erection of a number of public buildings reflecting

Figure 79 The east
side of Waghorn
Road, Snodland. In the
foreground are the
Drummond Almshouses
with a façade panelled
in red brick and flint.
Beyond them are the
earlier Eustace Hook
Almshouses and,
completing the row, the
Devonshire Rooms, used
as a Sunday school and
village hall.

their religious faith and philanthropic values, although most
were built after Charles Townsend's death in 1877. Perhaps
most prominent were the New Jerusalem Church erected on
the south side of the High Street in 1881-2 and the British
School in Holborough Road extended by the Misses Hook
in 1888. Five years later they made provision for some
secondary education for the more capable boys at the School
by establishing a Manual Training Classroom in the High
Street to the west of Mulberry Cottages. The largest collection
of public buildings lies on the east side of Waghorn Road
in a row extending northwards from the Manual Training
School: the Devonshire Rooms, half-timbered over polygonal
random stonework, built in 1895 as a Sunday School and
village hall; the Eustace Hook Almshouses, 1892-3, designed
for three residents by George R. Cobham of Gravesend and
erected by the Snodland builder Joshua Wilford for £830 (now
considerably altered); and the Drummond Almshouses of 1903,
for four residents.[260]

Housing the Workforce

The census returns suggest that housing was never provided exclusively for any particular type of worker, but it was natural that workers' cottages should be built as close as possible to their workplaces. From the mid-1850s the two growth points were at the east end of High Street, beside the paper-mill, and along Holborough Road between Providence Chapel and the lime and cement works.

Several cottages had been built close to the paper-mill before Charles Townsend Hook arrived in 1854. The 1841 tithe map shows a terrace between the mill and All Saints church. A second, longer terrace of 14 cottages, at right angles, is shown on the first edition Ordnance Survey map of 1865. They were of the early type without back extensions. These cottages were all cleared away when the mill was rebuilt on a larger scale after the disastrous fire of 1906. Railway Terrace, still largely surviving on the south side of High Street, must pre-date the coming of the railway in 1856, since it has been truncated by the track. Built of stock brick with rubbed brick detail, it originally had no back extensions, thus belonging to the early type of workers' housing.

Between 1854 and his death in 1877 Hook bought or built 91 cottages for his workers, at a cost of about £11,000. Initially he held only limited land close to the mill, so his first extensive cottage building took place beyond the western edge of the village in Birling Road and Constitution Hill. He is said to have erected 40 cottages here, but many cottages in this area have subsequently been demolished and it is no longer clear which ones were built for Hook. Those that survive in Birling Road are plain and unremarkable.[261]

The possibility of further building on the mill side of the village was opened up in 1867 when the Ecclesiastical Commissioners sold 24 acres of land east of Brook Street in order to fund the rebuilding of the National School. A north-south spine road, May Street, was laid out, with the much shorter East Street across its southern end. The houses and cottages erected for Hook in East Street by Snodland builders are fully documented. On the north side two villas for senior employees were built by Joseph Privett for £390 each by June 1868, and two cottages by Thomas Burgess and Robert Langridge for £115 each by September 1870. On the south side an unbroken terrace of 13 extremely plain cottages was built, seven by Privett for £113 each by October 1868, the rest by Burgess and Langridge by November 1869, for the slightly higher price of £129 each. All had been swept away by c.1980. The still surviving housing in May Street is slightly later, dating from between 1871 and 1875. Many of these were erected by Burgess and Langridge.[262]

William Lee's activities in building workers' housing are harder
to pin down. The estate which he had bought in 1846, centred
on Holborough, did not extend far southwards in the parish. The
scanty surviving evidence of subsequent purchases by Lee and
his heirs show them building up land holdings on both sides of
Holborough Road as far south as the *Bull Inn* crossroads, and then
selling off plots for building. However, the ribbon development on
the west side of Holborough Road north of Providence Chapel and
the two terraces on the east side, Prospect Place at the south end,
and Victoria Terrace (demolished *c.*1980), must all have been built
primarily for the labourers in Lee's lime and cement works. Almost
all this housing appears on the first edition of the Ordnance Survey
prepared in 1865.[263]

Earliest in character is Prospect Place, of stock brick with
rubbed brick dressings, and single-storey back extensions. The
cottages on the west side of the road are extremely miscellaneous,
in short terraces and pairs, with a couple of free-standing villas,
one of which, 'Bryncree' (No.115), was inhabited for a time by
the paper mill manager, William Dedrick. This was a desirable
location, with a wide view over the Medway valley to the North
Downs above Boxley, and the housing is set generously back from
the roadway to take advantage of the prospect. Two terraces,
Jessamine Cottages (numbers 117-131 odd) and Magnolia Terrace
– at first called Brown's Cottages (numbers 147-153 odd), are
designed, exceptionally, with wide upper and lower windows both
of three arched lights, and with arched dormers in the roof-slope.

At the north end were some post-1865 terraces. Of these the
two-part Holborough Terrace (numbers 191-205 odd) survives,
its southern half dated 1872. The whole terrace is in the decorative
style of the early 1870s, with red and yellow striped brickwork
and decorative terracotta heads to the windows and doorways in
front and even on the back extensions. The parlour windows here
are also unusually wide, acknowledging the view. Three further
terraces, Dorking Place, Walgrave Place and Orchard Cottages
of the 1880s lined the old road at Holborough as it ran west-east
beside the stream. They were demolished in the mid-20th century.

In the centre of Snodland village the first large-scale development
was of Bull Fields in the 1870s and 1880s. This rectangular area
bordered on the north by the upper High Street and on the east by
the turnpike road, and extending southwards to the parish boundary,
was by tradition the field where the village bull was tethered. It
formed part of Cox's Farm, owned by Lord Romney in the 18th
century, but released for building by the then owner, Edward Thomas
Luck of West Malling, before his death in 1877. Terraced cottages
were built on the west side of the turnpike (Malling Road) up to the

Figure 80 Clara Place, Snodland, a three-cottage terrace in Constitution Hill. Note the use of striped brickwork, decorative terracotta string course and door and window heads.

crossroads, and a parade of 12 shops in the upper High Street. In the middle of the Fields a short new road, Portland Place was laid out, and further west, as far as Birling Road, were allotment grounds.

The terraces throughout, whether of shops or cottages, include some elevations with decorative terracotta heads to windows and doorways. In the outward facing terraces the terracotta was combined with high quality 'white' gault brick striped with red. Portland Place, however, which was not visible to passers by, was given plain stock brick walling, though the details are of terracotta throughout. This was the only entirely uniform part of the development, though the north side of the street at least is known to have been built up piecemeal from at least 1877 until after 1881. Even in its much altered state it is possible to recognise Bull Fields as the largest development in Snodland involving the unidentified builder whose hallmarks were striped brickwork and decorative terracotta detail. The same person must also have been responsible for Faith Place, May Street, 1871, and Holborough Terrace, 1872, together with the most exuberant example of all, Clara Place, the three-cottage terrace in Constitution Hill dated 1875.[264]

The Coulson Estate

Ribbon development further south in Malling Road took place in Birling parish, although forming a continuation of the fabric of Snodland. The land belonged to the Revd Thomas Borlase Coulson, who had been given it by his father in 1862 as part of his marriage settlement. Building along Malling Road was under way by the mid-1880s; the date 1887 is prominently displayed on Wells Terrace (east side) and Stanley Terrace (west side). In 1892-3 the

Figure 81 Bramley Road, Snodland, laid out west of Malling Road in the 1890s as part of the Coulson development. The road, which runs east-west, has a short north-south arm (called Recreation Avenue since the 1900s) at its western end, which links through to Birling Road to the north.

church of Christ Church, Lower Birling was erected further down the road to serve the new residents.[265]

The Coulson development along Malling Road was aimed at a middle-class clientele. In June 1892 the Birling Building Society put 94 plots on the Coulson estate up for sale, along both sides of the road, closing the gap between the 1880s housing and the newly built church. Conditions were attached to the sale to ensure the erection of villas; most plots were intended for semi-detached pairs. The contrast between the houses built on these plots and those of the 1880s further north is still noticeable, even though details of construction and decoration suggest that the same builder, Joshua Wilford, may have erected them all. In 1888 the parish boundary was extended southwards to bring all the houses within Snodland.

The northern end of the Coulson estate was largely developed after the Revd T.B. Coulson's death in 1895, on the initiative of his widow and daughters. Here Bramley Road was laid out on the west side of Malling Road, 50 yards south of the Primitive Methodist chapel. Nelson Villa (No.23) on the south side of the road is dated 1891, anticipating the rest of the development, while on the north side Collingwood Villas (numbers 28-36 even), are dated 1897. As late as 1902 the development of this area was still patchy and incomplete.[266]

At the same time as the development of the Coulson estate was extending Snodland southwards, a compact layout of new roads north of High Street and east of Holborough Road was consolidating the centre of the village. After the death of Charles Townsend Hook's brother Eustace in 1890, Waghorn Road was laid out on part of the grounds of his house. Queen's Road and the dogleg Queen's Avenue, which makes the link into Holborough Road, were laid out on land which seems to have been part of the Holborough Court Estate.[267]

Joshua Wilford was the dominant housebuilder on Queen's Road and Queen's Avenue. At first he had his headquarters in Church Fields, conveniently beside the Medway for the transport of goods and materials, and there he built himself a showy house, 'Sunnyside', doubtless intended to impress potential clients. But *c.*1897 he built a large depot in Queen's Avenue, at the heart of the new development. The only house documented as having been built by him is No. 22 Queen's Avenue, of 1903. But the whole of Queen's Road, largely complete by 1901, is clearly by him, together with the similar housing in Queen's Avenue. Osborne Villas, his finest houses here, were erected after 1908.[268]

As Snodland's population grew during the second half of the 19th century, and as tentacles of housing spread out to west, north and south, High Street, the backbone of the village, was also gradually transformed. Old cottages in their garden grounds were pulled down and replaced by the houses of the increasing number of professionals, not only the ferryman and the coal merchant, but also the doctor and the solicitor, which a population of around 3,000 required. An increasing number of purpose-built shops took the place of shopkeepers trading from their cottages. A significant moment must have come in 1869 when a kerbed footpath was laid the full length of the street. Further street paving followed in 1877-8, and in 1878 the Hook sisters paid for street lighting, providing gas free of charge.[269]

Figure 82 Snodland. The handsome Italianate railway station, erected in 1856, set a new standard of modernity for Snodland's buildings. W.H. Poynder built the similarly Italianate *Queen's Head Hotel* adjoining, which was soon established as the venue for official village meetings.

The development of High Street can be traced chronologically from east to west. At the eastern extremity was the railway station of 1856, and adjoining this the *Queen's Head Hotel*, built at around the same time. Opposite the hotel, on the south side of High Street, are the earliest purpose-built three-storey shops, including the red-brick former post office of 1869, with a curved corner to May Street.[270]

To the west, in an area destroyed by the inner by-pass *c.*1980, came the Hook family residences. Charles Townsend Hook's 'Veles' stood on the south side, while his brother Eustace's Delamere House was set well back on the north side. All that is left of these residences is the former laundry and coachman's house of 'Veles' beside the *Queen's Hotel*, made imposing by full-height brick arcading. The next survivor on the north is the timber-framed Mulberry Cottages, with the rendered, and perhaps timber-framed, *Red Lion* on the south side. Beyond this are further three-storey shops, notably a stock brick parade of three, numbers 74-78 (even), with decorative terracotta dressings, built in 1878. These face towards Waghorn Road with its row of philanthropic buildings erected by the Misses Hook.[271]

The Hook enclave on the south side is completed by the New Jerusalem church, with Colonel Holland's large house, 'Ivymeath', in the same materials and also with a tower, at the rear. The extensive glebeland of the Rectory prevented any further development of the south side of High Street almost as far as the crossroads. In 1909 the Rector surrendered the streetward half to the villagers as a recreation ground and allotments. The Rectory itself, built in 1814, was greatly enlarged in 1865 to the design of the widely-employed London architect Arthur Blomfield, who went on in 1869-70 to restore All Saints church.[272]

Facing the New Jerusalem church on the north side of the street is Hope Terrace, a terrace of eight red-brick cottages of the 1860s, probably built as an investment by T.W. Peters, the village coal merchant. His handsome red-brick house, Anchor Place, *c.*1860-1, stands next door. This begins the group of late 19th-century villas for professional men, several of them double-fronted, but none separated from its neighbour by more than an alley. In the middle stands the Congregational Church of 1888, beside which Queen's Avenue squeezes its way to the High Street. Beyond is a purpose-built bank, dated 1900 (and now much enlarged), a sign that by the turn of the century Snodland was serving commercially not only its own residents, but those of surrounding villages, too. The final group on the north side before the crossroads has been demolished. It included a parade of shops and Nephalite Villa, built for the ferryman, Edward Baker, with a big columned porch.[273]

Figure 83   The *Bull Inn*, Snodland. An inn from at least the early 18th century, the *Bull Inn* was rebuilt in 1775 and again in 1881. The current structure of half-timber and red brick makes it one of Snodland's most impressive buildings.

In the years around 1900 the crossroads became confirmed as the hub of village activity. On the north-west corner, the *Bull Inn*, little altered since being rebuilt in 1881, is one of Snodland's best buildings. On the south-east corner, the baker's shop with a long bakery extending its flank down Malling Road, is also little altered. This is at the end of Snodland's most impressive parade, of six tall two-storeyed shops, of red brick with white-banded pilasters emphasising the upper storey and large hooded dormers in the roofslope. The parade was built in 1902, and the lower post office added at its eastern end in 1909.

In the early years of the 20th century shop development spread into the east side of Holborough Road. Here, in a parade of seven, three shops are crowned by bargeboarded gables, the other four by fantastic shaped and pedimented gables above bands of strapwork pargetting. Their exact date is not known. A little further north, opposite Covey Hall Farm, is a large plot which W.L.H. Roberts of Holborough Court Estate conveyed in November 1903 to the Rochester and District Co-operative and Industrial Society. The six-bay shop which the Society built on it survives greatly altered and shorn of its fanciful skyline, as Snodland Working Men's Club. Next door is Snodland's last pre-war public building, the cinema of 1912, in use as a Roman Catholic church since the 1940s.[274]

In Snodland as everywhere else, the First World War stopped new building in its tracks. After the end of hostilities the economic conditions had greatly changed, and when in 1919 the Holborough Court Estate advertised further building plots for sale on both sides of Holborough Road there were no takers. The high point of industrial development in the Lower Medway Valley had passed.[275]

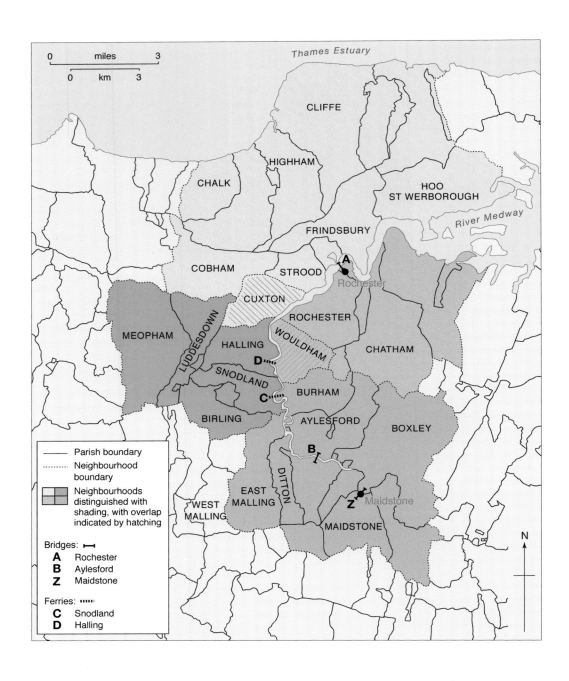

Thames Estuary

River Medway

CLIFFE

HIGHHAM

CHALK

HOO
ST WERBOROUGH

FRINDSBURY

COBHAM

STROOD

A
Rochester

CUXTON

ROCHESTER

MEOPHAM

LUDDESDOWN

HALLING

WOULDHAM

CHATHAM

D

SNODLAND

C

BURHAM

BIRLING

AYLESFORD

BOXLEY

B

DITTON

EAST
MALLING

Z
Maidstone

WEST
MALLING

MAIDSTONE

0   miles   3

0   km   3

N

—— Parish boundary

········ Neighbourhood
boundary

Neighbourhoods
distinguished with
shading, with overlap
indicated by hatching

Bridges: ⊢—⊣
A   Rochester
B   Aylesford
Z   Maidstone

Ferries: ┅┅┅
C   Snodland
D   Halling

The Lower Medway Valley and the Wider World

Figure 82 Neighbourhood areas in the Lower Medway Valley.

The Lower Medway Valley parishes formed part of a much wider world. They enjoyed strong ties with neighbouring parishes through family and kinship linkages and cross-parochial landholding. They were linked also to the county of Kent, bound together by the system of administration, transport routes and a shared agrarian and industrial heritage. Beyond the county boundaries there were close ties with London, the main source of finance and luxury goods, an important destination for migrants, and a market for locally produced foodstuffs and manufactured goods. Trade and long-distance migration brought connections with other parts of Britain and the world beyond the Kent coastline. In this chapter we face outwards to look at how the valley and its people connected both within the valley, and then through Kent, the south east, and into Continental Europe.

THE VALLEY

Although the parish was an important administrative and social focus during the 18th and 19th centuries, most local people had connections over a wider territory. Few people remained in the same parish throughout their lifetime; many held land or had business interests in a number of parishes. Within the valley we can tentatively identify four neighbourhoods based on surname distributions and marriage patterns (Figure 82). In the south, Burham and Aylesford had close ties with each other, and with Ditton, Allington, Boxley and Maidstone. Families such as the Brookers and Broomfields were found across this area and 96 per cent of the marriages recorded in the Burham registers were between people living within this 'neighbourhood'. Halling and Snodland were also strongly connected, and had links with neighbouring Birling and Luddesdown. These four parishes shared use of the workhouse at Halling until 1834.[276]

Further to the north, Cuxton, Strood and Frindsbury formed a larger, albeit rather looser, neighbourhood with the adjacent parishes of Cobham, Shorne, Higham and Cliffe and Chalk. The Earl of Darnley had substantial holdings in each of these parishes, helping to bind them together. On the other side of the Medway, Wouldham had close connections with Rochester, and from the mid-19th century growing links with Burham and Halling due to their shared interest in the cement industry.

NAME OF LANDOWNER	ACREAGE OWNED	NO. OF PARISHES	PARISHES WHERE MORE THAN 50 ACRES HELD
Charles Gustavus Whittaker	1390	10	Luddesdown, Strood, Meopham, Trottiscliffe, East Barming, Snodland, Paddlesworth, Ryarsh
Earl of Darnley	5577	6	Cliffe, Shorne, Cuxton, Strood, Luddesdown, Halling
Robert Turberville Bingham	539	4	Cliffe, High Halstow, Frindsbury
Mrs Sarah Comport	710	3	Frindsbury, High Halstow, Cliffe
Thomas Stephens	412	4	Paddlesworth, Snodland, Birling
Francis Bradley	607	7	Halling, Birling, Ryarsh
Earl of Abergavenny	1148	4	Birling, Ryarsh
Earl of Aylesford	2550	6	Boxley, Burham, Aylesford
Charles Milner	2477	5	Aylesford, Ditton, East Malling
Earl of Romney	2153	4	Boxley, Allington, Aylesford
Col. James Best	743	3	Boxley, Aylesford
John Golding	275	3	Ditton, Aylesford
Dean and Chapter of Rochester	1281	7	Wouldham, Cliffe, Aylesford, High Halstow, Boxley
Sir Joseph Henry Hawley	865	5	Leybourne, Cliffe

Figure 85 Table showing the distribution of landed property in the Lower Medway Valley

Defining neighbourhood areas in this way reminds us that the Lower Medway Valley was not a unified economic and social region in the late 18th century. Strong links existed between some parishes, but others were less closely affiliated. George Groombridge, the Aylesford baker, had customers in Burham and Wouldham and Snodland, but not in Halling or Cuxton. Also revealing are the connections between parishes suggested by cross-parochial landholding. Large tracts of land within the valley were held by aristocratic or gentry families with estates which stretched across a number of parishes (Fig. 85).[277]

The Earls of Darnley had substantial holdings in Cobham, Shorne, Chalk, Cliffe, Strood, Cuxton and Halling. On a slightly lesser scale, the Preston Hall estates of Charles Milner, spread from Aylesford into Ditton and East Malling. Workmen employed by the Earl of Darnley operated across his Kent lands: labour accounts from the 1850s record work done by the same team of builders at Whornes Place in Cuxton, and of Cobham Hall. The ties could also be seen in terms of tenancies, with land in several parishes often rented to the same tenants. In the 1840s William Pye leased extensive tracts of land from Lord Darnley in Cuxton, Strood and Halling, while William Lake was a tenant in Cliffe, Cuxton and Luddesdown. Large landowners such as Darnley and Milner played an important role in organising the local agrarian economy. Their estates and farms were not limited by parish boundaries.

Cross-parish landholding among lesser owners was also important. Evidence from wills shows that many testators held land in two or more parishes lying within the same neighbourhood area. The Strood saddler, John Gouge, had tenements in Frindsbury and Cliffe, while the Aylesford gentleman, William Kynaston Summerfield, held land in Maidstone, Sandgate and Burham. The economic interests of many households crossed parish boundaries, and this helped bind neighbourhoods together.[278]

Neighbourhoods were also shaped by the movement of people within them. People moved for a variety of reasons: in search of work, to take up an apprenticeship, on marriage, or when their circumstances changed. Many of these moves were over very short distances, often within the confines of the neighbourhood area. When leaving home to go into service Rebecca Lovett travelled only three miles from Aylesford to Burham. Both farm servants and rural day labourers appear to have moved within relatively limited spheres. Farm servants, in particular, tended to remain close to home, with moves of more than three to four miles uncommon in the late 18th century.[279]

Judging from the evidence of pauper settlements, Aylesford drew the majority of its in-migrants from the immediately adjacent area. The river Medway seems to have acted as a significant barrier to movement, since very few paupers were returned to parishes on the west bank of the river. Paupers removed *to* the parish had settled across a wider area, although Maidstone, which lay within the neighbourhood, accounted for the largest proportion. Similar

Figure 86 Map showing part of the Earl of Darnley's holdings in Strood, Cuxton and Cobham, colour-coded to identify different farms.

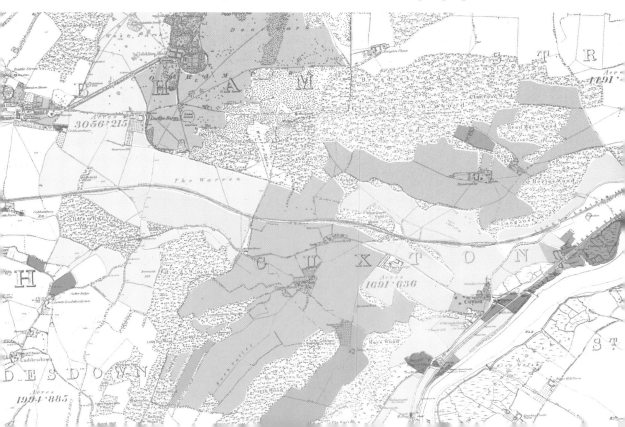

conclusions can be drawn from local apprenticeship records. Almost two-thirds of the apprentices assisted by Godden's Charity in Snodland were placed within five miles of the village, half of them in parishes within the same neighbourhood area.

Changing Patterns of Mobility

What was the impact of industrial change on movement within the valley? Parishes on both sides of the Medway shared in the industrial growth associated with the brick and cement industries, so we might imagine that they forged stronger connections during this period than had hitherto been the case. Could this have produced a more unified industrial community in the valley? To test this assumption we can use census data, which from 1851 included information about place of birth.

Industrialisation attracted incomers, most of whom came from neighbouring parishes which already had close ties to the area. Thomas Cubitt recruited brickyard workers for Burham from the under-employed agricultural labourers of the locality, with only skilled foremen brought in from further afield. Parishes lying a distance from the river failed to attract industrial development and labourers left them in search of work. Both Boxley and Luddesdown lost population between 1851 and 1901 due to this outflow of workers. The populations of riverside parishes increased markedly and became significantly more diverse. Most now contained large numbers of migrants, drawn primarily from the locality, but also from further away.[280]

Figures from the census for 1861, 1881 and 1901 confirm that the eight parishes had a large migrant population. Only around 36-38 per cent of people remained in their parish of birth, fewer than in the south-east more generally, where between 47 and 71 per cent of residents were native-born in 1851. However, census data also confirms the local origins of many migrants in the valley: in 1861, 34.4 per cent had been born within five miles of their current address, rising to 39.7 per cent in 1901. Parishes continued to be closely linked with others in their neighbourhood area. More migrants living in Aylesford had been born in Maidstone, Burham, East Malling and Boxley than anywhere else, while Strood retained close ties with Frindsbury and Rochester.[281]

There is evidence of increasing divergence in the migration patterns of the eight parishes. By 1881 clear distinctions were emerging between those parishes dominated by brick and cement manufacture, such as Burham and Halling, and those with a more mixed economy like Strood and Snodland, and these differences became more noticeable in 1901. Generally brick and cement parishes had a larger proportion of resident natives, suggesting that workers in these industries were becoming less mobile than those employed in other sectors, including agriculture. In the case of brick-making this can perhaps be explained by the structure of the industry. Brickmaking teams employed primarily family labour, reducing the need for children to leave the parish in search of work and limiting the opportunities for migrants. The 1861 census shows Henry Allum working in the brickfields at Strood with his 17-year-old son, and daughters aged 15 and 12. Another possibility is that the expansion of the brick and cement industries simply provided sufficient employment opportunities to discourage young people from leaving their parish of origin.

If we separate out the different industrial sectors it is clear that cement workers were slightly more likely to remain in their birthplace than agricultural labourers by 1881. Figures for brickmakers are more ambiguous, with a large proportion of resident natives in 1881, but fewer in 1861 and 1901. There are also interesting differences in the migration patterns of the various occupational groups. Farm labourers were more likely to have been born within the same neighbourhood area, whereas cement workers frequently came from another valley parish, showing how industrial workers helped to form new linkages between cement-producing parishes along the banks of the Medway, which cut across established neighbourhood boundaries. Thomas Stevens, a cement labourer born in Halling, was living across the river in Wouldham in 1881. Charles Rogers was born in Maidstone, raised three children in Aylesford, but had been living in Halling for at least six years at the time of the 1901 census.

Links between riverside parishes were less evident among brickmakers, probably because this was a seasonal occupation often combined with agriculture, ensuring that those born locally remained locked into established neighbourhood networks. During the rapid expansion of brick and tile making in the mid-19th century many recruits to the industry were drawn from further afield. Census listings for Aylesford, Burham, Frindsbury and Strood show substantial numbers of migrants from the brick-making parishes of the Medway and Swale estuaries, and also from the suburbs of London where the industry was well established. By 1901 recruitment to a declining industry appears to have become more localised, with only 38 per cent born more than five miles from their place of residence.

The papermaking industry was different again. Workers were recruited from other papermaking districts across the country, with significant numbers coming from Buckinghamshire, Hertfordshire and Scotland.[282]

Figure 87 Snodland Ferry enabled workers to get from Snodland to Wouldham.

Industrialisation brought about a reorientation of neighbourhood areas which became more pronounced as the decades passed. Increasingly interaction took place along and across the river Medway because employment opportunities for brick and cement workers were focused here. Whereas agriculture supported diffuse patterns of migration, the localised distribution of industry along the riverside encouraged more concentrated flows. In the 1850s and 1860s workers often moved into and out of these industrial activities as the demand for labour fluctuated. By the 1880s many cement workers had little experience of agriculture other than harvest work, and had become divorced from the old parish linkages of their forebears. Often several generations of the same family worked in the industry, forging new social networks based on their occupation. To some extent this must have led to the development of separate communities of industrial workers particularly among the brick workers and papermakers, although the rapidly expanding cement industry was more open to newcomers.

Census data does not tell the full story. Housing shortages in the valley meant that many workers travelled each day to the cement and brick works from surrounding rural parishes or nearby towns in the 1850s and 1860s. According to the Revd S. Hornibrook, many working in Burham and Aylesford came from as far afield as Maidstone. Twelve-year-old Thomas Fowler lived at East Malling, four miles from his workplace at the Burham brick and cement works. He got up at 4.30am each day and was not usually home by 8pm. Unsurprisingly he complained of being 'always very tired'.[283]

Closed parishes were controlled by a few large landholders who could restrict settlement of poor households by limiting the building of cottages. Open parishes, in contrast, tended to have dispersed land ownership so that control over settlement was more difficult. The tithe survey for East Malling shows that Sir Stephen Twisden, the largest landowner, held only 28 per cent of parish land, while another 13 people had holdings of over 50 acres. In contrast 56 per cent of land in Burham was owned by the Earl of Aylesford, and there were only four other substantial landowners.[284]

This may explain why housing was apparently in short supply in Burham, but more plentiful in East Malling. Certainly, the number of lodgers in Aylesford, Burham and Snodland in 1861 suggests that accommodation was seriously lacking here. The percentage of the parish population recorded as boarding or lodging was 12.1 per cent in Aylesford, 11.8 per cent in Burham, and 11.7 per cent in Snodland compared with an overall figure for the valley of 8.4 per cent. In 1861 ten adult lime works labourers in Burham were described as 'sleepers in ash holes'. All of them were migrants.

By the 1880s large numbers of workers' cottages had been erected in most of the cement parishes and housing shortages were less acute, but it is indisputable that in the early stages of industrialisation rural parishes adjacent to the main industrialising belt played a vital role in providing accommodation for many of the new brick and cement workers.

KENT CONNECTIONS

The valley and its environs lay within a broader hinterland stretching across much of west Kent, with many towns and villages having significant connections with the valley communities. Migration patterns influenced and reflected the shape and extent of this broader hinterland. Although most people moved only short distances, broader trends in mobility can be identified across Kent as a whole. Most notably there was a shift from the south and east of the county to the north and west, with the towns and industrialising villages of north Kent showing some of the highest rates of population growth. Many of the migrants came from the Weald and central Kent where the traditional woollen cloth and iron-working industries had been in decline since the late 17th century. Around 140 parishes witnessed falling populations between 1851 and 1901, the majority lying within this central belt.[285]

Although the valley parishes lay within the industrialising northern part of Kent, most experienced a net outflow of working people until the 1840s: Cuxton's population fell from 384 to 298 between 1821 and 1831, and Aylesford, Snodland and Halling all showed losses between 1801 and 1811. Across the valley population growth until the 1850s barely kept pace with rates for the county as a whole.

Many working people headed for the Medway towns, particularly Chatham dockyards, which were the driving force behind economic development across the region. The dockyard workforce grew from 797 in 1712 to 1,720 in 1758 and 2,321 towards the end of the French wars in 1814. Closure of yards at Deptford and Woolwich in 1869 led to renewed expansion, with around 3,500 artificers and labourers employed in 1875, rising to almost 5,000 by 1909. Dockyard workers recorded in the 1851 census had come from places such as Edenbridge, Hawkhurst, Maidstone and Woolwich. Higher wages were the main attraction, although working in the dockyards also enabled a young man to learn a trade which would confer status. On the other hand, dockyard work was unstable. Surges of expenditure during wartime led to the recruitment of additional temporary employees, 'extraordinary' men, who were laid off once peace returned.[286]

Figure 88 Chatham Dockyards, 1785-1794, by Joseph Farrington. In 1785 the Navy Board commissioned Nicholas Porlock and Joseph Farrington to paint panoramic views of the six royal naval dockyards, with the intention of capturing every building, dock and slipway in scenes bereft of people. Of the six dockyards only Deptford, Chatham, Woolwich and Plymouth were completed during the ten-year project. This image provides a graphic account of the royal yards at the end of the 18th century.

By no means all of those leaving the valley parishes headed for the dockyards or the Medway towns for that matter, as can be seen clearly from the pattern of apprenticeship. County-wide returns survive only for the period 1710-60, when a national register was kept for taxation purposes, but even at this early date these show a steady flow of apprentices from the study parishes, bound to masters in a range of different trades and resident across Kent and surrounding counties. There were particular clusters in the towns of west Kent, especially Maidstone, Rochester and Chatham, emphasising the importance of these places as destinations for migrants from the valley. Local registers, which cover a longer period, confirm that Maidstone attracted apprentices mainly from Aylesford, although five of the eight parishes were represented in the listings. Henry Hall, the son of a Frindsbury shipwright, was apprenticed to the Maidstone bricklayer, William Houghton, in 1769. Masters in the Medway towns recruited the majority of their apprentices locally, although a number came from Maidstone and the Hoo peninsula. Only Strood was a significant destination for apprentices, reflecting its urban status and significant concentration of tradesmen and artisans.[287]

Apprentices were typical of migrants – young, single and moving for employment reasons. Admittedly they represented the more upwardly-mobile sections of society, but it seems reasonable to presume that other migrants would have followed similar paths, and thus the patterns outlined here provide a good indication of the parts of Kent with which the Lower Medway Valley was most closely connected. Certainly, the distribution of paupers removed to Aylesford was broadly similar. The greatest number were returned from Maidstone (24), followed by Chatham (13) and Burham (6), with others coming from towns as far afield as Faversham, Cranbrook and Sevenoaks.[288]

Employment opportunities as a result of industrialisation intensified linkages between the valley and its wider hinterland, and altered the nature, volume and direction of migrant flows. The valley parishes changed from being net exporters of labour to being net importers on a significant scale, often drawing newcomers from well beyond the valley. Many migrants recorded in the 1861 and 1881 census returns were born in the greensand and Wealden parishes south and west of Maidstone, an area of mixed farming with relatively little industrial development and persistently low wages.[289]

A growing number of those arriving had been born in the brickmaking parishes of the Hoo peninsula and the coastal belt between Gillingham and Faversham. By 1881 there had also been a substantial influx from the cement-producing parishes of the Thames estuary between Dartford and Gravesend. These migration patterns suggest a considerable circulation of workers between the different industrial districts of north Kent in the mid-19th century. In part this must have stemmed from the instability of employment in the brick and cement industries at the time. Many small brickfields were short-lived speculative ventures, worked for a number of years until the brickearth was exhausted. In the lime and cement industry too, there were frequent bankruptcies, particularly in the 1850s and 1860s, leading to the laying off of workers who moved elsewhere in search of work.[290]

Perhaps typical was William Whatman, a brickmaker who was born in Hoo, baptised his children in Grays, Essex, and Frindsbury, and was living in Cuxton in 1861. Hardly surprisingly, the setting up of a new works usually attracted skilled workers from outside the immediate area. The large number of migrants in Eccles Row in 1861 can be linked to the establishment of the Burham brickworks nearby a decade earlier. Of the 183 inhabitants 32 were from Crayford and a further three from neighbouring Erith. All household heads are described as brickmakers, and they appear to have moved as family groups. By 1881 only three Crayford-born residents remained in the Row.

Links with a wider region were forged not only by permanent relocation, but also by seasonal migration to harvest hops and fruit. Many of the migrant workers came from towns and villages across north-west Kent. William Marshall noted that, during the hopping, 'The town of Maidstone is nearly deserted ... Tradesmen's daughters, even of the higher classes; and those of farmers and yeomen of the first rank, and best education, are seen busy at the hop bins'.[291]

Employers frequently complained that workers were hard to come by during the hopping season. In 1865 a Factory Commissioner visiting William Joynson's paper-mill in St Mary Cray reported that 'At the time of my visit (Sept) the full complement of hands were not present; about 100 more females were wanting in the rag room, and 50 more children in the glazing room, but could not be got; at that time of the year it is always difficult to get hands, as they prefer the chance of fruit and hop picking'.[292]

Most pickers lived within easy walking distance of the hop gardens; others were taken there daily by wagon or traction engine. With the coming of the railways travel to the hop-growing district became much easier, further increasing the flow of migrants. In September 1869 the *Chatham Journal* reported that 'About 12,000 hop-pickers have arrived at Maidstone from various parts. Two trains reached Maidstone on Monday and Tuesday last week from Gravesend and Strood conveying 1000 pickers. A few others arrived by ordinary trains, averaging 50 or 60 daily.'[293]

Retailing

It was not just the movement of people that tied the valley to a wider world; flows of goods and information were also crucial to the process. North-west Kent was covered by a network of towns and villages providing goods and services to the population. The social elite shopped at a variety of centres for different items. The Earls of Darnley bought tea and coffee, books, and furniture in London, ordered newspapers from Maidstone and Canterbury, but purchased bread and candles from local tradesmen. Generally, people were willing to travel further to purchase specialist, or high order, goods, whereas they expected to be able to buy lower value items locally. Tradesmen providing quality goods or services tended to be concentrated in a few larger towns since they needed to draw on customers from a wider area. By contrast shopkeepers selling everyday items relied mainly on local patronage and were more widely distributed.[294]

Maidstone, as the county town of west Kent, was the hub of a great deal of retailing. It also had an important administrative role, providing, amongst other things, a venue for quarter sessions and assizes, and it was also the main social centre in the western half of the county. Perhaps unsurprising, in the 1770s it was reputed to have the best shops in the county.[295]

At the next level in the hierarchy were places such as Chatham, Rochester and Gravesend. All had specialist functions in addition to their role as market centres. By the 1790s each could boast at least 30 retail and service categories. Chatham had an upholsterer, a silversmith and a chinaman, Gravesend a wine merchant, and Rochester a musical instrument maker. Below them were locally important market centres such as Ashford, Tonbridge and Tenterden and, at the bottom of the hierarchy, small market towns such as West Malling, Goudhurst and Wrotham, which served only a limited area. Here the only tradesmen to be found in the late 18th century were butchers, bakers, grocers, shoemakers and the like.[296]

Several larger towns competed for the custom of people in the valley. The areas of influence of Maidstone, Rochester and Chatham substantially overlapped, and subsumed those of lesser towns like Strood, West Malling, and later, Snodland. Those living in the south of the study area tended to look towards Maidstone, those in the north towards Rochester, Chatham and Strood, but there was no clear dividing line between these market areas. The Strood carpenter, Henry Dixon Edmeades, drew his customers from across the valley and further afield in the early 19th century.

The circulation patterns of newspapers published in Maidstone and the Medway towns emphasise this overlap. The *Maidstone Journal* had agents throughout the south-east of England. Indeed, the proprietor, John Hall, claimed in 1817 that the paper was 'extensively circulated … throughout the counties of Kent, Sussex, Middlesex, Surrey and Essex'. The residence of those placing advertisements suggests the effective circulation of the newspaper may have been rather less extensive. Places mentioned in early 19th-century editions stretch from Dartford to Hastings and Ashford to Sevenoaks, indicating an area covering most of west Kent and extending into East Sussex. The *Rochester and Chatham Journal*, published from 1855, had a more limited circulation within the Medway towns and 'Mid-Kent generally', although it did include some advertisements for tradesmen in places such as Maidstone, Faversham and Gravesend. This and the Maidstone newspaper were within the sphere of the London press, whose network of agents extended nationally.[297]

Advertisements and news stories relating to the study parishes appeared in both sets of local newspapers, reflecting the overlap in their circulation areas, although the level of coverage for each parish varied. Aylesford, Burham and Wouldham regularly featured in the Maidstone papers, while Cuxton and Frindsbury appeared more often in Rochester and Chatham-based publications. Over time people in the Medway towns turned increasingly to their local newspapers and the influence of the Maidstone press in the northern part of the valley almost certainly declined. The *Maidstone Journal* abandoned a separate section for news reports relating to the Medway towns, entitled 'Rochester and Chatham reporter' after about 1840. Indeed, across the region the choice of newspapers increased during the later decades of the century as new titles appeared. By 1890 there were at least nine publications circulating in the Lower Medway Valley, including the *Chatham News*, *Kent Messenger* and *South Eastern Gazette*.[298]

The distribution of customers served by particular tradesmen reveals a remarkably similar pattern. The hinterlands of Maidstone shopkeepers were principally oriented towards the south and west, whereas tradesmen in the Medway towns looked for customers in the towns themselves and the Hoo peninsula to the north. The ledger of an unknown Maidstone draper, dating from 1768-73, reveals a network of customers extending along the greensand parishes of central Kent and southwards into the Weald, but very few north of the town. In contrast more than 50 per cent of Henry Dixon Edmeades' customers came from Strood, where his carpentry business was based, with another 20 per cent from Rochester, Chatham and Frindsbury.[299]

These distribution patterns suggest that of the valley parishes only Aylesford lay clearly within Maidstone's area of interest. Residents of the other parishes seem to have looked increasingly to Rochester and Chatham for their goods and services. For those living in Frindsbury and Cuxton, Strood must also have been an important shopping centre, and by the late 19th century Snodland was growing in importance. By contrast, dependence on Maidstone declined, as is clear from the reduced circulation area of the Maidstone papers after rival publications were founded in Rochester and Chatham, and in the widening horizons of tradesmen based in the Medway towns. In turn this reflected a general re-orientation of linkages within west Kent, as industrialisation linked the valley more firmly with the port of Rochester, and with the Medway towns in general.

THE PULL OF THE CAPITAL

The whole of south-east England felt the tentacles of London. The economic vitality of the region was determined largely by the capital's huge demand for food, agricultural products, manufactured goods and labour. The intensity of this relationship increased over time as transport improvements made the capital more accessible. Road links improved markedly in the decades after 1770, with the spread of turnpikes and a considerable expansion of carrying services. By the 1830s only a few scattered parts of Kent were more than five miles from a coach stop offering direct links to the metropolis. The Medway towns alone had 16 services a day by 1836.[300]

SPEEDY CONVEYANCE OF HOPS TO LONDON,
FROM THE
Bridge Wharf, Maidstone,
BY WAY OF THE
THAMES AND MEDWAY CANAL.

SIMMONDS & CO's
VESSELS SAIL EVERY DAY, during the HOP
SEASON, to KENT WHARF, BOROUGH, making a
certain and safe passage in about 24 hours, passing regularly
through the THAMES AND MEDWAY CANAL.
A constant supply of COAL, COKE, WOOLLEN
RAGS, OIL and RAPE CAKE.
Bridge Wharf, Maidstone,
Sept. 12th, 1831.

Figure 89 An advertisement for a water carrying service via the Thames-Medway Canal, printed in the *Maidstone Journal and Kentish Advertiser*, 13 September 1831. High tolls and congestion in the tunnel section meant that many barge skippers continued to follow the longer route round the Nore.

For all this movement overland, the economy of the valley depended far more on its water-borne traffic. By the 18th century a fleet of hoys, hatch-boats and barges provided a regular service to London: an arduous journey of almost 24 hours passing down the Medway, around the Nore and then up the Thames estuary. Attempts to reduce journey times by cutting a canal across the Hoo peninsula proved unsuccessful, but by the early 19th century a number of paddle steamers were offering a daily service to the capital.

The development of railways from the 1840s enabled greater numbers to travel and reduced journey times considerably. The Thames and Medway Canal was converted to a railway in 1845, providing links to the steamer service from Gravesend pier. In the second half of that year there were 7,118 train services through the Medway tunnel carrying some 253,867 passengers. By 1849 the line had been extended to Dartford, offering a direct link to central London. Further lines extended the network to Maidstone (1856) and across the Medway to Rochester, Chatham and Faversham (1858). By 1900 few places in Kent were more than three miles from a railway station, and cheap-day excursion tickets enabled working families to go shopping in the West End and Londoners to have a day by the sea for their annual holidays.[301]

Imports and Exports

In all of this the linking feature was London, and trade links from the valley to the capital were already well established in 1750. The river Medway had long provided an important conduit for goods from the Kentish interior, a role enhanced by improvements during the 1740s which extended navigation as far as Tonbridge. Exports consisted primarily of timber, iron and munitions from the Weald, and cereals, hops and fruit from the rich agricultural belt around Maidstone. Imports from the capital included groceries, manufactures and goods of foreign origin such as wine and tobacco, reflecting London's role as the country's leading entrepôt. Indeed, the account books of local tradesmen reveal that their supplies were mainly from wholesalers and merchants in the capital.

Much of this trade was carried by barges of 40 tons or less, as larger vessels were unable to pass under Rochester Bridge. Amongst the barge owners in the 1810s was Charles Heathorn of Maidstone. His account books record numerous consignments of rag stone shipped to Vauxhall, and lime from the works at Whornes Place in Cuxton. Return cargoes included coal, ashes and on one occasion a 'steam engine and iron rails'. Another Maidstone carrier, William

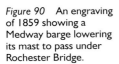

Figure 90 An engraving
of 1859 showing a
Medway barge lowering
its mast to pass under
Rochester Bridge.

Hayward, active between 1838 and 1841, carried several loads of
cherries to London, returning with rags for the paper-mill at Tovil.
By the 1830s a number of carriers offered a regular service to the
capital. Simmonds and Co. advertised 'speedy conveyance of hops
to London' from Bridge Wharf, Maidstone, 'by way of the Thames
and Medway canal'. They promised certain and safe passage in
under 24 hours.[302]

Industrialisation substantially increased the volume of trade
and the range of goods transported, although the extent of growth
is hard to calculate as most shipments were not subject to customs
duties. Evidence from trade directories reveals a considerable
expansion of both barge building and carrying services from
the 1840s, coinciding with the expansion of the brick and lime
industries. Between 1840 and 1849 at least 15 barge yards were
operating on the river compared with only five in the 1820s, while
the number of carriers also rose substantially. The number of vessels
registered at Rochester also increased from the mid-19th century,
the majority being barges and lighters of less than 50 tons.[303]

The growth in traffic was such that the first effective count of
vessels entering the port of London in 1872-3 indicates an inward
coasting trade of nearly 17,000 voyages, carrying 780,000 tons
of cargo. Much of this expansion was due to the bulk shipment
of building materials including timber, lime, ragstone, bricks
and tiles. By the early 19th century it is estimated that several
hundred million bricks were transported by barge from the
Medway to London each year. House building swallowed up
much of this output, but many of the larger brickmakers, such as
William Webster of the Burham Brick, Lime and Cement Co. Ltd,
were also government contractors, supplying materials for large

infrastructure projects such as the London sewers and Thames embankment.[304]

We know from Parliamentary reports that the Aylesford Pottery Company provided 256,000 Aylesford bricks for 'Main Drainage Works' in October 1862. Shipments of lime and cement were also increasingly significant. By the 1860s many of the larger cement manufacturers had their own fleet of barges: William Peters of Wouldham Hall operated 80 vessels in 1881, while the mud contractor Solomon J. Brice had over forty.[305]

London was also the source of much of the investment which financed industrial development. Many of the manufacturers who set up works in the valley were previously based in the capital. Thomas Cubitt moved his main brickmaking operations to Burham in 1852, as existing sites at Caledonian Road and Thames Bank had become exhausted. William Margetts, the leading figure in the West Kent Gault Brick and Cement Co. was a London stockbroker, while William Lee was the youngest son of a Lewisham building contractor.[306]

The majority of shareholders in lime and cement companies were also Londoners. For example, at the Burham Brick, Lime and Cement Company in 1887, 1,079 shares were in the hands of Londoners, 450 in the hands of Kent shareholders and 470 held elsewhere. Londoners contributed towards the funding of major infrastructural projects in the region such as the Thames and Medway Canal and the South Eastern Railway. It was London-based contractors who were the driving force behind the development of brick and cement making in the valley since it was they who generated the demand for building materials and had the finances necessary for success in this capital intensive sector.[307]

Figure 91 This late 17th-century prospect of Rochester by J. Collins clearly demonstrates the reliance of the lower Medway parishes on the river for the movement of people and materials. By the 1880s, river traffic on the Medway had grown exponentially, largely to satisfy the capital's insatiable demand for timber, bricks, lime, cement and other building materials.

London was also crucial to the functioning of the local labour market. In the period before industrialisation the capital absorbed much of the surplus agrarian population from the valley. This influx of people continued once manufacturing had taken root, but at a somewhat reduced level, and just as importantly London now turned provider, dispatching an army of itinerant workers to the hop and fruit growing districts during the harvest period.

Apprenticeship was a common route into the capital's workforce. Most apprentices came from middling social backgrounds because of the high premiums charged by London masters, which may explain why few valley children were involved. Of the *c.*1,500 Kent-born apprentices bound to masters in 49 London livery companies between 1700 and 1805 only nine came from the valley: five from Strood and four from Aylesford. Among them was Francis Furmager, son of an Aylesford bargeman, who was apprenticed to Robert Browne of the Tylers' and Bricklayers' Company in 1757, and James Maiden, son of a Strood linen draper, who was bound to John Leach of the Needlemakers' Company in 1783.[308]

Another important, though less well-recorded, group of London in-migrants was female domestic servants. Girls in their late teens often made their way to the capital in search of work, usually after a spell of employment with a country family or in a nearby market town. Some of those who moved to the capital were sent back again when they fell on hard times. Rosamond Cutbath (31) was removed to Aylesford in 1853 with her two bastard children when, unable to find work, she was admitted to the workhouse in the parish of St Mary, Islington. Of all those removed to Aylesford parish between 1760 and 1860 only six were from London, but four of these were women.[309]

Leaving the Valley

Industrialisation in the valley may have reduced the incentive to migrate to London for work, but even after 1850 the capital continued to attract young ambitious people from the valley. A survey of the place of residence in 1901 of people born in Aylesford and Frindsbury confirms that a significant proportion had moved to London or its environs. Women outnumbered men by almost two to one among these in-migrants reflecting the imbalance in work opportunities they must have found in the valley, and the many openings that were available in London's service sector. Of the 36 women whose occupation is known, 27 had gone into domestic service. Others were working as dressmakers or shop assistants. Men moving to the capital took up a wider range of trades: six were general labourers, three were police officers, two were schoolmasters and one was an upholsterer.[310]

Moving in the opposite direction were seasonal migrants who streamed out of London during the late summer to help with the hop and fruit harvest. William Marshall observed that 'a few days before the picking begins, the lanes, and village greens, swarm with these strolling pickers; men, women, children, and infants'. In 1908, an estimated 75,000 hoppers were at work in Kent, 25,000 of them in the Maidstone area alone. Many came from the poorer districts of the capital: costermongers, washerwomen, bricklayers, general labourers and match girls from Whitechapel, Limehouse, Stepney, Bethnal Green and Lambeth.[311]

By the 1860s the majority of seasonal migrants travelled by rail, boarding special trains to Maidstone and Tonbridge laid on by the South-Eastern Company with reduced fares. The much criticised 'gang' system was widespread, with buyers in the capital recruiting teams of pickers and then paying for their travel expenses and providing food and accommodation. Occasionally things went badly wrong: the *Maidstone Journal* reported in September 1869 that the Medway Union workhouse at Chatham had been overwhelmed by an influx of around 2,000 'destitute and forlorn' pickers in a single week, whose behaviour was so disorderly that the master had to call in the police to subdue them.[312]

As well as playing a crucial role in the industrial and agrarian economy of the region, London was also the prime source of specialist services and consumer goods. The capital was considered the leader of fashion, and shopping place of choice for the wealthy. Like most people of their social standing, the earls of Darnley were avid consumers. From their accounts we can trace numerous shopping expeditions to London. In November 1825 the 4th earl purchased a 'Mapp of the Roman Empire' from the geographer James Wyld of Charing Cross. In the same year be bought cream vases, bowls and a tea set from Josiah Wedgwood & Son, and in 1830 a 'wainscott frame and glass for a print of the Reverend Thomas Goodall' from George Cooper, a carver, gilder and looking glass manufacturer of Piccadilly.[313]

With transport improvements the delights of the West End were opened up to a wider audience, although the cost of a coach or train fare to the capital remained outside the reach of many working families. In 1845 a second-class rail ticket from Strood to Gravesend cost 6d. and a combined steamer and rail ticket to London was 1s. 6d., equivalent to a day's wages for an agricultural labourer. We know from diary evidence that ordinary families were shopping in the capital by the close of the century.[314]

London was also the best place to go for entertainment.
During the 18th century the winter season was a central part
of the social calendar for the nation's elite. Lavish events were
held across the capital in the pleasure gardens, assembly rooms
and theatres. By the early 19th century leisure facilities and
social events were spread more widely across the provinces,
but the greatest spectacles were still to be found in the capital.
From its opening in 1851 the Crystal Palace proved a draw
for visitors from all over the country, including Kent. Edward
Ladd Betts used it as the venue for his son's coming-of-age
celebrations in 1865, inviting all his tenants and estate workers
to the event. The excitement generated by the train journey
from Aylesford and the celebrations themselves suggest that
such excursions remained an occasional treat for most Medway
valley residents.[315]

BEYOND SOUTH-EAST ENGLAND

The Medway valley also had extensive links with the rest of
the United Kingdom and the wider world. Rochester was an
important trading centre, involved not just in the coasting
trade but also trade with continental Europe. The jurisdiction
of the port extended from the Isle of Grain to Sheerness, and
it had the deepest and most sheltered harbour in Kent and
Sussex, capable of handling large ocean-going vessels. By the
mid-18th century half the shipping of Kent was registered here.
In 1789 this amounted to 177 vessels, displacing 6,712 tons. The
extent of trade with other parts of Britain, and with Europe, is
clear from Figure 92.[316]

Foreign ships also visited Rochester, many of them mooring
at Strood Docks. On census day in 1881 the *Norafield* from
Norway with a crew of five was moored at Strood, together
with the *Othello* and *Tetta Margaretha* from Germany with
crews of nine and four respectively, and the *Sophia* from the
Netherlands, carrying five crew members, plus the wife and
two daughters of the master. Bulk cargoes were unloaded at
Rochester quay, and then carried upriver in barges and lighters
of 40 tons or less.

In the mid-18th century the main imports into the Medway
were coal, malt and barley for the expanding brewing and
distilling industries of Maidstone and Chatham. By the
1800s coal was the dominant trade due to its widespread use
for domestic heating and in the manufacture of lime and
cement. Shipments came mainly from the north-east ports of
Hartlepool and Middlesbrough. Duties collected at Rochester

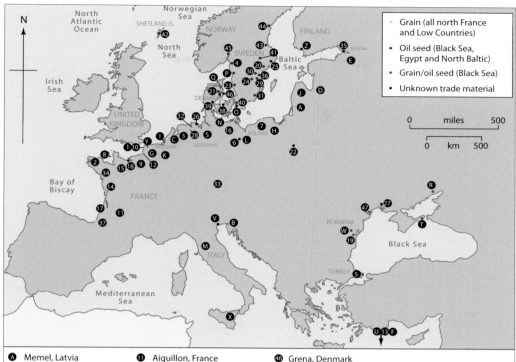

Ⓐ	Memel, Latvia	⑪	Aiguillon, France	㊹	Grena, Denmark
Ⓑ	Trieste, Italy	⑫	Le Tréport, France	㊼	Odessa, Ukraine
Ⓒ	Amsterdam, Neth.	⑬	Damietta, Egypt		
Ⓓ	Riga, Latvia	⑭	Nantes, France		
Ⓔ	St Petersburg, Russia	⑮	Caen, France		
Ⓕ	Archangel, Egypt	⑯	Straisund, Germany		
Ⓖ	Ostend, Belgium	⑰	Bordeaux, France		
Ⓗ	Danzig (Gdánsk), Poland	⑱	Le Vivier-sur-Mer, France		
Ⓘ	Rotterdam, Neth.	⑲	Ibrail, Romania		
Ⓙ	Libau, Latvia	⑳	Stockholm, Sweden		
Ⓚ	Antwerp, Belgium	㉑	Randers, Sweden		
Ⓛ	Stettin, Poland	㉒	Apins, Poland		
Ⓜ	Leghorn, Italy	㉓	Gothenburg, Sweden		
Ⓝ	Oldenburg, Germany	㉔	Linköping, Sweden		
Ⓞ	Malmo, Sweden	㉕	Söderköping, Sweden		
Ⓟ	Uddervala, Sweden	㉖	Carolinesiel, Germany		
Ⓠ	Aardus, Denmark	㉗	Nikolayev, Ukraine		
Ⓡ	Taganrog, Russian Fed.	㉘	Emden, Germany		
Ⓢ	Hamburg, Germany	㉙	Norrköping, Sweden		
Ⓣ	Kerch, Ukraine	㉚	Lidköping, Sweden		
Ⓤ	Alexandria, Egypt	㉛	Kalmar, Sweden		
Ⓥ	Venice, Italy	㉜	Hooksiel, Germany		
Ⓦ	Galati, Romania	㉝	Waldemarswith, Germany		
Ⓧ	Messina, Italy	㉞	St Malo, France		
Ⓨ	Nieuport, Belgium	㉟	Cromstradt, Russia		
Ⓩ	Abo, Finland	㊱	Nykoping, Sweden		
①	Dunkirk, France	㊲	Bayonne, France		
②	Sables, France	㊳	Korsør, Denmark		
③	Groningen, Neth.	㊴	Fredericia, Denmark		
④	Frederickstadt, Norway	㊵	Helsingborg, Sweden		
⑤	Constantinople, Turkey	㊶	Westeras (Västerås), Sweden		
⑥	Rugenwalde, Germany	㊷	Westerwick, Shetland Is.		
⑦	Stolpmünde (Ustka), Pol.	㊸	Soderhami, Sweden		
⑧	Jersey, Channel Is.	㊹	Sundsvall, Sweden		
⑨	Abbeville, France	㊺	Christiana (Oslo), Norway		
⑩	Calais, France				

㊹	Blyth	
㊺	Hartlepool	
㊻	Newcastle	
㊼	Sunderland	
㊽	South Shields	
㊾	Middlesbrough	
㊿	Seaham	

Port of Rochester	
⑥	Llanelli
⑥	Goole
⑥	London
⑥	Swansea

suggest imports of around 80,000 chaldrons per year in the 1820s rising to 330,000 in the 1860s.[317]

Most exports from the Medway valley went to London, although some goods were shipped elsewhere: fullers earth to the textile centres of eastern England, especially Colchester; oysters to Holland and Flanders. By the late 19th century, exports of bricks, paper and particularly cement were more important. There was also a good deal of clandestine trade with the continent until duties were reduced in the 1840s: smugglers exported wool and coin, returning with tea, wine, spirits, tobacco and a myriad of other foreign commodities. The small creeks of the Medway estuary and Hoo peninsula were ideal for landing this illicit cargo: Quarry Wharf in Frindsbury was often used for the loading and unloading of corn during the 1730s, much to the annoyance of the Bridge Wardens at Rochester who lost out on toll duties.[318]

Many residents of the valley also had personal experiences of foreign climes. Some were sailors or fishermen, with contacts

Figure 93 Strood Dock with ships moored and unloading. Strood dock originally marked the Thames and Medway Canal entrance to the tunnel to Higham (visible in the background of the photograph).

in distant ports. Seafarers were concentrated in the parishes above Rochester Bridge, Strood and Frindsbury. Others had been born overseas or in distant parts of the United Kingdom. Census data reveals a substantial contingent of 'foreigners' concentrated in Frindsbury, Strood and Snodland. In 1901 the largest group were 95 people from Ireland and 92 from Scotland, the latter including 18 Scottish papermakers. There were also substantial numbers from Europe (42), North America (30) and the East Indies (30), along with 45 mainly European mariners listed with their vessels in Frindsbury and Strood. Many long-distance migrants, particularly those from Ireland, worked in unskilled manual jobs as general labourers, navvies or cement workers, though a few were employed in skilled occupations, such as engineer, surgeon and schoolmaster.

Many of the key industries in the Lower Medway Valley had links well beyond the immediate area. Paper manufacturers had connections outside the region through their trade organisation, the Master Paper Makers Committee, which met on an *ad hoc* basis from the 1780s. The Committee, which was dominated by producers from London and the Home Counties, sought collectively to control prices, oppose rises in excise duty and resist demands for higher wages. Skilled workers in the industry also had a nationally organised trade union from the 1790s, the Original Society of Papermakers.[319]

The cement industry operated within a national and international environment. Investors in the Medway valley works were drawn not only from London and the Home Counties, but from other parts of the United Kingdom and overseas. A.D. Robertson and Edward Howard, who established the Wouldham Cement Company in 1863, came from Bombay, while Otto Trechmann, who acquired the Whornes Place works around 1900, was Danish-born and based in West Hartlepool, where he owned another works.[320]

Technical innovations were also imported from foreign competitors: the rotary kiln, for instance, which was developed in the United States, revolutionised cement production in the 1900s. Furthermore, the formation of Associated Portland Cement Manufacturers in 1900 brought together producers from across Kent and other parts of the United Kingdom into a single organisation.[321]

The changing environment, economy and society of the Lower Medway Valley can be properly appreciated only through an awareness of its wider geographical context. The valley remained closely tied to its immediate hinterland throughout the 18th and 19th centuries, although the nature of that relationship changed. Old ties forged over centuries of farming the land were overlain and later overtaken by new industrial connections. This was reflected in riverside parishes becoming distanced from their rural hinterland as a distinctive industrial culture began to take root. Industrialisation was a symptom of the region's growing integration into the metropolitan economy. The industries that grew up along the Medway – cement, bricks, paper, barge building – were all geared primarily towards supplying the needs of the capital. Proximity to this centre of nation and Empire also helps to explain growing international connections.

Chapter 9

Industrial Decline and Landscape Change

There is a magic in the morning,
There's a tang about the air.
O here, up here, is the place to be.
The sun's right up,
But the world's not there!
O here, up here, is the place for me.
We look upon a billowy lake
Of vapours, white as snow,
As gold-topped chimneys sticking up
From the busy world below

There is a magic in the noonday
And the tide is at a flood
O here, up here, is the place to be.
Cement is turned to ivory:
There's gold instead of mud.
O here, up here, is the place for me.
I saw the marsh become a land
Where crystal rivers flowed;
And I've seen the Walls of Sion
From the top of Borstal Road.[322]

The strong bond between people and locality in the Lower Medway Valley is encapsulated in these stanzas of Donald Maxwell's poem 'Medway Heights' which glories in the scenery of the valley in the early 20th century and its Turnerian inspiration to the senses. That landscape has the power to evoke feelings of belonging is well known. For many people their sense of identity is bound up with a particular place. Features in the landscape act as cultural markers which help to define home territory. In the Lower Medway Valley these markers included many of those objects in the landscape most often captured in paint or prose: Aylesford Bridge, Kits Coty House, the ruins of the Bishop's Palace at Halling, Rochester Castle and Temple Manor in Strood. All of these symbolised continuity and long tradition; they tied residents into a shared cultural heritage.

LANDMARKS IN A LOST LANDSCAPE

Each parish, too, had its landmarks; memorable locations through which villagers understood their locality. These could be the parish

Figure 94 Halling. Bishop's Palace when in use as a poorhouse. Based on a print of 1772, this view shows the dwelling house after the repairs necessary after a storm of 1720 in which parts of the hall had been blown down. The house is divided into two distinct parts: a north end with gabled north wall and a hipped roof south end, the two being divided by a tall gabled wall. Note the tower projecting into the court and a ruined wall to the south. The latter forms one wall of a west-to-east range. The north wall of this range is regarded as being in line with the tall dividing wall.

church, the village school, the local inn, or even a particular road junction or well-frequented shop. These personal landmarks helped define the space within which people went about their daily lives. Important, too, were boundary markers, those features in the landscape that represented the edge of a particular territory. Traditions such as beating the parish bounds were an attempt to fix such markers in the minds of local people particularly in an era before the widespread use of mapping.

Over the past two centuries the landscape of the valley has undergone two periods of profound change during which earlier landscapes were partially erased: industrialisation and deindustrialisation. Each transformation has been marked by a need to remember lost landscapes and to commemorate change. This can be seen in the many images of rustic Medway on the eve of industrialisation, and in the record of industrial decline documented by local artists and authors such as Donald Maxwell and more recently John Austin. It is no surprise that there are almost as many photographs of the demolition of the cement works as there are of these sites in full operation.

Landscape change could erase many of the cultural features that gave a place meaning for its inhabitants, leaving them feeling rootless. Demolition of large parts of the Bishop's Palace in Halling to make room for Hilton, Anderson and Co.'s cement works severed an important link with the community's past. The quarrying of chalk led to the loss of local landmarks such as Quarry House in Frindsbury, while the building of workers' cottages changed many villages out of all recognition. Over time new cultural markers emerged: chimneys, rail lines and the docks which industrial development brought to the valley. These have now also largely disappeared, hence the keen interest locally in preserving these sites as part of a local cultural heritage.

Perhaps unexpectedly, it was only in the 20th century, when the industries of the valley went into decline that they were portrayed in a more positive light. Donald Maxwell's evocative watercolours of 'cement land' depict a world that would have been familiar to people at the time, but was rapidly disappearing. The same sense of nostalgia can be picked out in the work of those early 20th-century photographers who set out to document the everyday landscapes of the cement villages. They provide us with a rich record of daily life in the valley when cement was still king, something that ceased to be true in the decades after the First World War.

Equally unexpectedly, what we also see in late 19th- and early 20th-century accounts of the area is a preoccupation with antiquities; with links back to an ancient past before the valley was 'despoiled' by industry. Descriptions of Aylesford usually focused not on the brick and pottery works and paper-mill which provided employment to many of the parishioners, but on Kits Coty House and the Countless Stones, two Neolithic chambered long barrows on Blue Bell Hill in the north of the parish. This prehistoric landscape was often given mythical significance through the identification of the barrows as the resting place of Catigern and Horsa, believed to have been killed in battle between the Britons and Saxons nearby.[323]

Other landscape features picked out consistently by writers in the 19th century included the parish church, the Friars, formerly a Carmelite Priory, and old Aylesford bridge. All are ancient structures with a long and varied history. This preoccupation with ancient things reflected a long-standing tradition of Kent antiquarianism which can be traced back to Lambarde, Pepys and Stukeley, but it may also reveal an aversion to modernity. Many of the writers seem to have drawn comfort from being able to dwell on the description of familiar landmarks such as Rochester Castle and Aylesford Bridge: they provided elements of reassuring continuity in a fast changing world.

For many residents today the valley is still the 'land of cement', but at the same time each community has its own strong local identity, which draws on the landscape, institutions, history and folk memory of the particular locality. Aylesford continues to draw

Figure 95 Aylesford. The 14th-century bridge across the Medway. The distinctive central arch was created in 1824 when a pier was removed and the arch widened to allow the passage of larger river traffic. The other four arches are of a four-pointed order and are double chamfered with stone dressings. Aylesford Bridge, a fine example of the type, is scheduled as an ancient monument.

on its mythologised druidical past, and on its long history as a bridging point over the Medway, reflected in many of the buildings which line the High Street. This is a landscape dripping in history: a rich heritage in which industry plays only a fleeting role. Eccles, by contrast, seems proud in its identity as a modern community, founded on bricks and cement. Set back from the river it appears self-contained; a place apart. Its relatively uniform terraces in grid-iron pattern speak of self-sufficiency and an egalitarian spirit.

Snodland is different again. The relative grandeur of its public buildings such as the clock tower, Devonshire rooms and bath house suggest the makings of a civic culture. Strood appears as the poor relation of Rochester, but with its own identity founded on fishing and engineering. Collectively these places form a landscape with a single identity, but many personalities.

REMINDERS OF AN INDUSTRIAL PAST

The scenes depicted in Sonny Hanson's 1938 film of the Medway valley were of an intensely industrial landscape, but the cement works which dominated the landscape in 1938 have mostly gone, leaving only scattered fragments along the riverside. In many cases these remains are now buried under new housing estates or tons of spoil dumped during flood defence work.

Some substantial remains survive, although often shrouded beneath vegetation. At Burham it is possible to make out the foundations of several banks of bottle kilns, raised tramways and

Figure 96 Footprint of William Lee's barge dock at Halling and the wall of a kiln bank, now covered in light brush behind it. The dock is choked with silt and reeds, but still clearly defined by a shuttered concrete wall. A survey of the site in the 1990s also described a large derelict brick shed with steel beams, identified as an engineering workshop, but this has since been demolished.

Figure 97 Halling. Raised tramway, near the Bishop's Palace. The site of Hilton, Anderson and Co's nearby works at Halling Manor is another that has now been redeveloped for housing. Here the main survival is a short section of the tramway which linked the cement works with its quarries to the west of the modern A228. This runs adjacent to the old Bishop's Palace on a raised embankment, the northern end of which is constructed of brick with concrete cladding.

slurry backs, as well as the footprint of slurry mixers from the later phase of the works when four rotary kilns were in operation. As elsewhere the riverside quay is probably the best preserved structure. Further downstream the brick bases of chamber kilns can be traced at both the West Kent works of William Margetts, and Peters' works at Wouldham Hall, immediately to the north. At the latter the site of 16 bottle kilns is also marked by heaps of destruction debris.[324]

It is the dozens of chalk and clay pits scarring the landscape which provide the most powerful reminder of a lost industrial past. In the late 19th-century heyday of Medway cement these excavations covered around five per cent of the land surface of the eight parishes, and spread out along both sides of the valley. Today many are overgrown with vegetation: prime brown-field sites for redevelopment. Those pits on the east bank of the Medway can best be viewed from the high vantage point of Blue Bell Hill. From here the landscape stretches out a patchwork of scrub-covered hollows, rich green pastures and straggling villages.

The two Culand pits lying directly below the scarp are probably the most prominent. Here there is still evidence of the tramways which carried the chalk down to the riverside works, along with the rusted remains of several wagons. From the riverside quarrying is evident from the line of white chalk cliffs running intermittently along the valley sides from Aylesford to Wouldham and Snodland to Frindsbury. The immense size of these features can only truly be appreciated from close quarters. Houlder pit, associated with Lee's

Halling Then and Now: comparative use of historic and modern photographs

During the spring of 2006 one of the Kent Volunteers, Margaret Crowhurst, unearthed a collection of glass plate negatives showing street scenes of Halling dating from the early 1900s. These early photographs of the village, thought to have been taken by local photographer, Stephen James Foreman, were kept in a box at Halling School along with a variety of other archives, and remained in good condition.

With permission from the school the glass negatives were loaned to another of the volunteers, Roger Smoothy, who had been working with Maidstone Camera Club on a project to digitise the glass plate negative collection of Maidstone Museum. He was able to achieve remarkable results by rephotographing the slides using a specially adapted lighting rig. By blowing up the resulting digital images it is now possible to read shop signs and even the serial numbers of some pieces of equipment newly installed in Halling cement works.

What the collection of 40 negatives shows is a picture of everyday life in the village at the beginning of the 20th century. There are several views of the High Street, images of the new workers' housing such as Poynder and Hilton Terraces, and close-up shots of the

post office, Beaney's barber's shop, the parish church and village school. Additionally there is a fascinating group of images showing rebuilding work in progress at Hilton and Anderson's Halling Manor cement works.

By comparing these images with modern photographs taken from the same vantage point it is possible to see how much, or in some cases, how little has changed. For instance, other than repainting, Formby Terrace looks much as it did in c.1915. Only

the hedges and shrubs in the front garden look different and the wrought iron gate and railings have been replaced by a wooden fence. A view of the High Street looking north from the junction with Ferry Lane reveals more obvious changes. A number of shop fronts have been removed and the buildings reverted to residential use, a reflection of the sharp decline in village shops in the age of the motor car. Indeed, the street is now lined with parked cars, whereas in the early 1900s the

only traffic in evidence was two horse-drawn carts. Poynder and Hilton Terraces have lost the uniformity they displayed in the 1900s with the addition of porches, paint or render and UPVC windows. The high walls in front of the terraces have also been largely removed and road space allocated for parking.

Overall what these 'Then and Now' images reveal is a transition from working village to dormitory settlement. In many of the 1900s pictures the chimneys of Halling Manor cement works are visible in the distance, and the dust which they produced can be seen coating the streets and buildings. Most of the villagers would have worked here, or in other nearby cement works which lined this section of the Medway. Today only one works remains, and most Halling residents have to commute to work in Maidstone, the Medway towns or further afield. This greater mobility and the faster pace of life explains the loss of village services and intrusion of the motor car into most of the modern photographs. Whereas aspects of the streetscape from the 1900s remain recognisable, the cultural landscape of the village in 2009 has been utterly transformed.

Figure 98 This tunnel took the tramway from the Culand pits under the Rochester Road. The track from the upper chalk pit passes through a further half-mile-long tunnel, which survives in a good state of preservation.

works at Halling, covered some 500 acres and was in places more than 100 yards deep. It was used as a bomb and ammunition store by the RAF during the Second World War.[325]

Just how pervasive an impact the lime and cement industry has had can best be illustrated from Frindsbury Ness, where chalk quarrying has transformed the whole topography of the area. What was described in the early 19th century as a gently sloping promontory affording scenic views of Rochester Castle and Cathedral is now a low lying industrial estate, bounded to the north by a sheer cliff of chalk some 95 feet high, on the top of which Frindsbury's All Saints church sits rather precariously. South of the church formerly stood a mansion called Quarry House, which Hasted commended for its beautiful views of the river and surrounding country. This house was described by an officer stationed at Upnor Castle in 1750 as the Kentish Vauxhall as it had become a favourite place of resort for the people of Rochester and Chatham. On fine days, crowds of fashionable promenaders would walk the circuit of paths that criss-crossed its grounds.[326]

By the mid-19th century the crowds of visitors had gone as the shoreline took on a more industrial tone. Shipyards and quays lined the water's edge, while a number of quarries steadily ate into the peninsula, feeding the seven cement works which were erected along the shoreline between 1851 and 1888. In 1897, with much of the chalk reserves of the area exhausted, Quarry House itself was demolished for the chalk upon which it stood.[327]

Not all quarrying activity was associated with the large lime and cement manufacturers. The many deneholes and chalkwells which litter the area remind us that there were also many small producers. Deneholes were dug mostly by farmers from at least the 13th century to provide chalk for marling acidic soils. They generally consist of a narrow circular shaft up to 80 feet deep, at the bottom of which chambers were cut into the chalk in the shape of a double trefoil. Chalkwells are similar to deneholes, though usually later in date, with wider shafts and a simpler arrangement of chambers. Although often filled in with rubble, disused deneholes and chalkwells were sometimes simply covered over and forgotten.[328]

This neglect could have disastrous consequence decades later in areas such as Frindsbury where housing estates were built over former quarry sites. In one notorious incident on 21 November 1967 Mrs Jean Thompson fell to her death down a 150ft shaft after the ground subsided beneath her feet as she was walking down an alleyway between West Street and Bill Street Road with her young son, Mark. Many other cases of subsidence have occurred in Frindsbury over the years reflecting the intensity of mining in this area. Fortunately many former shafts can now be identified by shallow circular depressions, or their location traced from old maps. There is now known to be a chalkwell under the football pitches at Temple School in Frindsbury.[329]

Cement manufacture required not only chalk, but also river mud or clay. Extraction of clay has, like chalk quarrying, left a profound impact on the valley's landscape, although one that is

Figure 99 An article from the *Chatham, Rochester and Gillingham News* of 22 March 1985 reporting the opening up of a large chasm which threatened the home of a Frindsbury couple. The Frindsbury Peninsula was quarried extensively and subsidence has become a serious issue. In an ironic twist in this case, the hole was later filled with 125 tons of concrete.

initially less apparent to the casual observer. Much of the mud came from the saltings of the Medway estuary: low-lying coastal salt marshes used primarily for grazing sheep. It was dug out by teams of men known as 'muddies', who beached barges on the marshes, loaded them up at low tide, and then floated them off as the tide rose. Today we can see evidence of their activities all round the estuary in the form of shallow depressions cut into the sediments.[330]

Where digging was particularly extensive, such as Upchurch marshes, and the south side of the Hoo peninsula, the saltings still have a distinctive pock-marked appearance. Some sense of the scale of these operations can be gained by looking at the activities of S.J. Brice and Sons, one of the larger mud contractors on the Medway at the turn of the century. They dug out 1,356,000 tons from East Hoo Creek between 1881 and 1911, and 557,000 tons from nearby West Hoo Creek between 1881 and 1907.[331]

By the late 19th century the level of extraction was such that Rochester Corporation, and later the Medway Conservancy Board and Admiralty, began to raise serious concerns about the impact on navigation. Clay diggers commonly breached sea defences to beach their barges, and the depressions they dug enabled water to flood over a wider area. This reduced the rate of flow in the river causing silting of the channel. The estuary that we see today, with its many marshes, mud banks, creeks and channels, is a legacy of this period of intense exploitation.[332]

Brickfields have left a less visible imprint on the landscape, because they contained few permanent structures and often

Figure 100 The artificial landscape on the north bank of the Medway in Cuxton parish created by removal of brick earth, leaving generally lower ground surfaces. The cottages in the foreground were formerly occupied by brickmakers.

Figure 101 Burham. Although most of the Lower Medway brick and cement works have been demolished or redeveloped, a number of structures survive on the river banks and masked in the undergrowth. At the Burham works, the remains of a riverside wharf for the cement works are still visible.

existed for only a few years until the brickearth of the area was exhausted. Once a brickfield was abandoned the site was often reclaimed for cultivation. Orchards, in particular, thrived on the Thanet sands exposed once the brickearth had been removed. Today the sight of flat fields up to six feet below road level is one of the clearest indications of brickmaking. These lower ground surfaces can be found across the valley, particularly in Frindsbury, Strood and Cuxton where many of the larger brickmakers were based. One substantial site lies between the modern A228 and river Medway north of Cuxton. Another, around Temple Manor in Strood, is now the location of an industrial estate.[333]

In Frindsbury the search for evidence is hampered by the fact that housing now covers many of the former brickfield sites, but the many localised changes in ground level are suggestive. The steep drop behind numbers 17-45 Iden Road almost certainly reflects the removal of brickearth and Thanet sand when this area was part of the substantial Nursery Brickfield. Other evidence of brickmaking comes from the glass, china or other detritus washed up on beaches and coastal marshes around the Medway estuary. This material was part of the household refuse shipped up from London to provide the 'rough stuff', a mixture of coke and ashes, used for firing the bricks.[334]

Substantial remains of brickfield buildings are found only in the south of the area where businesses were larger and more mechanised. At Burham the foundations of Cubitt's large pottery and engine shed can be traced in the undergrowth, along with kiln bases, washbacks and the remains of an elaborate tramway system which linked the different parts of the site. When established in 1852 the Burham works were the most advanced in the world. Situated on a gentle slope, the buildings were arranged along the tram lines so that each stage of production moved closer to the quay, ensuring only coke to fuel the engines and kilns had to be carted uphill.[335]

Piped water was provided to the works from a large reservoir which still survives, as does the massive river wall from where the bricks were loaded on to barges. There were also extensive buildings at the Aylesford Pottery Company's works including the pottery, 'a large square building of three floors, with six circular pottery kilns, each with six furnaces', two Hoffman kilns, six Scotch kilns and numerous drying and making sheds. This site has now been lost under Forstal industrial estate, although traces of the clay pit can be seen at the edge of Cobtree Manor Park.[336]

It was the natural resources of the Lower Medway Valley that drew the attention of entrepreneurs, and its proximity to

Figure 102 A panoramic view of the Medway from Blue Bell Hill in 2008. A hive of industry less than a century before, the 21st-century Medway Valley bears more resemblance to the agrarian landscape of the 18th century, with only the exposed chalk scarp in the foreground and distance, the enlarged settlement of Burham (centre) betraying the area's industrial past.

London, the main market for manufactured goods of every variety. The fluctuating fortunes of different industries were determined by government policy, market conditions and the pace of technological change. The place of the valley as an industrial region was secured by the internal synergies generated by the concentration of so much manufacturing endeavour in this restricted area. After 1900 exposure to competition and the restructuring of the UK economy highlighted the region's over-reliance on a few staple sectors. They could not compete, decline set in, and new industries did not develop in place of those which were lost. Today many of its inhabitants commute to London and travellers pass by on the M20, opened in 1961. The valley in the early 21st century is not so far removed from the rural world of this area in the 18th century.

Endnotes

CHAPTER 1 Introducing the Lower Medway Valley pp. 1-8

1   C. Dickens, *Pickwick Papers* (1868), 99.
2   J.C. Cox, *Rambles in Kent* (London, 1913), 198.
3   C. Dickens jnr (ed.), *All the Year Round* (London, 1893); W. and M. Wyllie, *London to the Nore Painted and Described* (London, 1905), 192, 227; E. Harris, *The Riverside: An Itinerary of the Medway within the City of Rochester and Memories it Recalls* (Rochester, 1930), 41-2.
4   J.H. Richardson, 'Watery Trail: River Medway' (Screen Archive South East, 1938), 22 mins, black and white silent, 9.5mm film.
5   D. Maxwell, *Unknown Kent* (London, 1921), 99; R.H. Goodsall, *The Medway and its Tributaries* (London, 1955), 182.
6   CKS U234/E21.
7   H. Smetham, *History of Strood* (Chatham, 1899), 353-8.
8   A. Pearce and D. Long, 'Chalk Mining and Associated Industries of Frindsbury', *Kent Underground Research Group: Research Report 3* (1987), 18-22, 55-6.
9   Smetham, *History of Strood*, 205-6.
10 K.E. Wells, *Preston Hall and its Owners* (unpublished pamphlet).
11 G. Mingay, 'Agriculture' in A. Armstrong (ed.), *The Economy of Kent, 1640-1914* (Woodbridge, 1995), 53-4.
12 A. Ashbee, 'The Toll Road', www.snodlandhistory.org.uk/localhis/tollroad [accessed 15/08/2006].
13 Mingay, 'Agriculture', 54-63; M. Overton *et al.*, *Production and Consumption in English Households* (London, 2004), 39-47.

CHAPTER 2 Land and Farming pp. 9-22

14 Mingay, 'Agriculture', 52-3.
15 J. Boys, *General View of the Agriculture of the County of Kent* (2nd edn, London, 1805), 18-19.
16 C.W. Chalklin, *Seventeenth Century Kent* (Rochester, 1978), 76; Overton *et al.*, *English Households*, 43-4.
17 E. Hasted, *The History and Topographical Survey of the County of Kent*, Vol. III, (Canterbury, 1797-1801), 525; CKS DRb/Pi57/12; DRb/Pi45/7.
18 Overton *et al.*, *English Households*, 45.
19 Boys, *General View*, 169-71, 180-1; CKS DRb/Pi44/11 A,B; DRa/Pi 25/1.
20 *Ibid.*, 84-5.
21 *Ibid.*, 14.
22 M. Overton, *Agricultural Revolution in England* (Cambridge, 1996), 121-5; *South Eastern Gazette*, July 1867; 22 Oct. 1867.
23 J.M. Preston, *Aveling and Porter Ltd* (Rochester, 1987), 4-7, 29; *South Eastern Gazette*, 10 Feb. 1868; J. Phippen, *New and Enlarged Directory for Maidstone and its Environs* (1850) [adverts].
24 R. Arnold, *A Yeoman of Kent* (London, 1949), 185-6; CKS DRB/Pi45/7; DRB/Pi57/23.
25 D.W. Harvey, 'Locational Change in the Kentish Hop Industry and the Analysis of Land Use Patterns', *Transactions and Papers (Institute of British Geographers)*, 33 (Dec. 1963), 123-44; *Account of Number of Acres under Cultivation of Hops, 1858 and 1861* (Parl. Papers 1859 (175) [XXV], 269; Parl. Papers 1862 (163) [Vol. LV], 671).
26 Mingay, 'Agriculture', 77.
27 Information derived from J.M. Preston, 'Summary and assessment of the industrial archaeology of the Medway Gap', unpublished paper commissioned by the steering committee of the Valley of Vision project (Aug 2006).
28 A. Bignell, *Hopping Down in Kent* (London, 1977), 144-5; CKS U234/E21.
29 J.Y. Stratton, *Hops and Hop-pickers* (London, 1883), 43-52.
30 PP 1868-9 XIII.1, *Royal Com. Employment of Children, Young Persons and Women in Agriculture, Second Report,* (Parl. Papers 1868-9 [XIII.1], Appendix, 42, 58).
31 Stratton, *Hop-pickers*, 148-9.
32 Chalklin, *Seventeenth Century Kent*, 88-90.
33 P. Barfoot and J. Wilkes, *Universal British Directory* (1792), 501; *Finch's Directory* 1803; Pearce and Long, 'Chalk Mining', 68.
34 Hasted, *History and Topographical Survey*, Vol. IV, 399, 409, 463.
35 CKS U234/E21.
36 CKS DRb/Pi/56/5, DRa/Pi/25/1.
37 D. Church, *Cuxton: A Kentish Village* (Sheerness, 1976), 100; Pearce and Long, 'Chalk mining', 7.
38 Pearce and Long, 'Chalk Mining', 46.
39 Holborough Court itself replaced an earlier house, Holloway Court, which was located close to Holborough water mill; A. Ashbee, *Town Talk*, Sept. 2005, 28-9.

40   S. Bagshaw, *History, Gazetteer and Directory of the County of Kent*, Vol. 1 (1847), 253; J.H. Sephton, *Around Aylesford* (Stroud, 1999), 73-82.

41   Pearce and Long, 'Chalk mining', 42.

42   D.H. Fletcher, 'Mapping and estate management on the early 19th century estate: the case of the Earl of Aylesford's estate atlas', *Arch. Cantiana*, 109 (1991), 85-109.

43   CKS U234/T5.

44   F.M.L. Thompson, 'An Anatomy of English Agriculture, 1870-1914' in B.A. Holderness and M. Turner (eds), *Land, Labour and Agriculture, 1700-1920* (London, 1991), 226, 233.

45   MALSC U565 A3, A9, A314, A320.

46   CKS P12/13/A/5; Boys, *General View*, 1st edn (London, 1794), 85-6.

47   MALSC U565 A9.

48   MALSC U565 A3, U565 A6.

49   *Reports of special assistant Poor Law Commissioners on the Employment of Women and Children in Agriculture*, 131 (Parl. Papers 1843 [XII]).

50   MALSC U565 A3; Boys, *General View*, 2nd edn, 191.

51   J. Whyman, 'Agricultural developments 1700-1900' in T. Lawson and D. Killingray (eds), *An Historical Atlas of Kent* (Chichester, 2004), 108.

52   T. Richardson, 'Labour' in A. Armstrong (ed.), *The Economy of Kent, 1640-1914* (Woodbridge, 1995), 243-4.

CHAPTER 3 Industry and Manufacturing pp. 23-52

53   J.M. Preston, *Industrial Medway: An Historical Survey* (Rochester, 1977), 33, 42-3.

54   Pearce and Long, 'Chalk Mining', 45-6; MALSC U565 A49.

55   D. Barnard, *Merrily to Frendsbury: A History of the Parish of Frindsbury* (Rochester, 1996), 51-6.

56   CKS U234/E21; CKS P12/28/5; Preston, *Industrial Medway*, 55-7.

57   Preston, *Industrial Medway*, 36.

58   *VCH Kent* Vol. III, 391-2, 396; CKS U234 P12/28/4.

59   Pearce and Long, 'Chalk Mining', 26-9.

60   Preston, *Industrial Medway*, 56; MALSC U565 A49; CKS Q/CI 410/1-7; TNA PROB 11/962.

61   J. Woodforde, *Bricks to Build a House* (London, 1976), 103; CKS U234/E21.

62   Pearce and Long, 'Chalk Mining', 45, 49; CKS U234/T5.

63   Registrar General, Census of 1831, *Enumeration Abstract* (1833), 264-5.

64   Bagshaw, *History, Gazetteer and Directory*, 327-8, 338-41; Preston, *Industrial Medway*, 54.

65   CKS U234/E21; H. Hobhouse, *Thomas Cubitt: Master Builder* (London, 1971), 310-12; Post Office Directory (1855), 264.

66   Preston, *Industrial Medway*, 71-3.

67   *Illustrated News of the World*, 8 Oct. 1859.

68   Bagshaw, *History, Gazetteer and Directory*, 276; J. Tallis, *A Comprehensive Gazetteer of Gravesend with its environs* (London, 1839).

69   Barnard, *Merrily to Frendsbury*, 51-7.

70   W.R. Craske, 'The cement industry – its rise and progress on the Medway', *Chatham, Rochester and Brompton Observer*, 7 May 1898, 8C.

71   Barnard, *Merrily to Frendsbury*, 88-9.

72   Preston, *Industrial Medway*, 99-125.

73   Bagshaw, *History, Gazetteer and Directory*, 276.

74   P. Pugh, *The history of Blue Circle* (Cambridge, 1988) 38.

75   Preston, *Industrial Medway*, 80-4.

76   Preston, *Industrial Medway*, 54, 71, 93-5; W. Coles-Finch, *The Foords of Rochester* (Rochester, 1917); A. Ashbee, 'The lime and cement industry', www.snodlandhistory.org.uk/localhis/cement [accessed 15/03/2006], 7.

77   A.J. Francis, *The Cement Industry 1796-914: A History* (Newton Abbot, 1977), 47-52.

78   R. Lucas, 'The tax on bricks and tiles, 1784-1850: its application to the country at large, and, in particular, the county of Norfolk', *Construction History*, 13 (1997), 45; Pugh, *Blue Circle*, 18.

79   G.R. Redgrave, *Calcareous Cements, Their Nature, Manufacture and Uses* (London, 1895), viii.

80   Francis, *Cement Industry*, 19-159; *The Builder*, 22 May 1880, 643.

81   *The Builder*, 22 May 1880, 643; Preston, *Industrial Medway*, 75-7.

82   Harris, *The Riverside*, 41.

83   W.R. Craske, 'The cement industry – its rise and progress on the Medway', *Chatham, Rochester and Brompton Observer*, 7 May 1898, 8C; *Report from the Select Committee of the House of Lords on Injury from Noxious Vapours* (Parl. Papers 1862 [XIV.1], 239-42); Preston, *Industrial Medway*, 109-13.

84   Smetham, *History of Strood*, 347.

85   *Blue Circle*, July 1958 quoted in Preston, *Industrial Medway*, 85.

86   Preston, *Industrial Medway*, 166-75; Pugh, *Blue Circle*, 65-8.

87   Preston, *Industrial Medway*, 36-7.

88   J. Mokyr, 'Demand vs. supply in the Industrial Revolution', *Journal of Economic History* (1977), 107; D.C. Coleman, *The British Paper Industry, 1495-1860* (Oxford, 1958), 217-26.

89   Post Office Directory (1855), 264; 1851 census.

90   Preston, *Industrial Medway*, 39; A. Ashbee, 'Early Snodland papermakers' (*c.*1740–1854)', *Snodland Historical Society* (2003), 29.

91 K.J. Funnell, *Snodland Paper Mill: C. Townsend Hook and Company from 1854* (2nd edn, Townsend Hook Ltd, 1986), 21-4.

92 Census 1861, *Kelly's Directory* 1867, 1874, 1878, 1882, 1899. The figures in Kelly's are approximate and make no distinction by sex or age. See Funnell for the productivity of the paper mill.

93 *Royal Comm. on Employment of Children in Trades and Manufactures not Regulated by Law: Fifth Report, Appendix* (Parl. Papers 1866 [XXIV], 140-2); Pearce and Long, 'Chalk Mining', 64-73.

94 Francis, *Cement Industry*, 183; J. Rochard, *Historical Chatham and Rochester* (Chatham, 1894), 45.

95 Preston, *Industrial Medway*, 48, 140-5.

96 F.G. Wilmott, *Bricks and Brickies* (1972), 1-2.

97 Francis, *Cement Industry*, 130-46; Pugh, *Blue Circle*, 36-8.

98 Pugh, *Blue Circle*, 34-40, 65-74.

99 E.J. March, *Spritsail Barges of Thames and Medway* (Newton Abbot, 1970).

100 *South Eastern Gazette*, 10 Feb. 1868.

101 *Children in Trades and Manufactures* (Parl. Papers 1866 [XXIV], 128); CKS P12/13/A/4; P12/13/A/7; CKS Q/CI/441/1.

102 Richardson, 'Labour', 258-9; *Royal Commission of Labour fourth report, minutes of evidence and appendices* (Parl. Papers, PP 1893 [XXXVII]) Pt.2, 139; G. Crossick, *An Artisan Elite in Victorian Society: Kentish London 1840-1880* (London, 1978), 78-84.

103 The resolutions are printed in full in T. Balston, *William Balston, Paper Maker, 1759-1849* (London, 1954), 159-63; Coleman, *British Paper Industry*, 299-300; E.H. Hunt, *Regional Wage Variations in Britain, 1850-1914* (Oxford, 1973), 62.

104 *Royal Comm. on Employment of Children in Trades and Manufactures not Regulated by Law: Fourth Report, minutes of evidence and appendices* (Parl. Papers, 1865 [XX], 142).

105 *Children in Trades and Manufactures* (Parl. Papers 1866 [XXIV], 127-9).

106 F.G. Willmott, *Cement, Mud and 'Muddies'* (Sittingbourne, 1977); *Children in Trades and Manufactures*, (Parl. Papers, 1866 [XXIV], 140-1).

107 Preston, *Industrial Medway*, 92-3; C. Hadfield, *The Canals of South and South East England* (Newton Abbot, 1969), 81-101; D. Brooke, *The Railway Navvy* (Newton Abbot, 1983), 20.

108 *Report from the Select Committee of the House of Lords on Injury from Noxious Vapours*, (Parl. Papers, 1862 (486), 239-42).

109 Hasted, *History and Topographical Survey*, Vol. III, 547; Preston, *Industrial Medway*, 11-13; R. Marsh, *The Conservancy of the River Medway 1881-1969* (Rochester, 1971), 14.

110 G.P. Bevan, *Handbook to the County of Kent* (6th edn, London, 1887), 58; A.R. Hope Moncrieff (ed.), *Black's Guide to West Kent* (London, 1901), 27.

111 See, for instance, W. Coles Finch, *The Medway, River and Valley* (London, 1929); Bagshaw, *History, Gazetteer and Directory*, 249-50.

112 W.G. Hoskins, *The Making of the English Landscape* (London, 1955), 299.

113 Bagshaw, *History, Gazetteer and Directory*, 323.

114 Maxwell, *Unknown Kent*, 98.

115 *Black's Guide to Kent* (Edinburgh, 1885), 80-120.

116 Quoted in Church, *Cuxton*, 135.

117 E. Harris, *A Trip down the River Medway* (Rochester, 1897).

118 Maxwell, *Unknown Kent*, 99.

119 Maxwell, *Unknown Kent*, 102, 105; D. Maxwell, *History from a Sketch Book* (London, 1926), 160.

CHAPTER 4 The Landowners and Industrialists pp. 53-66

120 Information taken from the Tithe Apportionments held on microfilm at CKS. Originals are in TNA, IR 29/17/14, 59, 103, 145, 160, 285, 336, 404.

121 Hasted, *History and Topographical Survey*, Vol. IV, 436-9; CKS U886/T1/Bundle 7; TNA, IR 29/17/14.

122 Church, *Cuxton*, 56, 100-1. See also 168-9 for a table showing who worked each of the 11 farms in the parish from 1665-1938; Cuxton Tithe Award schedule, 12 May 1842, as transcribed at www.kentarchaeology.org.uk. [accessed 12/01/2007].

123 www.snodlandhistory.org.uk/localhis/cement [accessed 09/02/2007].

124 *The Builder*, 25 Sept. 1886 with illustrations.

125 CKS P12/28/9, *Handy Book for the Villagers of Aylesford*, (2nd edn, Maidstone, 1866); *Kelly's Directory*, 1882.

126 *South Eastern Gazette*, 20 Aug. 1867; J. Woolmer, *Historical Jottings of the Parish of Snodland* (1894), 10, 47. Text accessible on www.snodlandhistory.org.uk/; *Kelly's Directory of Kent* (1882), 505.

127 Francis, *Cement Industry*, 181-3.

128 Smetham, *History of Strood*, 215, 345-6; Hasted, *History and Topographical Survey*, Vol. IV, 464. www.snodlandhistory.org.uk/localhis/cement [accessed 26/08/2006].

129 P. Clark and L. Murfin, *The History of Maidstone: the Making of a Modern County Town* (Stroud, 1995), 107-10.

130 MALSC 09S/2/2/1; MALSC 09S, Rochester Book Society, 1797-1965; J.B. Hewitt, 'The History of the Rochester Book Society' (unpublished, 1932). Thanks to Ann Lyons for providing this information.

131 CKS P12/28/9, *Handy Book*.

132 National Archives, PCC, PROB 11/1858, 20 February 1836, Will of Charles Milner. See also in CKS U886 five documents dated 1766-1773, relating to the building of a new school at Aylesford. www.snodlandhistory.org.uk/localhis/schools [accessed 15/11/2006].

133   E.S. Gowers and D. Church, *Across the Low Meadow: Halling, a Village on the Medway* (Maidstone, 1979), 107; *Kelly's Directory*, 1874.

134   www.snodlandhistory.org.uk/localhis/schools [accessed 15/11/2006].

135   *Chatham News*, 24 June 1865.

136   Gowers and Church, *Low Meadow*, 108-18, extracts from the school log.

137   Gowers and Church, *Low Meadow*, 24.

138   CKS P12/28/9, *Handy Book*, 42; Hasted, *History and Topographical Survey*, Vol. IV, 442; A. Maccrerie, *Knowing Aylesford* (Hadlow, 1964), 5.

139   www.snodlandhistory.org.uk/localhis/hook [accessed 27/03/2007].

140   CKS P12/28/9, *Handy Book*, 42-3.

141   Church, *Cuxton*, 92.

142   CKS P12/28/9, *Handy Book*, 29-31; *Kent Messenger*, 10 Dec. 1881; The Temperance Tavern is listed in *Kelly's Directory*, 1882.

143   Church, *Cuxton*, 59; *Chatham Observer*, 14 July 1894.

144   N. Yates and J. Gibson (eds), *Traffic and Politics: The Construction and Management of Rochester Bridge AD 43-1993* (Woodbridge, 1994), Appendix A, 'Wardens and Assistants of Rochester Bridge', 289-310 for a list of all Rochester Wardens and the public offices they held.

145   Marsh, *River Medway*, 20-1, 161.

146   *Maidstone Telegraph*, 6 Aug. 1859.

CHAPTER 5 House, Home and Community pp. 67-90

147   A. Quiney, *Kent Houses* (Woodbridge, 1993) 182-9; http://www.imagesofengland.org.uk/ [accessed 10/11/2006].

148   CKS DRA/Pi/25/1.

149   CKS DRB/Pi/44/11B, DRB/Pi/58/6.

150   Boys, *General View*, 1st edn, 30-1; *ibid.*, (2nd edn, revised, London, 1813), 33.

151   J. Burnett, *A Social History of Housing, 1815-1985* (2nd edn, London, 1986), 34-6.

152   CKS XK/Aylesford, Sales particulars for the Preston Hall estates, 1867; *Employment of Children*, (Parl. Papers 1868-9 [XIII.1]), 44).

153   *Employment of Children*, 46; Burnett, *Social History*, 47-53.

154   CKS XK/Aylesford, 1867.

155   PP 1868-9, XIII.1, *Employment of Children*, 43, 46; *Comms. on Sanitary Condition of the Labouring Population of England: Local Reports- Kent and Sussex* (Parl. Papers 1842 [XXVII.1], 44).

156   *The Builder*, 10 Dec. 1852.

157   CKS K333 Kent.

158   *Kent Messenger*, 30 Aug. 1892.

159   N. Pevsner and A. Clifton-Taylor, 'Building materials' in J. Newman, *The Buildings of England: West Kent and the Weald* (Penguin, 1969), 23-9; Article by Donald Maxwell in *The Church Times*, 26 July 1929, quoted in M. Ffinch, *Donald Maxwell* (Kendal, 1995), 103.

160   CKS XK/Rochester, 1890.

161   S. Williams, 'Earnings, poor relief and the economy of makeshifts', 29; see the relieving books for Malling Union - CKS G/ML/R/A2.

162   H. Boys, 'On the Kentish corn-scythe and binding rake', *Journal of the Royal Agricultural Society*, I (1840), 446-7; *Women and Children in Agriculture*, (Parl. Papers 1843 [XII], 171,185; Boys, *General View* (1st edn) 86.

163   *Children in Trades and Manufactures* (Parl. Papers 1865 [XX], 143-4; *Children in Trades and Manufactures*, (Parl. Papers 1866 [XXIV], 128-9).

164   Gowers and Church, *Low Meadow*, 52; *Employment of Children* (Parl Papers 1868-9 [XIII.1], 41); Hunt, *Regional Wage Variations in Britain*, 118-28.

165   *Children in Trades and Manufactures*, (Parl. Papers 1866 [XXIV], 127).

166   S. King and A. Tomkins (eds), *The Poor in England 1700-1850: An Economy of Makeshifts* (Manchester, 2003); NA MH12/5227; CKS G/ML/R/A2.

167   Mingay, 'Agriculture', 51-3; R. Wall, 'Some implications of the earnings, income and expenditure patterns of married women in populations in the past', in Henderson and Wall (eds), *Poor Women and Children in the European Past* (London, 1994); *Commissions of Inquiry into Charities in England and Wales: Thirtieth Report* (Parl. Papers, 1837 [XXIII.1], 350-2, 357).

168   CKS P12/5/A/3; *Commissions of Inquiry into Charities in England and Wales: Twenty-sixth Report*, (Parl. Papers, 1833 [XIX.1], p. 200); CKS P12/25/A/1.

169   B. Keith-Lucas, *Parish Affairs: the Government of Kent under George III* (Maidstone, 1986), 111; Smetham, *History of Strood*, 261-76; Gowers and Church, *Low Meadow*, 35.

170   CKS P12/12/A/4.

171   D.A. Baugh, 'The cost of poor relief in South-East England, 1790-1834', *Economic History Review*, 2nd Series, xxviii:1 (1975), 67; CKS P12/12/A/7.

172   NA MH12/5226.

173   T. Buss, 'Recollections of Eccles' (unpublished article); *Chatham Observer*, 9 Feb. 1895.

174   NA MH12/5228; *Chatham Observer*, 9 Feb. 1895.

175   *Report of Chief Registrar of Friendly Societies, 1877: Appendix* (Parl. Papers 1878 [LXIX.3], 69-75). In 1803 only seven such groups are recorded with a combined membership of around 400; *Abstract of Answers and Returns under Act for procuring Returns relative to Expense and Maintenance of the Poor in England* (Parl. Papers 1803-4 [XIII], 222-3); CKS P12/13/A/5; *Abstracts of Quinquennial Returns of Sickness and Mortality experienced by Friendly Societies*,

1855-75, (Parl. Papers 1880 [LXVIII.517], 220).

176   CKS G/ML/R/A2.

177   *Minutes of Evidence taken before the Select Committee on the Combination Act of 1824 in respect of the Conduct of workmen in the United Kingdom* (Parl. Papers 1825 [417], 594-5).

178   *Royal Commission of Labour: Answers to Schedules of Questions* (Parl. Papers 1892 [XXXVI.5], 234-5).

179   *Return of Prosecutions in England and Wales under the Game Laws, 1857-62* (Parl. Papers 1864 [XLIX.33], 143-5); *Chatham News*, 27 Aug. 1881; *Chatham News*, 10 Dec. 1859.

180   *Rochester Gazette*, 27 Jan. 1857; *Chatham News*, 21 Jan. 1860; *Chatham News*, 1 Mar. 1862.

181   CKS P12/13/A/7.

182   N. Yates, R. Hume and P. Hastings, *Religion and Society in Kent* (Woodbridge, 1994), 117-8; TNA MH12/5226; Buss, 'Eccles'.

183   Church, *Cuxton*, 54.

184   Smetham, *History of Strood*, 217.

185   G.M. Arnold, *Robert Pocock* (Gravesend, 1883), 83.

186   Smetham, *History of Strood*, 208; Clark and Murfin, *History of Maidstone*, 108-9.

187   Church, *Cuxton*, 109.

188   Church, *Cuxton*, 104.

189   Barnard, *Merrily to Frendsbury*, 139; Halling School Logbook, May 1881. See also N. Miners, 'Snodland's civil parish boundary and the boundary walk', *Snodland Historical Society Newsletter*, Vol. 3:2 (April 2000).

190   Buss, 'Eccles'; Gowers and Church, *Low Meadow*, 76.

191   *South Eastern Gazette*, 16 July 1867.

192   *Chatham Observer*, 11 Aug. 1900.

193   *Kelly's Directory of Kent* (1882), 29.

194   Information from Dean Jones; CKS P12/24/6; Gowers and Church, *Low Meadow*, 94-5; *Chatham Observer*, 24 Sept. 1898.

195   *Kent Messenger*, 12 Jan. 1884; information from Andrew Ashbee.

196   A. Ashbee, *Notes from Snodland Rectory, 1865-1882* (Snodland, 1993), 11, 37.

197   *Kent Messenger*, 10 Dec. 1881; Funnell, *Snodland Paper Mill*, 48; a more comprehensive account of the Hook's benefactions can be found on www.snodlandhistory.org.uk/localhis/hook [accessed 19/02/2007].

198   CKS P12/28/9, *Handy Book*; Church, *Cuxton*, 59-60.

199   P. Gosden, *The Friendly Societies in England 1815-1875* (Manchester, 1961), 10, 17; *Chatham News*, 22 Aug. 1868; CKS P12/24/1.

200   *Kent Messenger*, 16 Jan. 1897; Gowers and Church, *Low Meadow*, 74.

201   *Rochester and Chatham Journal*, 14 Nov. 1891.

202   Gowers and Church, *Low Meadow*, 75.

203   J. Clancy, *Cinemas of the Medway Towns* (Wakefield, 2006), 67, 75.

CHAPTER 6 Church, Chapel and People pp. 91-8

204   M. Roake, 'Religion and the 1851 Census', in Lawson and Killingray, *Historical Atlas*, 168-9; CKS p12/8/1, Vestry Minute Book, 1736-1916.

205   Roake (ed.), 'Religious worship in Kent: The Census of 1851', *Kent Records* (1999), XXVII, 110.

206   *Children in Trades and Manufactures* (Parl. Papers 1866 [XXIV]), 149-50).

207   CKS P165 7/1; *Chatham and Rochester News*, 9 Oct. 1886.

208   CKS 1851 Religious Census.

209   Smetham, *History of Strood*, 60-86.

210   CKS 1851 Religious Census; CKS P108 5/4; *Bromley Journal and West Kent Herald*, 25 Feb. 1870.

211   CKS 1859 Visitation document; H. Smetham, *Rambles round Churches* (Chatham, 1928).

212   Roake (ed.), *Religious Worship*; unpublished diary of Rosamund Nash Spong of Mill Hall, Aylesford, 1835 (private collection).

213   CKS, P12/28/43-4, *Aylesford Parish Magazine* for 1886-7; information from present owner.

214   P. McDougall, *Chatham Past* (Chichester, 1999), 49; A. Whiteman and M. Clapinson (eds), *The Compton Census of 1676: A Critical Edition* (London, 1986), 407; A.H. Shorter (ed.), *Studies on the History of Papermaking in Britain* (Aldershot, 1993), Smetham, *History of Strood*, 249-53; Roake (ed.), *Religious Worship*, 85; MALSC RG4/1189.

215   Whiteman and Clapinson (eds) *The Compton Census*, 407; MALSC N/URC/432.

216   Ashbee, 'Snodland papermakers', 15-23.

217   F.L. Cross and E.A. Livingstone (eds), *The Oxford Dictionary of the Christian Church* (2nd edn 1974), 1327-8; A. Ashbee, *The Early History of the New Church in Snodland*, 4-6; *The Monthly Observer and New Church Record*, Vol. VIII (1864), 280.

218   *Kent Messenger*, 23 Mar. 1881, 11 Feb. 1882.

219   The church was designed by 'Mr Bridge of Maidstone', who can be identified as Henry Bridge, surveyor and valuer, of 37 Week Street. The builder was J.W. Walker and Sons of Francis Street, Tottenham Court Road. *Kent Messenger*, 11 Feb. and 1 July 1882; *Kelly's Directory*, 1882; *Illustrated London News*, 29 July 1882, 124; Funnell, *Snodland Paper Mill*, 46-7, 51.

220   *Kent Messenger*, 19 Oct. 1878; Woolmer, *Historical Jottings*.

221   Woolmer, *Historical Jottings*.

222   Smetham, *History of Strood*, 254.

223   Roake (ed.), *Religious Worship*, 108; A.D. Gilbert, *Religion and Society in Industrial England*

(London, 1976), 17-22; R. Homan, *The Victorian Churches of Kent* (Chichester, 1984), 92; Smetham, *History of Strood*, 258-9; CKS, M6/2D/1/1 *passim*. Stroud designs are M6/2D/1/2/1-3.

224   Church, *Cuxton*, 66.

225   *Kelly's Directory*, 1882, 28; Gowers and Church, *Low Meadow*, 21.

226   Gilbert, *Religion and Society in Industrial England*, 205-6.

CHAPTER 7 Aylesford, Eccles and Snodland pp. 99-128

227   Hasted, *History and Topographical Survey*, Vol. IV, 427-9.

228   CKS U442/P4.

229   CKS U234/E21, 2.

230   CKS U234/E21; For the development of the back extension see S. Muthesius, *The English Terraced House* (London, 1982), 88-97.

231   CKS U886/P9 and P10 (1849); U886/P11 (1855).

232   Hasted, *History and Topographical Survey*, Vol. IV, 438-9; CKS U886/T1/Bundle 7.

233   CKS Q/C1/453.

234   H. Colvin, *A Biographical Dictionary of British Architects 1600-1840* (1995), 1041. In the schedule of the conveyance of the Preston Hall estate, 19 August 1848 (CKS U886/T1/Bundle 8 Pt.2) there are listed at Little Preston Farm 'ornamental cottages capable of conversion into a farmhouse'. These may have been to Whichcord's design, but had been demolished by 1867. Successive maps of the estate clearly show that a surviving set of ornamental cottages are on a different site, and were probably built after the others were taken down (c.f. CKS U886/P9 and P10 with U886/P13).

235   CKS U866/T1/Bundle 8 Part 2.

236   The outline plan of the new Hall is shown on the estate map of 1849, CKS U886/P10. The date 1857 occurs on a weathervane; Sephton, *Around Aylesford*, 73-82; Post Office Directory (1855), 264; 1867 Sale brochure, CKS XK/Aylesford; English Heritage, *Images of England*, IoE numbers 179246, 179263, 179264, 179265.

237   They all appear on a map of the Preston Hall estate dated c.1855 (CKS U886/P11).

238   W. Finlay, Notebook 1850-1 (privately owned); R. Hunt, *Mining Records* (1860), mineral statistics for 1858.

239   J.H. Sephton, *Preston Hall, Aylesford* (Aylesford, 1997), 24. The fountain was removed c.1928.

240   *Kelly's Directory*, 1874. E.W. Stephens's undated designs for this phase are CKS DE/S/1/12/1-5. *Kelly's Directory*, 1878. The Pratling Street school was demolished in 1905.

241   CKS XK/Aylesford/Too. Particulars of 32 plots for sale on 14 June 1900.

242   'Aylesford in the 1930s'. Typescript memoir by A.J.N., Feb. 2004. The accompanying sketch map also indicates Danes Brewery at the foot of Mount Pleasant, where late 20th-century blocks of flats now stand.

243   CKS U234/E4.

244   Hobhouse, *Thomas Cubitt*, 308-15.

245   Buss, 'Eccles'; *Kelly's Directory*, 1855, sub Aylesford; census, 1861.

246   Ordnance Survey six inches to one mile, 1st Edition, 1869; Censuses, 1871-1901; Buss, 'Eccles'; The Inland Revenue Returns for 1908 record his son Frederick Hart as owning five houses in Alma Road, four in Belgrave Street and two in Victoria Street.

247   Census 1861; Buss, 'Eccles'.

248   T. Buss, 'Eccles', calls Varney's holding 'two meadows'. The piece of land in question is clearly identifiable just outside the somewhat fragmented north-east corner of Eccles (i.e. Rowe Place) Farm in R.K. Summerfield's map of 1804 (CKS U234/E21/map no. 2). Varney's name also occurs in 1884 as owner of the residue of land when building was complete (CKS U234/E19, particulars of sale of properties from the Earl of Aylesford's estate, map accompanying lots 21-24).

249   The houses in Varnes Street first appear in the 1881 census, as does the east side of Victoria Street. The west side of Victoria Street and the whole of Belgrave Street are first listed in the census of 1891.

250   Annotated sale particulars, CKS, U234/E19, lots 22-4; *Aylesford Parish Magazine*, 1886.

251   Flyer exhibited in Eccles Church in July 2007. Conveyances owned by Mr D. Stoner of Eccles show Varney in December 1881 selling a plot in Belgrave Street to Thomas Driver, carpenter, and Thomas Fullman, bricklayer: on it they built four houses which they sold on in November 1882 to a Maidstone timber merchant's clerk, who presumably rented them out. This must represent the normal method of development.

252   P. Morgan (ed.), *Domesday Book: Kent* (Chichester, 1983), 4.9. Two other mills in the parish are also mentioned. A Topographical Map of the County of Kent by J. Andrews, A. Dury and W. Herbert (1769; facsimile, Lympne, 1968).

253   DCMS List description; see also www.snodlandhistory.org.uk/localhis/papermill [accessed 12/04/2006]; *Archaeologia Cantiana*, 1876, 321.

254   www.snodlandhistory.org.uk/localhis/tollroad [accessed 30/02/2007].

255   www.snodlandhistory.org.uk/localhis/19thcentury [accessed 18/06/2006].

256   'National School in Brook St' – www.snodlandhistory.org.uk/localhis/cement [accessed 19/11/2006]; *South Eastern Gazette*, 20 Aug. 1867.

257   *The Builder*, 25 Sept. 1886 with illustrations. The house was built of red brick with dressings of red concrete and moulded bricks.

258   www.snodlandhistory.org.uk/localhis/papermill [accessed 23/11/2006]; A. Ashbee, 'Snodland papermakers'.

259   Funnell, *Snodland Paper Mill*, illustration on 28.

260 It was only the second of its type in the country; inscription on the building transcribed in
     Woolmer, *Historical Jottings*. See also *The Builder*, 29 Oct. 1892.
261 Information from Hook's ledger, cited in Funnell, *Snodland Paper Mill*, 35; A. Ashbee, *Snodland
     in Old Picture Postcards* (The Netherlands, 2001), caption to fig. 65.
262 *South Eastern Gazette*, 20 Aug. 1867. Bills preserved in Snodland Museum.
263 CKS U2102/T12-18, 35-36, P2-3.
264 Ashbee, *Old Picture Postcards*, caption to fig. 63. Snodland Millennium Museum Doc. Hse. 009 is
     a copy of a conveyance in December 1877 of no. 12 Portland Place to Walter Mole, a bricklayer,
     who subsequently resided in the house.
265 Ashbee, *Old Picture Postcards*, caption to fig. 62. Information on the Coulson family inheritance
     is in SMM Doc. Hse. 019.
266 Ashbee, *Old Picture Postcards,* caption to fig. 64; CKS U2102/T36.
267 CKS U2102/P3. The interpretation of this undated map of part of the Holborough estate is not
     straightforward.
268 The title deeds of Wilford's depot begin in 1897. Snodland Millennium Museum, Doc.Lan.05,
     Doc.Hse.013.
269 As late as 1891, so the census shows, Mulberry Cottages were occupied by a blacksmith, the
     proprietor of a sweet shop, and a chimney sweep; C. de R. Wall, *Snodland and its History, 55 B.C.
     to A.D. 1928* (1928), 23; D. Petty, 'Victorian Philanthropy: A Case Study of the Hook family of
     Snodland', SHS pamphlet 29 (Snodland, 2007), 29, 44.
270 MALSC P342/8/1, Vestry Minute Book, 12 Sept. 1856; Woolmer, *Historical Jottings*, 42.
271 Snodland Millennium Museum, Doc.Hse.041.
272 Wall, *Snodland and its History*, 33; *Building News*, 1870. The Rectory was demolished *c.*1969.
273 Ashbee, *Old Picture Postcards*, caption to figs 2, 11.
274 CKS U2102/T18.
275 CKS U2102/T19, particulars of 'choice and ripe building plots' for sale on 19 July 1919, and P7,
     an undated sketch map roughly indicating the location of plots.

CHAPTER 8 The Lower Medway Valley and the Wider World pp. 129-50

276 Gowers and Church, *Low Meadow*, 35.
277 CKS Q/CI/14.
278 TNA PROB 11/2101, PROB 11/1781.
279 CKS P12/13/6; C.G. Pooley and J. Turnbull, *Migration and Mobility in Britain since the Eighteenth
     Century* (London, 1998), 54-70.
280 Hobhouse, *Thomas Cubitt*, 312; T. Lawson, 'Rural population trends to 1901', in Lawson and
     Killingray, *Historical Atlas* , 103.
281 D.R. Mills and K. Schurer, 'Migration and population turnover', in D.R. Mills and K. Schurer
     (eds), *Local Communities in the Victorian Census Ennumerators' Books* (Oxford, 1996), 222-6.
282 Coleman, *British Paper Industry*.
283 *Employment of Children*, (Parl. Papers 1868-69 [XIII.1], 46); *Children in Trades and
     Manufactures*, (Parl. Papers 1866 [XXIV], 141).
284 TNA IR29/17/59 and IR 29/17/238.
285 A. Armstrong, 'Population: 1831-1914' in Armstrong (ed.), *Economy of Kent*, 46-7; T. Lawson,
     'Rural population trends to 1901', in Lawson and Killingray, *Historical Atlas*, 103.
286 Preston, *Industrial Medway*, 20; J.C. Coad, *The Royal Dockyards, 1690-1850, Architecture and
     Engineering Works of the Sailing Navy* (Aldershot, 1989); Richardson, 'Labour', 251, 252.
287 TNA IR1; CKS MD/Ra/1/2-3; MALSC RCA/2/18-19.
288 For a discussion of how representative apprentices were of all migrants see I.D. Whyte, *Migration
     and Society in Britain, 1550-1830* (London, 2000), 17-18.
289 Richardson, 'Labour', 258-9.
290 Pearce and Long, 'Chalk Mining', 33. Preston, *Industrial Medway*, 77-80; Francis, *Cement
     Industry*.
291 W. Marshall, *The Rural Economy of the Southern Counties* (London, 1798), Vol. I, 242.
292 *Children in Trades and Manufactures* (Parl. Papers 1865 [XX], 151).
293 Stratton, *Hop-pickers*, 132; *Chatham News*, 25 Sept. 1869.
294 MALSC U565/H1-13.
295 C. Seymour, *A New Topographical, Historical and Commercial Survey of the County of Kent*, 545.
296 *Universal British Directory*, vols 2-5 (1790-1797).
297 *Maidstone Journal*, 18 Nov. 1817; *Rochester and Chatham Journal*, 24 April 1880.
298 D. Killingray, 'Newspaper', in Lawson and Killingray, *Historical Atlas*, 184.
299 CKS U1823/35; CKS Q/CI/29.
300 T.P. Smith, 'The geographical pattern of coaching services in Kent in 1836', *Archaeologia
     Cantiana*, XCVIII (1982), 195-9.
301 Hadfield, *Canals*, 99-110; F. Andrews and G. Crompton, 'Development of railways and roads
     since 1830', Lawson and Killingray, *Historical Atlas*, 124-5.
302 CKS Q/CI/410; Q/CI/409; *Maidstone Journal*, 13 Sept. 1831.
303 Preston, *Industrial Medway*, 58-9.
304 R. Craig and J. Whyman, 'Kent and the sea' in Armstrong, *The Economy of Kent*, 171-2; Preston,
     Industrial Medway, 51; Francis, *Cement Industry*, 186-7.
305 *Report of the Metropolitan Board of Works, 1862-3* (Parl. Papers 1864 [L.67], 27); Preston,
     Industrial Medway, 100-1.

306   Hobhouse, *Thomas Cubitt*, 309-12; Preston, *Industrial Medway*, 82; Francis, *Cement Industry*, 181.
307   TNA BT31/1670/5913.
308   M. Kitch, 'Capital and kingdom: migration to later Stuart London', in A.L. Beier and R. Finlay
       (eds), *The Making of the Metropolis: London 1500-1700* (London, 1986), 224-51. London livery
       company apprentice records taken from www.originsnetwork.com. Kitch suggests that London
       apprentices most commonly came from ports and market towns since trading contacts made it
       easier to find a position. In this case 57 apprentices hailed from Maidstone, 54 from Chatham and
       38 from Rochester.
309   CKS P12/13/5.
310   This dataset was compiled by tracing the 1901 residence of all people born in Aylesford, whose
       surname appears in the 1881 census listing for that parish, using the National Archives website
       census index. The procedure was then repeated for those born in Frindsbury.
311   Marshall, *Rural Economy*, 242-3; Richardson, 'Labour', 257.
312   *Maidstone Journal*, 13 Sept. 1869.
313   MALSC U565/H2-4.
314   Hadfield, *Canals*.
315   CKS P12/28/9, *Handy Book*.
316   D. Ormrod, 'Rochester Bridge, 1660-1825' in Yates and Gibson (eds), *Traffic and Politics*, 167-8;
       Craig and Whyman, 'Kent and the sea', 169.
317   MALSC RCA/N2/1-78.
318   D. Ormrod, 'Rochester Bridge', 168-9; Craig and Whyman, 'Kent and the sea', 175-81, 192-3.
319   Coleman, *British Paper Industry*, 262-74.
320   Francis, *Cement Industry*, 183-6.
321   Preston, *Industrial Medway*, 166; Francis, *Cement Industry*, 258-67.

CHAPTER 9 Industrial Decline and Landscape Change pp.151-62

322   D. Maxwell, 'Medway Heights' in *The Enchanted Road* (London, 1927).
323   Bagshaw, *History, Gazetteer and Directory*, 249-50.
324   Preston, 'Medway Gap'.
325   Gowers and Church, *Low Meadow*, 54, 62.
326   Barnard, *Merrily to Frendsbury*, 51.
327   Barnard, *Merrily to Frendsbury*, 100-6.
328   Pearce and Long, 'Chalk Mining', 26-9.
329   *Chatham, Rochester and Gillingham News*, 24 Nov. 1967; 1 Dec. 1967; Pearce and Long, 'Chalk
       Mining', 56-9.
330   Willmott, *Cement, Mud and Muddies*.
331   Preston, *Industrial Medway*, 74-5.
332   Marsh, *River Medway*, 53-6; R. Simper, *The River Medway and the Swale* (Woodbridge, 1998), 5,
       caption for fig. 9.
333   Preston, 'Medway Gap'.
334   Pearce and Long, 'Chalk Mining', 71; Willmott, *Bricks and Brickies*, 21-2.
335   Hobhouse, *Thomas Cubitt*, 310-12; *The Illustrated News of the World*, 8 Oct. 1859.
336   *South Eastern Gazette*, 11 June 1867.

Bibliography and Sources

This section gives information about the sources used in writing this volume and suggestions for those wishing to undertake their own research. The list of record repositories that hold Kent material includes a brief description of the categories of records held. After the name of each, the abbreviation used appears in brackets.

RECORD REPOSITORIES

Blue Circle Archive, Snodland (BC)
Records of the cement companies that combined to form APCM and later Blue Circle in the 20th century (limited access - managed by the Gravesend Historical Society).

British Library (BL)
Property deeds; church plans; maps and plans; views and engravings; local newspapers (Newspaper Library), papers relating to navigation on the Medway and the oyster fishery.

Centre for Kentish Studies, Maidstone (CKS)
Local authority records; parish records for Aylesford; probate records; poor law; quarter sessions; charities; enclosure; tithes; family and business records; property deeds; maps and local history books and periodicals.

Halling School (HS)
Collection of archives and ephemera assembled by local historian Ted Gowers including school log books and archive photographs (limited access).

House of Lords Record Office
Includes records of Private Acts of Parliament.

Maidstone Library (ML)
Local newspapers; trade directories; parish registers.

Medway Archives and Local Studies Centre (MALSC)
Parish records; parish registers and other diocesan records; records of the Dean and Chapter of Rochester; local authorities; apprentice registers; family and business papers; local newspapers; records of canal and navigation companies; poor law; charities; tithes; turnpikes; nonconformist records; port records; maps; archive photographs and film, and local history books and periodicals.

Public Record Office, since 2003 part of the National Archives (TNA)
Records of national government relating to the Lower Medway Valley: wills and inventories; taxation records; bankruptcy; poor law administration.

Rochester Bridge Trust (RBT)
Title deeds and administrative records relating to land owned by the Trust particularly in Frindsbury parish.

BIBLIOGRAPHIES, DICTIONARIES AND GUIDES TO ARCHIVAL SOURCES

Bennett, G., *The Kent bibliography: a finding list of Kent material in the public libraries of the county and the adjoining London boroughs* (London, 1977)

Bergess, W., *Kent maps and plans in the libraries of Kent and the adjoining London boroughs : a finding list* (London, 1992)

Dictionary of National Biography (*DNB*) (CD searchable) and *The Oxford Dictionary of National Biography.*

Goulden, R.J., *Kent town guides, 1763-1900: a bibliography of locally-published Kent town guides, together with accounts of the printing, publishing, and production of town guides in certain towns in Kent* (London, 1995)

Hull, F., *Kentish maps and mapmakers, 1590-1840* (Maidstone, 1973)

Norton, J.E., *Guide to the National and Provincial Directories of England and Wales* (before 1856)

Shaw, G. and Tipper, A., *British directories: a bibliography and guide to directories published in England and Wales (1850-1950) and Scotland (1773-1950)*, (2nd edn, London, 1997)

ON-LINE SEARCHES

A range of material relating to the Medway valley, including transcripts of documents, photographs and articles, is available on the England's Past For Everyone website: **www.englandspastforeveryone.org.uk**

A2A – Access to Archives: www.a2a.org.uk
This site describes many of the archival holdings of the repositories listed above.

British History Online: www.british-history.ac.uk

British Library Manuscripts Catalogue: www.bl.uk/catalogues/manuscripts.html

Chronological Table of Local Acts 1797-2003: www.opsi.gov.uk/chron-tables/chron-index. htm

Cityark: http://cityark.medway.gov.uk/
Website of Medway Archives and Local Studies Centre. As well as archive listings this includes digitised parish registers, an ImageBase containing thousands of archive photographs and a MovieBase of archive film.

Here's History Kent: www.hereshistorykent.org.uk/
Innovative website managed by Kent County Council offering guidance for local historians and a wide range of source materials for towns and parishes across Kent.

Kent Archaeological Society: http://www.kentarchaeology.org.uk/
Website includes downloadable books and articles, and datasets including tithe award transcripts.

Kent Photo Archive: http://www.kentphotoarchive.org.uk/site2009/index.php
Archive photographs covering the whole of Kent accessed through a clickable map and subject or placename index.

National Register of Archives:
(now incorporated into The National Archives website) **www.nationalarchives.gov.uk**

PRIMARY SOURCES NOT IN PRINT

Maps
Lyon Alexander, J. Map of the Preston Hall estate – Aylesford and Burham, 1854 (CKS U886/P15)

Baker, F., Frindsbury, Manor, 1768 (MALSC CCRc P16)

Gouge, J., Map of Frindsbury Manor, 1792 (MALSC CCRc P18)

Gouge, J., Plan of Frindsbury Manor Farm, 1811 (MALSC DRc EP10)

Gouge, J., Plan of Hawkins Manor, Strood, 1825 (MALSC DRc EP18)

Gouge, J., Plan of Strood, part of Newark estate, c.1849 (MALSC DRc EP19)

Hodkinson, J., Estate map of Cuxton and Halling, 1774 (CKS CCRb/P/1)

Joy, J., Estate map of Halling, 1731 (CKS CCRb/P/3)

Summerfield, R.K., Aylesford Estate Atlas 1805, with later additions (CKS U234/E21)

West, I.J., Maps of the Preston Hall estate – Aylesford, Boxley, Ditton and East Malling, 1849 (CKS U886/P9&10)

Tootell and Sons, Maidstone, Map of the Preston Hall estate, 1860 (CKS U886/P13)

Tithe maps, c.1840 - copies for all parishes on CD-Rom from CKS

Estate map of Frindsbury and Strood, 1778 (MALSC CCRc P22)

Estate map of Halling and Snodland, c.1800 (CKS CCRb/P/6)

Plan of Wouldham Court Farm, c.1740 (MALSC DRc EP20)

Map of the Holborough estate, undated (CKS U2102/P3

For details of other categories of manuscript and archival primary sources used in the preparation of this volume please consult the endnotes.

PRIMARY SOURCES IN PRINT

Place of publication is London unless otherwise stated.

Maps
Ordnance Survey Maps

Official Publications
References to the Medway valley will be found in many of the parliamentary papers and commission reports, census returns etc., on such topics as the relief of the poor, education, charities, public health, agriculture. Many of these can now be accessed through British History

Online: www.british-history.ac.uk

Parliamentary debates can be searched at: www.hansard.millbanksystems.com

Census
Online Historical Population Reports: www.histpop.org/ohpr/servlet
Many census enumerators' books are now available online. Copies of the Kent ones 1841-1901 are available at CKS and MALSC.
1831 *Abstract of the Answers and Returns on Population 1831*, HC 1833 Abstract HC 1833 Vol. 1

Newspapers and Journals
Chatham News 1-1357 (1859-1885)
Chatham and Rochester News 1358-2302 (1885-1903)
Chatham, Rochester and Gillingham News 2303-6703 (1903-1989)
Chatham Observer 1-164 (1870-1873)
Chatham and Rochester Observer 165-1437 (1873-1897)
Chatham, Rochester and Brompton Observer 1438-1749 (1897-1903)
Chatham, Rochester and Gillingham Observer 1750-3479 (1903-1937)
Rochester Gazette 459-746 (1830-1835)
Rochester, Chatham and Strood Gazette 747-2460 (1835-1868)
Maidstone Gazette 1501-2748 (1830-1851)
South Eastern Gazette 2749-12629 (1952-1936)
Maidstone Journal and Kentish Advertiser 1-3503 (1786-1853)
Maidstone and Kentish Journal 3504-11409 (1853-1911)
Maidstone and Kent County Standard 1-1159 (1873-1885)
Kent County Standard, Tunbridge Wells Standard and Southborough and Tonbridge Journal 1160-2630 (1886-1912)
Maidstone Telegraph, Rochester and Chatham Gazette 1-137 (1859-1861)
Maidstone Telegraph, Malling Chronicle and West Kent Messenger 138-666 (1861-1871)
Kent Messenger and Maidstone Telegraph 667-6257 (1871-1931)

Directories, Gazetteers and Year Books
Bagshaw, S., *History, Gazetteer and Directory of the County of Kent*, Vol. 1-2 (1847)
Black's Guide to Kent (1885)
Black's Guide to West Kent (1901)
Finch's Directory 1803
Kelly's Directory of Kent 1867, 1874, 1878, 1882, 1899, 1903, 1905, 1911, 1913, 1915, 1918
Percy and Co., *Rochester Chatham, Strood, New and Old Brompton and Gillingham Directory* (1871-1873)
Phippen, J., *New and Enlarged Directory for Maidstone and its Environs* (1850)
Phippen, J. and J.F., *A Directory of Rochester, Chatham, Strood and their vicinities* (Rochester, 1858)
Pigot and Co.'s National London and Provincial Commercial Directory (1832-1834)
Pigot & Co.'s Directory of Kent (1840)
Post Office Directory (1855)
Simpson's Rochester, Chatham, Strood and Brompton Directory (1865)
Tallis, J., *A Comprehensive Gazetteer of Gravesend with its environs* (London, 1839)
Universal British Directory (1790-8)
Wright's Topography of Rochester, Chatham and Strood (Chatham, 1838)

Records and primary sources
Bevan, G.P., *Handbook to the County of Kent*, 6th edn (London, 1887)
Boys, J., *General View of the Agriculture of the County of Kent*, 2nd edn (London, 1805)
Denne, S., *The History and Antiquities of Rochester and its Environs*, 2nd edn (Rochester, 1817)
England's Topographer: or a New and Complete History of the County of Kent (1828-1831)
Harris, E., *A Trip Down the River Medway* (Rochester, 1897)
Harris, E., *The Riverside: An Itinerary of the Medway within the City of Rochester and Memories it Recalls* (Rochester, 1930)
Hasted, E., *The History and Topographical Survey of the County of Kent*, 1st edn, 4 vols (Canterbury, 1778-1790); 2nd edn, 12 vols (Canterbury, 1797-1801)
Ireland, S., *Picturesque Views of the River Medway* (London, 1793)
Marshall, C., *Select Illustrated Topography of Thirty Miles Round London* (London, 1837-1838)
Marshall, W., *The Rural Economy of the Southern Counties* (London, 1798)
Maxwell, D., *Unknown Kent* (London, 1921)
Maxwell, D., *History from a Sketch Book* (London, 1926)
Maxwell, D., *The Enchanted Road* (1927)

Roake, M. (ed.), 'Religious worship in Kent: The Census of 1851', *Kent Records* (1999), XXVII
Rochard, J., *Historical Chatham and Rochester* (Chatham, 1894)
Seymour, C., *A New Topographical, Historical and Commercial Survey of the Cities, Towns and Villages of the County of Kent* (Canterbury, 1776)
Smetham, H., *History of Strood* (Chatham, 1899)
Stratford, J., *London; being an Accurate History and Description of the British Metropolis and its Neighbourhood* (London, 1805-1810)
Tombleson, W., *Tombleson's Views of the Thames and Medway* (London, 1833-1834)
Whiteman, A., *The Compton Census of 1676: a critical edition* (Oxford, 1986)
Woolmer, J., *Historical Jottings of the Parish of Snodland* (Snodland, 1894)
Wyllie, W. and M., *London to the Nore Painted and Described* (London, 1905)

SECONDARY SOURCES IN PRINT: BOOKS, JOURNALS AND ARTICLES

Place of publication is London unless otherwise stated. The following list concentrates on local material. Other printed secondary sources are cited in the endnotes.

Andrews, F.W.G., 'Railways and the community: the Kentish evidence', *Archaeologia Cantiana*, 123 (2003), 185-202
Armstrong, A. (ed.), *The Economy of Kent, 1640-1914* (Woodbridge, 1995)
Armstrong, W.A., 'The population of Victorian and Edwardian Kent' (1), *Archaeologia Cantiana*, 112 (1993), 1-16
Armstrong, W.A., 'The population of Victorian and Edwardian Kent' (2), *Archaeologia Cantiana*, 114 (1994), 17-38
Arnold, R., *A Yeoman of Kent: an Account of Richard Hayes, 1725-90, and of the Village of Cobham* (London, 1949)
Ashbee, A., 'Notes from Snodland Rectory, 1865-1882', SHS pamphlet (Snodland, 1993)
Ashbee, A., 'The Early History of the New Church in Snodland', SHS pamphlet
Ashbee, A., 'Snodland in Old Picture Postcards', SHS pamphlet (2001)
Ashbee, A., 'Early Snodland papermakers (c.1740-1854)', (Snodland, 2003)
Austin, J.K., *Yesterday's Medway from Rochester Bridge to Chatham Intra* (Rainham, 2006)
Austin, J.K., *The Medway Shore as it was from Burham to Borstal* (Rainham, 2007)
Balston, T., *William Balston – Paper Maker* (London, 1954)
Barnard, D., *Merrily to Frendsbury* (Rochester, 1996)
Bergess, W. and Sage, S., *Five Medway Villages* (Kent, 1983)
Bignell, A., *Hopping Down in Kent* (Hale, 1977)
Black, S.B., 'Swing: the years 1827-1830 as reflected in a west Kent newspaper', *Archaeologia Cantiana*, 107 (1989), 89-106
Bower, J., 'Probate accounts as a source for Kentish early modern economic and social history', *Archaeologia Cantiana*, 109 (1991), 51-62
Bower, J., 'The Kent yeoman in the seventeenth century', *Archaeologia Cantiana*, 114 (1994), 149-64
Boys, H., 'On the Kentish corn-scythe and binding rake', *Journal of the Royal Agricultural Society*, I (1840)
Chalklin, C.W., *Seventeenth Century Kent: A Social and Economic History* (Longman, 1965)
Chalklin, C.W., 'Sources for Kentish history: trade and industry', *Archaeologia Cantiana*, 108 (1990), 73-89
Church, D., *Cuxton: A Kentish Village* (Sheerness, 1976)
Clark, P. and Murfin, L., *The History of Maidstone: the Making of a Modern County Town* (Stroud, 1995)
Coad, J.C., *The Royal Dockyards, 1690-1850, Architecture and Engineering Works of the Sailing Navy* (Aldershot, 1989)
Coleman, D.C., *The British Paper Industry, 1495-1860* (Oxford, 1958)
Coles-Finch, W., *The Foords of Rochester* (Rochester, 1917)
Coles-Finch, W., *The Medway, River and Valley* (Daniel, 1929)
Crossick, G., *An Artisan Elite in Victorian Society: Kentish London 1840-1880* (London, 1978)
Ellis, D., *Medway Yacht Club: the first hundred years 1880-1980* (Maidstone, 1979)
Ffinch, M., *Donald Maxwell* (Maxwell Estate, 1995)
Fletcher, D.H., 'Mapping and estate management on the early nineteenth-century estate: the case of the Ear of Aylesford's estate atlas', *Archaeologia Cantiana*, 109 (1991), 85-109
Francis, A.J., *The Cement Industry 1796-914: A History* (Newton Abbot, 1977)
Funnell, K.J., *Snodland Paper Mill: C. Townsend Hook and Company from 1854*, 2nd edn (Snodland, 1986)
Goodsall, R.H., *The Medway and its Tributaries* (Kent, 1953)

Gower, E.S. and Church, D., *Across the Low Meadow: Halling, a Village on the Medway* (Maidstone, 1979)

Hadfield, C., *The Canals of South and South East England* (Newton Abbot, 1969)

Harvey, D.W., 'Locational Change in the Kentish Hop Industry and the Analysis of Land Use Patterns', *Transactions and Papers (Institute of British Geographers)*, 33 (Dec. 1963), 123-44

Hobhouse, H., *Thomas Cubitt: Master Builder* (Macmillan, 1971)

Homan, R., *The Victorian Churches of Kent* (Chichester, 1984)

Kain, R.J.P., 'The tithe commutation surveys', *Archaeologia Cantiana*, 89 (1975 for 1974), 101-18

Keith-Lucas, B., *Parish Affairs: the Government of Kent under George III* (Maidstone, 1986)

Lawson, T. and Killingray, D. (eds.), *An Historical Atlas of Kent* (Chichester, 2004)

McCrerie, A., *Knowing Aylesford* (Hadlow, 1964)

McDougall, P., *Chatham Past* (Chichester, 1999)

March, E.J., *Spritsail Barges of Thames and Medway* (Newton Abbot, 1970)

Marsh, R., *The Conservancy of the River Medway 1881-1969* (Rochester, 1971)

Melling, E. (ed.), *Kentish Sources, III. Aspects of Agriculture and Industry*, (Maidstone, 1961)

Melling, E., 'Kentish tradesmen in the early 19th century', *Archaeologia Cantiana*, 66 (1953), 98-102

Mitchell, I., 'The public markets of some north-west Kent towns, 1700-1850', *Archaeologia Cantiana*, 117 (1998), 173-88

Newman, J., *The Buildings of England: West Kent and the Weald* (Penguin, 1969)

Overton, M., Whittle, J., Dean, D. and Hann, A., *Production and Consumption in English Households 1600-1750* (Routledge, 2004)

Pearce, A. and Long, D., *Chalk Mining and Associated Industries of Frindsbury*, Kent Underground Research Group: Research Report 3 (1987)

Petty, D., 'Victorian Philanthropy: A Case Study of the Hook family of Snodland', SHS pamphlet 29 (Snodland, 2007)

Preston, J.M., *Industrial Medway: An Historical Survey* (Chatham, 1977)

Preston, J.M., *Aveling and Porter Ltd Rochester* (Rochester, 1987)

Pugh, P., *The History of Blue Circle* (Cambridge, 1988)

Quiney, A., *English Domestic Architecture: Kent Houses* (Suffolk, 1993)

Redgrave, G.R., *Calcareous Cements, Their Nature, Manufacture and Uses* (London, 1895)

Sephton, J.H., *Preston Hall, Aylesford* (1997)

Sephton, J.H., *Around Aylesford* (Stroud, 1999)

Shorter, A.H. (ed.), *Studies on the History of Papermaking in Britain* (Aldershot, 1993)

Simper, R., *River Medway and the Swale* (Lavenham, 1998)

Smith, T.P., 'The geographical pattern of coaching services in Kent in 1836', *Archaeologia Cantiana*, XCVIII (1982)

Stratton, J., *Hops and Hop-pickers* (1883)

Tatton-Brown, T., 'Cobham Hall: the house and its gardens', *Archaeologia Cantiana*, 122 (2002), 1-28

Wall, C. de R., *Snodland and its History, 55 B.C. to A.D. 1928* (1928)

Willmott, F.G., *Bricks and Brickies* (1972)

Willmott, F.G., *Cement, Mud and 'Muddies'* (Kent, 1977)

Yates, N. and Gibson, J.M. (eds), *Traffic and Politics: The Construction and Management of Rochester Bridge AD 43-1993* (Woodbridge, 1994)

Yates, N., Hume, R. and Hastings, P., *Religion and Society in Kent, 1640-1914* (Woodbridge, 1994)

SECONDARY SOURCES NOT IN PRINT: THESES, DISSERTATIONS, REPORTS

Baker, D.A., 'Agricultural prices, production and marketing, with special reference to the hop industry: North East Kent 1680-1760' (University of Kent PhD thesis, 1976)

Buss, T., 'Recollections of Eccles' (unpublished pamphlet, 1908)

Cordle, C.E., 'Hop cultivation and marketing: Wealden Kent and Southwark, 1744-2000', (University of Leicester PhD thesis, 2005)

Hewitt, J.B., 'The history of the Rochester Book Society' (unpublished pamphlet, 1932)

Hood, M.A., 'The historical geography of the River Medway Navigation: including its relationship to the national history of inland waterways, the economic situation of the local area and wider aspects of trade and investment' (Bedford College, London PhD thesis, 1979)

Rees H., 'The Medway Towns – their settlement, growth and economic development' (University of London PhD thesis, 1954)

'River Medway: Historical and general Account' (typescript 1911, reprinted 1975)

Wells, K.E., 'Preston Hall and its owners' (unpublished pamphlet, 1983)

Index

Page numbers in italics refer to pictures or their captions

Picture Credits

The authors and publishers wish to thank the following for permission to reproduce their material. Any infringement of copyright is entirely accidental: every care has been taken to contact or trace all copyright owners. We would be pleased to correct in future editions any errors or omissions brought to our attention. References are to page numbers except where stated.

B.M. Thomson, 33
British Newspaper Library, 30
Centre for Kentish Studies, Kent Archive and Local History Service, Kent County Council, 9, 43
Chatham News, 159
Crosby Lockwood & Son, 41
Dover Publications, 42
E.S. Gowers & D. Church, 22, 86
Halling Primary School (originals held at Medway Archive, digitised by R. Smoothy), 3 (Fig. 5), 62, 72, 93, 141, 156, 157
English Heritage (Derek Kendell), x, 4, 7, 16, 88, 96, 104, 106, 107, 119 (Fig. 77), 120 (Fig. 78), 158, 160, 161, 162
Getty Images (Radio Times Hulton Picture Library), 28
Peter Higginbotham www.workhouses.org.uk, 78 (Fig. B)
Images of England, (M.K. Lofthouse) 15, (Sue Spice) 18, (Dr Henry Teed) 68, (Richard Hall) 75 (Fig. D)
Lafarge Cement UK, 40, 44, 112/13
Maidstone Library, 46
Maidstone Museum, 59 (Fig. 41)
Medway Archives and Local Studies Centre, 11, 32, 57, 131, 148, (Couchman Collection) 5, 14, 26, 49, 66, 74 (Fig. B), 142, 143
Museum of English Rural Life, 12
National Maritime Museum, 136
National Portrait Gallery, 54
Ordnance Survey, 27, 78 (Fig. A), 113 (Fig. B)
Private Collection/Bridgeman Art Library, 59 (Fig. 40)
R. Smoothy, 63 (Fig. 44), 98, 103, 108, 114, 116 (Fig. 74), 123, 125, 127
Routledge, 71
SAPPHIRE, 47
Snodland Historical Society, 13, 53, 55, 58, 81, 89, 94, 119 (Fig. 76), 120 (Fig. 79), 124, 133, 152
Amanda Thomas, 74 (Fig. A), 75 (Fig. C)
The National Archives, 82
Untraceable, 116 (Fig. 73)
University of London, 1, 3, 61, 63 (Fig. 45), 64, 97, 100, 101, 102, 130, 154, 155
F.G. Willmott, 29

The following maps were drawn by Cath D'Alton Figs 3, 18, 22, 35, 61, 71, 75, 84, 92, Panel 2 (Fig. A), © University of London,